STILL NOWHERE IN AN EMPTY VASTNESS

HISTORY + METAPHOR

STILL

NOW

IN AN

VAST

HISTORY +

ROBERTO TEJADA
NOEMI PRESS
BLACKSBURG, VIRGINIA

iNꟼIDEꟼ
POETICS
#4

HERE

EMPTY

NESS

METAPHOR

*...a continuity
that questions /
and a rift
in response*

JOSÉ LEZAMA LIMA

book cover & interior design: Douglas Kearney
text set in Alegreya + Fira Sans Condensed; display in Futura Condensed

published by Noemi Press, Inc.
A Nonprofit Literary Organization.

www.noemipress.org

This book is for Ramón A. Gutiérrez
—historian, pluralist, friend

CONT

NENTS

LIST OF ILLUSTRATIONS

Adolphe Jean Baptiste Bayot (1810–1866) and Louis Pierre-Alphonse Bichebois, (1801–1850) after Carl Nebel, (1805–1855), Genl. Scott's Entrance into Mexico, 1851, p 133, bottom.

Frederick Catherwood (1799–1854), Scene of ancient Mayan Indian monument in the Yucatan Penninsula of Mexico, 1843, Library of Congress F1435.C361 folio, p 139 .

Alan Diaz (1947–2018), photograph of Elián González held in a closet by Donato Dalrymple, one of the two men who rescued the boy from the ocean, right, as government officials search the home of Lázaro González for the young boy, in the early morning, in April 22, 2000 file photo, in Miami. (AP Photo/Alan Diaz, File), p 133, top .

Harry Gamboa Jr. (1951), *Roberto Bedoya*, 1994, from *Chicano Male Unbonded* series ©1994, Harry Gamboa Jr., gelatin silver print, 14 inches x 11 inches, edition of 6, p 141.

Laura Gilpin (1891–1979), *Steps of the Castillo, Chichen Itza, Yucatán*, 1932, photograph, Library of Congress, 93503240, p 138.

Marsden Hartley (1877–1943), *Earth Cooling*, 1932, oil on cardboard mounted on masonite, 24 1/2 x 33 7/8 inches, Amon Carter Museum of American Art, Fort Worth, Texas. p 132, bottom.

José Montoya (1932–2013), *Calendario '77*, 1977, silkscreen print, 15 x 21 inches, Sacramento Art Department Art Collection, p 132, top.

George Oppen (1908–1984), cradle or bassinet, photographer unknown, photographs of furniture and wood relief carvings from Mexico, Mary Oppen Papers (MSS 0125, flatbox 109, folder 2), Special Collections & Archives, UC San Diego Library, p 136, top.

George Oppen (1908–1984), Industrial scene with workers, wood relief carving, 18 x 22.5 inches, Mary Oppen Papers (oversize AB-06-D02), Special Collections & Archives, UC San Diego Library, p 145.

George Oppen (1908–1984), Two figures beside tree, wood relief carving, 22.5 x 27 inches, Mary Oppen Papers (oversize: AB-02-F01), Special Collections & Archives, UC San Diego Library, p 144.

Jackson Pollock (1912–1956), *Coal Mine, West Virginia*, c. 1936, lithograph in black on wove paper; image 11 3/8 x 15 1/2 inches, sheet 14 3/16 x 17 7/16 inches; Reba and Dave Williams Collection, Gift of Reba and Dave Williams National Gallery of Art, Washington, p 136, bottom.

James Walker (1818 or 1819–1889), *The Storming of Chapultepec, Sept. 13th. 1847 1848*, chromolithograph with applied watercolor, 23 9/16 x 35 15/16 inches, Amon Carter Museum of American Art, Fort Worth, Texas, p 135.

Edward Weston (1886–1958), *Woman Seated on a Petate*, 1926, [photograph, Collection] Center for Creative Photography © 1981 Center for Creative Photography, Arizona Board of Regents, p 137.

Edward Weston (1886–1958), *Los Changos Vaciladores*, 1926, [photograph, Collection] Center for Creative Photography © 1981 Center for Creative Photography, Arizona Board of Regents p 142–43

Edward Weston (1886–1958), *Juguetes, Doll and Sombrero*, 1926, [photograph, Collection] Center for Creative Photography © 1981 Center for Creative Photography, Arizona Board of Regents, p 140

Map, Routes of Cabeza de Vaca, Coronado, and De Soto and Moscosco. University of Texas Perry-Castañeda Library Map Collection, from Atlas of Texas, published by The University of Texas at Austin, Bureau of Business Research, 1976, p 134

LIMIT
ROPHE

1 WHAT DOES IT MEAN TO ENGAGE AN ADVANCED POETIC language of authentic interest and public imperative? Is it possible to further complicate the forgery of statement for an implied readership, articulated at once by an actual person and surrogate self aspiring to matter, method, and music of a kind? To suspend the conflict between transparent properties still longed for in the now of art making and a multiplicity bestowed to poetic speech as determined by a successive reader's active voice? Is social engagement necessarily manifest, specified, awaiting notice or, by contrast, created elsewhere in the interpretive task over time? For the inheritor of avant-garde legacies, questions old and new surface to unsettle assumptions unique to the teleology of progress imagined by the modernist enterprise, especially as end-of-millennium developments in U.S. avant-garde poetics recede into the usable past. Even as I remain indebted in part to the pedagogies of that specific cultural moment—one of whose aims was to underline complex patterns and experimental relationships animated in immediate or historic context between author, writing, institution, and reader: breaking the spell, so to speak, of human-made things and their means of circulation—I accept lyric drive as that unfamiliar vitality in which personhood can or cannot know itself as an axiomatic proposition of the historical uncanny.

That drive seeks residence in drifting sounds consigned to oblivion but so rekindled in the tangible present as to coalesce into that voice Michel de Certeau describes as moving "through an intermediary zone between body and language... strange interval, where the voice gives speech without 'truths', and proximity a presence without possession."[1] An aspect of what I write advocates for sensation itself as a legitimate topic of inquiry; to underscore the private and collective dimensions of culture by way of a body-mind caught between a will-to-paradise and dystopian inertia, between the conflicting desires of whereabouts and exile, between individual resolve and social pessimism, rendered through the historically contingent events by which a subject is shaped; to produce at the limit by welcoming the uncertainty of ends, cultural contradiction, and public ambivalence.[2]

---

[1] Michel de Certeau. *The Writing of History*, trans. Tom Conley (New York: Columbia University Press, 1988) pp 230; 241.

[2] The term "limitrophe" points back to political uses in advance of the U.S. War with Mexico. In 1840, Juan Nepomuceno Almonte (1803–1869), Mexican Secretary of War, addressed the National Congress concerning the "usurpers of Texas," in a resolution to "offer peace or war, pardon or punishment" to its "perfidious inhabitants [who] seek to promote their fortunes by the ruin of Mexico." He enumerated as follows: "1. That the Government be authorized to incur any expense for the reduction of the department of Texas to the National Union. 2. That all politico-military measures be authorized with respect to this province and its limitrophe States, that may be deemed necessary to effect its pacification." These demands were published in "Projected Invasion of Texas by Mexico," *The New Yorker*, Feb 1, 1840, vol. 8; no. 20, p 315. The events that led to the U.S. War with Mexico resulted in the signing of the Treaty of Guadalupe Hidalgo, and Mexico's forfeiting of more than half of its national territory. Rehearsed in this book is my conflict with an uncritical U.S.-centric avant-garde, sectarian nativism, and the inclination to territorialize. Offered in the histories, essays, and manifestos that follow are the limitrophe spaces of poetry and art in alternate geopolitical imaginations; borderland eventualities and hemispheric desires that enliven a capacious Latinx poetics.

2   Jack Spicer: "No one listens to poetry"[3]—a condition fueled by the boundaries imposed between poetic practice and culture as separate activities in opposition to the role played by available institutions and the "aesthetic democracy" to which they give way: inescapable components in a continuing self-definition of the avant-garde.

•   The contested artifice of self-expression contrary to estrangements in the material fact of language, the attributes of medium, and the aporias by which radical practice devolves into mere style.

•   A way out of the crisis of representation—the stable, centered self ghosted through a repeatedly refigured subjectivity, or one forever displaced, as in the art of Mary Kelly—by the fact "that the production of authenticity requires more than an author for the object"[4] so much as to call for the occasion of a surrogate self.

•   The monolithic subject of Western history in light of demands on the autonomy or contingency of avant-garde writing in a racialized and relational world habitus.

•   The general "expansion of art"—and its fascination with the language of newer technologies, materials of industry, design, communication, publicity, spectacle, and mass consumption—as though in fear of public forgetting and personal oblivion. Susan Howe: "If history is a record of survivors, Poetry shelters other voices."[5]

---

[3]   Jack Spicer. "Thing Language," *My Vocabulary Did This to Me: The Collected Poetry of Jack Spicer*, eds. Peter Gizzi and Kevin Killian (Middletown, Conn: Wesleyan University Press, 2008) p 373.

[4]   Mary Kelly. "Re-Viewing Modernist Criticism," *Art After Modernism: Rethinking Representation*, ed. Brian Wallis (New York: New Museum of Contemporary Art; Boston: David Godine, Publishers, 1984) p 95. Originally published in *Screen*, Volume 22, Issue 3, 1 September 1981, pp 41–52.

[5]   Susan Howe. *The Birth-Mark: Unsettling the Wilderness in American Literary History*

3 A record of survivors unsettled by the semidarkness of the undersea night, the velodrome cradle undertow, and marveled by these monuments in place of the invertebrate culture unique to saltwater, rewarded as we were with a glimpse into a landscape few of us will ever know, even with these spastic infant limbs, these urges you want to go away, modes of guiding us down a current where—damselfish, triggerfish, lion fish—high quantities of oxygen help to break down the organic molecules into simpler forms for chemical filtration removal, while maintaining an environment conducive to the culturing of large populations of aerobic bacteria in reference to the future of the continent, or so he says, the fundamental problem now being not one of self-recognition, not here or elsewhere, but of union, the duty to combat isolation despite the economic and social difficulties or so we're convinced, of health and energy for the increasingly complex functions of the state where women will comprise nearly 60 percent of the country's technical force, hold jobs, earn good salaries, and be free and less dependent on men than in a past where news of each house they built was received here as good news, made us proud because we knew the hardships they faced in the construction, truly very difficult for us all, the town we had intended to build there, a project of great social benefit to the entire population for whom pleasure is derived in being spoon-fed and so benign that one may lead a normal life through the looking glass of aquatic containment—*sargassum, cabomba, vallisneria*—now that, to counter silicates producing micro-algae growth and heavy metals causing invertebrate meltdown, traditional methods will be applied, like those throughout history in cases of highly dangerous diseases, namely the quarantine of those infected, as in the case of cholera, leprosy, and so on, he added, meaning a slow death, a couple of pumps to hum and gurgle in trying to simulate an analogous system of life for those of us inhabitants still left.[6]

(Hanover: University Press of New England, 1993) p 47.

[6]   The language here borrows freely from speeches made by Fidel Castro, and the section was originally published in Sandra Ramos, *Autorreconocimiento del pez* (México City: Galería Nina Menocal, 1997). It serves a twin purpose as "Self-Recognition of the Fish" in Roberto Tejada, *Exposition Park* (Middletown, Conn: Wesleyan University Press, 2010) p 27.

An aspect
of what I write advocates for
sensation itself
as a legitimate topic
of inquiry;

◆

... and dystopian inertia
a will-to-paradise
caught between
by way of a body-mind
sions of culture
the private and collective dimen-
to underscore

STILL NO
IN AN

VASTNESS

WHERE EMPTY

O N JUNE 17, 1527, chief commander Pánfilo de Narváez set off from the port of San Lúcar de Barrameda, Spain, on a royal expedition with five ships and 600 men. Second in command was Álvar Núñez Cabeza de Vaca who, at the seasoned age of 37, had already achieved a considerable military career; and the undertaking of this voyage was to settle a colony in "Spanish Florida," from the southern tip of modern-day Florida along the Gulf Coast to the Río de las Palmas [or Río Grande] in the northernmost reaches of New Spain.

The Narváez expedition landed on the island of Hispaniola in mid-September, where, after three months at sea, 140 crewmembers were allured by the outpost amenities of Santo Domingo—and so deserted. Those remaining sailed further on to southwestern Cuba where—in a gripping initial episode—nearly the entire company was wiped out by a series of hurricanes. In their attempt to reach the city of Havana, contrary winds finally drove the expedition to what is now known as Florida. With the royal standard raised there, the six months that followed were a combination of first contact and tentative interactions with the native peoples, taking some captive as guides and interpreters, resolving disputes among the ranking officers on the question of what was to be done with the ships, which were eventually left behind, embarking on reconnaissance forays into the interior, fending off attacks, provoked and unprovoked, as well as staving off hunger and diseases such as malaria, and dysentery. Finally, with their numbers significantly reduced and having returned to shore with the assistance of the native inhabitants of that coastal region, the company pushed out to sea again, having remarkably constructed five 30-foot barges with which to head west along the Gulf Coast toward Pánuco.[1] On November 5 and 6, 1528, with this makeshift flotilla having been separated in the search for gold, two barges and eighty men landed on what is now Galveston Island, or an island just west of Galveston. The barges eventually perished, and all but fifteen of the men fell victim to various fates: cold, hunger, disease, drowning, injuries, violence at the hands of Native Americans, and even cannibalism—to the horror of local inhabitants, famished Spaniards were eating their deceased.

At this point, Álvar Núñez Cabeza de Vaca and three other survivors—Andrés Dorantes, Alonso del Castillo Maldonado, and Esteban[2]—proceed as the sole protagonists of the subsequent narrative that accounts for the six years of captivity, separation, reunion and wandering from one native people to another before their eventual reinsertion into viceregal life. The remarkably detailed cultural description and some of the extraordinary episodes related in the narrative are important early traces of that violent space emerging from the New World encounter itself: between founding fact and fiction along the intercultural frontier that separates precarious credibility from imaginable verisimilitude.

♦ ♦ ♦

Though separated by geographies of language, historical time, political location, and by versions of colonialism and religious context, in what follows, I superimpose onto Cabeza de Vaca's *La Relación of Álvar Núñez Cabeza de Vaca* (1542) Mary Rowlandson's posterior New England *A Narrative of the Captivity and Restoration*

---

[1] Now Tampico, on the coast of Central Mexico.

[2] Dorantes' slave, also known as Estevan or Estevanico, identified by some as a black African from Azemmour, or Azamor, Morocco.

of Mrs. Mary Rowlandson (1682) in a cross-cultural trans-American poetics indebted to William Carlos Williams' *In the American Grain* and José Lezama Lima's *La expresión americana*, among other cultural descriptions that seek to experiment with the uncertain historical processes of contact. In the later sections of *The Maximus Poems*, Charles Olson too envisioned a surrogate self as the situated effect and cause of events that give meaning to the technological present. "I have been an ability—a machine—up to / now. An act of 'history', my own, and my father's… completing something […] visionary… [akin to] lantern-slides, on the sheet, in the front-room Worcester, / on the wall…"[3] With Cabeza de Vaca as one of that expansive poem's figural forces, Olson chronicled evolutionary descent as the contingency of persons, places, and memory entrusted to survivals made possible in the present of exalted speech. One slide projected from *The Maximus Poems*' lantern of history describes Olson's contemporaries, the poet Leroi Jones (Amiri Baraka) and Malcolm X, as castaways on this "desperate / ugly / cruel / Land this Nation / which never / lets anyone / come to / shore."[4] A successive image projects the spectacle of history as determined by what the poem views to be a foundational shipwreck and wandering:

> As Cabeza de Vaca was
> given the Guanches gift
> and so could cure
> And did, at Corazone,
> New Mexico, remembered
> in the name
>
> From Fuerteventura crossing
> by the Dog, Gran Canaria, Gloucester
> is nearly Guanche too
> And may she too have
> as well-thought, and felt
> a place in men's minds[5]

---

[3]   Charles Olson. *The Maximus Poems*, ed. George F. Butterick (Berkeley: University of California Press, 1983) p 495.

[4]   *Ibid.*, p 497.

[5]   *Ibid.*, p 602.

Accounts of captivity like those by Cabeza de Vaca and Rowlandson produced governing narratives about Native Americans as Other, in testimonies that effected a two-fold transfiguration of the captive's subjectivity, a sort of twin conversion, both juridical and literary: in the case of Cabeza de Vaca, a misfired expedition of conquest, and subsequent years of wandering, enslavement, extraordinary happenings, and final reincorporation into the viceregal world; in the case of Rowlandson, a series of removes away from her ambit of stability, and her ultimate deliverance from a Narragansett massacre and capture. In each respective encounter, the shifting power-relations of a regenerate alterity are so rehearsed as to encompass the outward barbarism of massacre and annihilation, as well as those brutalities that resist portrayal in document form—together resonant with all the violence and collision that brought the entire New World project into being.

Extreme incidents portrayed in these works mirror the anxieties and differences to do with conquest, settlement, occupation and displacement. The formal and political consequences of these individuating experiences so persist, from the colonizing spheres of New England and the far reaches of New Spain, now the American Southwest, as to confuse these accounts with modernist attitudes and actions.[6]

---

[6] For the meaning of Cabeza de Vaca's *Relación* to the contemporary moment, see the feature film *Cabeza de Vaca*, directed by Nicolás Echeverría, Mexico, 1991; and Kathryn Mayers, "Of Third Spaces and (Re)localization: Critique and Counterknowledge in Nicolas Echeverria's *Cabeza de Vaca*," *Confluencia: Revista Hispánica de Cultura y Literatura*, vol. 24, no. 1, 2008, pp 2–16:

> By means of departures from the narrative structure of the original *Relación*, opaque images of Amerindians, and a surreally symbolic close to the film, Echevarría evokes an epistemic outside to the event of the Encounter that at the same time acknowledges the inevitable weight of Western hegemonic discourse on the film's enunciation.... Echevarría recognizes the impossibility of a discursive space divested of local perspective, yet asserts the value of a space crossed by opposing sites of enunciation as a record of the ideological paradoxes that constitute some of Latin America's most urgent cultural problems.

♦ ♦ ♦

A Narrative of the Captivity and Restoration of Mrs. Mary Rowlandson (1682) has served Early-American literary studies as a counter-example to that first-generation of founding fathers who, as Susan Howe remarks, "asserted the sacred and corporate success of their pioneering errand-enterprise."[7] Rowlandson also inaugurated an authorial persona in response to the frontier experience of colonist occupation that had consisted primarily of violent contact and counter-contact between the indigenous peoples and settlers, and displacement in the form of Native American assaults in search of human ransom.

In the U.S. poetic imagination, see Dale Smith, *American Rambler* (Austin, Texas: Thorp Springs Press, 2000), a book-length poem that collapses temporalities in a *relación* of "stripmall America / & smallpox/ before missions (Catholic & Capital) / Europe compressed itself / in Spanish Adam / Álvar Nunez / was delivered / a relic / of modern times." Interviewed, Smith discusses the function of Cabeza de Vaca as a cultural image that survives the historical figure:

> He was washed naked into the New World. He became a trader and healer, and lived among his native lords for eight years. He is Cortés' shadow in a sense. Like Cortés, he was trained to conquer. His grandfather exterminated a large portion of the population of the Canary Islands for God and King, not to mention his own wealth and honor... He fought in some bloody European battles before going west. So he wasn't heading to the New World with any but the standard ideals, to take gold and, if possible, extend the domain of his Catholic God. // But right from the start, things went wrong. He left Cuba in 1527 with more than 500 men and was one of four to return nine years later to Mexico City. His years in the wilderness, and his very careful relation of this wandering to King Charles V of Spain, struck me as very significant and demanded a closer look from me. Despite modernity's dominion, I believe that wilderness remains an active force in the New World. Yes, it remains a force as a subliminal image.

In "To Be a Good Finder: Dale Smith in conversation with Kent Johnson," *Jacket* 15, December 2001 <http://jacketmagazine.com/15/john-iv-smit.html>. Too, the poet Jay Wright, in his 1976 book-length poem, *Dimensions of History*, performs a journey akin to the castaway wandering of Cabeza de Vaca and his company, described in a section of the following essay "The Logic of Elsewhere."

[7] Susan Howe. *The Birth-Mark: Unsettling the Wilderness in American Literary History* (Hanover: University Press of New England, 1993) p 91.

To compare Rowlandson's *Narrative* with Cabeza de Vaca's chronicle is to explore the differences these two accounts activate—the subjectivities they render and the attendant belief systems and politics they perform. If, as Mary Louise Pratt has suggested in *Imperial Eyes: Travel Writing and Transculturation*, that "women protagonists tend to produce ironic reversals when they turn up in the contact zone,"[8] some of the symbolic reversals inscribed in Mary Rowlandson's *Narrative* so collocate to those in Cabeza de Vaca's *Relación*.[9]

The form of address in Cabeza de Vaca's *Relación*, as with Rowlandson's *Narrative*, continually oscillates between two registers: on the one hand, the post-factum description of a compelling struggle for survival under extreme conditions of duress; and, on the other, an ethnographic account of these experiences internalizing the newness of the natural surroundings and cultural phenomena.[10] To greater or lesser degrees, the accounts were generated in response to the belief or convention that, owing to their respective fate and deliverance, each author had so procured divine favor as to lend teleological authority to the text. Both narratives are complex performances in rendering truth-value through the rhetoric of virtue and example, of testimonial amending, eyewitness redress, and historical editing.

We can appreciate the significance of these elements when viewed through the lens of poetics. James Clifford has noted, "Cultural *poesis*—and politics—is the constant reconstitution of selves and others through specific exclusions, conventions, and discursive practices."[11] Cabeza de Vaca's *Relación* and Rowlandson's *Narrative* are formative to

---

[8]   The figure of Isabel Godin des Odonais is a case in point. See: Mary Louise Pratt. *Imperial Eyes: Travel Writing and Transculturation* (London: Routledge, 1992) p 21.

[9]   Also known by the title *Naufragios* (which translates to "Shipwrecks" in English), and rendered by one translator from the original Spanish into English as *Adventures in the Unknown Interior of America*.

[10]   This, in terms of the final cause of Christianity, politically embodied, in the former, by the Spanish Crown and Catholicism, or in the latter by Puritan religiosity and its establishment in the Massachusetts Bay Colony. See Lisa Voigt, *Writing Captivity in the Early Modern Atlantic: Circulations of Knowledge and Authority in the Iberian and English Imperial Worlds* (Chapel Hill: University of North Carolina Press, 2009).

[11]   James Clifford. *Writing Culture*, ed. James Clifford and George Marcus (Berkeley, University of California Press, 1986) p 24.

poets like Charles Olson and Susan Howe and, as I describe elsewhere in these pages, belated particulars eclipse authoritative design. This interposition—now an in-between-ness of transcribed events, now a twofold analogy of the hemispheric condition—appears in Olson's "The Kingfishers" and the poem's direct reference to Cabeza de Vaca's account.[12]

Cabeza de Vaca's *Relación* also forms an unlikely association with Rowlandson's, reading across the political imaginary of what might be referred to as trans-historical "border thinking."[13] This is a far-reaching project to be developed only provisionally here; an undertaking that aims to refigure the borders of the Americas and its modernities as an intricate series of "unsuspected relationships."[14] These range from

[12]   Charles Olson. *The Collected Poems of Charles Olson: Excluding the Maximus Poems*, ed George F. Butterick (Berkeley: University of California Press, 1987) pp 90–1.

> a state between the
> origin and the end,
> between
> birth and the beginning
> of another fetid nest
>
> of the two who first came,
> each a conquistador, one
> healed, the other tore the
> eastern idols down,
> toppled
>
> the temple walls, which,
> says the excuser were black
> from human gore)
>
> hear
> hear, where the dry blood
> talks where the old
> appetite walks

[13]   Walter Mignolo. *Local Histories / Global Designs: Coloniality, Subaltern Knowledge and Border Thinking* (Princeton, New Jersey: Princeton University Press, 2000) pp 49–88.
[14]   José E. Limón. *American Encounters: Greater Mexico, the United States and the*

the double movement of immigration and modernist exile to the imaginary or all-too-real translations and mistranslations that are the psychological patterns of metropolitan or settler colonialism, especially those that press against the historically charged confines of the actual geo-political line drawn, for example, between the United States and Mexico.

Mary Rowlandson's account "can be seen in the context of nineteenth century Manifest Destiny and the efforts to 'clean up' the plains and the Southwest to make way for the 'civilizing' of the frontier,"[15] precisely the geography of Cabeza de Vaca's sixteenth-century wanderings.

◆ ◆ ◆

"[As] if they would have torn our very hearts out..." writes Mary Rowlandson in the brutal opening description of the Narragansett massacre at Lancaster "on the tenth of February 1675." She is writing this a hundred years after the Narváez expedition shipwreck but concurrent with the writing of other captivity narratives in the Americas, even one penned in 1673 by military captain Francisco Núñez Pineda y Bascuñán, after living peaceably among the Auracanos of what is now Chile, entitled *Blithe Captivity*[16].

From the outset, Rowlandson's *Narrative* stages a formal and thematic immediacy, in stark contrast to the wandering episodes and textual eventualities of the *Relación*. The Lancaster siege attains a powerful economy of phrasing as it posits a dramatic visual field. This is accomplished by way of a distinct image: that of Rowlandson and others (presumably her children) looking out from a window or door to survey the rapidly approaching doom that takes the form of either one of two possible destinies awaiting those inside:

Erotics of Culture (Boston: Beacon Press, 1998) p 9.

[15] Richard Van Der Beets. *The Indian Captivity Narrative: An American Genre* (Lanham: University Press of America, 1984) p ix.

[16] Francisco Núñez Pineda y Bascuñán, *El cautiverio feliz*, Ángel C. González, ed. (Santiago: Ediciones Zig- Zag, n/d).

...came the Indians with great numbers upon Lancaster. Their first coming was about sunrising. Hearing the noise of some guns, we looked out; several houses were burning and the smoke ascending to heaven. There were five persons taken in one house; the father and the mother and a sucking child they knocked on the head; the other two they took and carried away alive.[17]

In this same passage, Rowlandson describes still another man "knocked on the head," stripped naked and disemboweled by Metacomet's[18] warriors. Infanticide, bloodstained nudity, and sacrifice ("they would have torn our very hearts out...") are the troubling backdrop anxiety informing the totality of the narrative whose figure-ground relation in this landscape is the legitimacy of writing itself. To reinforce the authority of her narrative, both at the level of socio-religious and narrative rhetoric, Rowlandson makes a curious disavowal of previous, possibly public, claims in favor of her own oblation over any eventual captivity:

I had often before this said that if the Indians should come, I should choose rather to be killed by them than be taken alive, but when it came to the trial my mind changed; their glittering weapons so daunted my spirits, that I chose to go along with those (as I may say) ravenous beasts, than that moment to end my days, and that I may the better declare what happened to me during that grievous captivity.[19]

The passage is salient on a number of levels. Susan Howe has argued that Rowlandson—contrary to a rendering of the events by Increase Mather[20]—was certainly "eager and able to save herself."[21] There is also the suggestion that at the crucial moment in the facts as described

---

[17]   Alden T. Vaughn and Edward W. Clark, eds., *Puritans Among the Indians: Accounts of Captivity and Redemption*, 1676–1724 (Cambridge, Massachusetts, 1981) p 35.

[18]   King Philip, his adopted English name.

[19]   Alden T. Vaughn and Edward W. Clark, eds., *Puritans Among the Indians: Accounts of Captivity and Redemption*, 1676–1724 (Cambridge, Massachusetts, 1981) p 35.

[20]   Puritan minister involved in the government of the colonies, primarily remembered for his part in the Salem witch trials.

[21]   Susan Howe. *The Birth-mark: Unsettling the Wilderness in American Literary History* (Hanover: University Press of New England, 1993) p 92.

above ("when it came to the trial"), Rowlandson employs the devise of envisioning the literary genesis of the present work in which the reader and Rowlandson are now continuous. A parenthetical remark ["(as I may say)"] draws her provisionally outside of the narrative as if to render, *après coup*, authority to the text ("to better declare what happened to me during that grievous captivity"). In seeking to represent an election, or subjective agency ("I should choose rather to be killed by them... that I chose to go along..."), Rowlandson's *Narrative* only further makes manifest a world, both actual and fictive, in which voluntarism does not, or cannot, exist.

Providence as the progenitor of a text in the New World landscape has been discussed by Djelal Kadir in his *Columbus and the Ends of the Earth: Europe's Prophetic Rhetoric as Conquering Ideology*. In his analysis of texts by Christopher Columbus, Bartolomé de las Casas, John Smith, and Roger Williams, among others, Kadir writes that the providentialist account

> ...functions as a philosophy of history, as a formulaic spectrum whose reflections shed a particular light, thereby making history meaningful in a particular fashion. That meaningfulness is, above all, deterministic in nature, and the force of its determinacies serves not only to 'explain' and justify historical events but, also, to imbue those occurrences with metaphysical and transcendental significance.[22]

The eventualities that occur both in Cabeza de Vaca's *Relación* and Rowlandson's *Narrative* are a kind of mutual befuddlement on the occasion of the encounters recorded by captive and unwitting ethnographer whose cultural description seeks to serve on two important levels: as personal testimony of hardship and deliverance, but also as broader *récits* bearing witness to the fact that the settler future is always "at a high premium and the ultimate prize."[23] In this respect, all occasions—be they by a series of removes, or by aimless wandering—are "penultimate emergencies"[24] that prefigure the final future.

---

[22]   Djelal Kadir. *Columbus and the Ends of the Earth: Europe's Prophetic Rhetoric as Conquering Ideology* (Berkeley: University of California Press, 1992) p 18.

[23]   *Ibid.*, p 18.

[24]   *Ibid.*, p 4.

In the case of Cabeza de Vaca, that final future is one predicated on the enterprise of occupation—this, despite the conflicting or contradictory compassion for which he argues on behalf of the Native Americans in later sections of the *Relación*. If Rowlandson's and Cabeza de Vaca's testimonies can be read in part as a kind of user's manual to personal redemption, genocide is nevertheless the ghost that haunts both these guidebooks. Writes Cabeza de Vaca:

> ...I had always the greatest care and diligence to remember everything particularly, so that at some time God Our Lord would be pleased to bring me thither where I am now, my account could testify to my good will and be of service to Your Majesty. Since the report of it is, I believe, advice of no little use to those who in your name will go to conquer those lands and bring them to the knowledge of the true Faith...[25]

Writing—whether equated with Cabeza de Vaca's contingent occupation or Rowlandson's removes into "the vast and desolate wilderness"—imparted "a knowledge of usages and artifices which would be of value to those who might sometime in the future find themselves among these people."[26] As written discourse, chronicles like that of Cabeza de Vaca participate in the metaphorics of cultural violence eroticized as a "projection of possible futures onto the structure of the lived present."[27] This compensatory masculine dissembling that equates a sexualized newfoundland with domination of a female body is relevant to the underlying but unnamed foreboding that informs Rowlandson's *Narrative*.

There are several suggested rape-threats as witnessed and elsewhere related by Rowlandson, from the opening intimidations posed by her Native American captors ("What, will you love English men still?") to the more visually graphic menace of the following scene related in the opening passages of the Fourth Remove:

[25] *Castaways, The Narrative of Álvar Núñez Cabeza de Vaca,* Enrique Pupo—Walker, ed., Frances M. López—Morillas, trans. (Berkeley: University of California Press, 1993) p 4.

[26] Álvar Núñez Cabeza de Vaca. *Adventures in the Unknown Interior of America,* trans. Cyclone Covey (Albuquerque: University of New Mexico Press, 1983) p 97.

[27] Elizabeth Grosz. *Volatile Bodies: Toward a Corporeal Feminism* (Bloomington: Indiana University Press, 1994) p 109.

> Amongst them also was that poor woman before mentioned who came to a sad end, as some in the company told me in my travel. She, having much grief upon her spirit about her miserable condition, being so near her time, she would often ask the Indians to let her go home; they, not being willing to that and yet vexed with her *importunity*, gathered a great company together about her and stripped her naked and set her in the midst of them. And when they had sung and danced about her (in their hellish manner) and as long as they pleased, they knocked her on [the] head and the child in her arms with her.[28] [Emphasis mine]

Other captives relate this description to Rowlandson, after she herself recalls being separated from her daughter Mary and "four little cousins and neighbors." There is a line of feminist philosophy and critical thinking, from Laura Mulvey to Iris Marion Young and others since, that has outlined the condition of female sexual difference as a divided subjectivity aware of itself as both a subject *and* as an object on view for another subject's viewing—a looked-at-ness whose violent underpinning is a continual menace to the dividing line that makes possible the conditions of any spatiality. The aim of this gaze in Rowlandson's account, is to obliterate all examples of "importunity" or demands as unfettered subject:

> The threat of being seen is, however, not the only threat of objectification that the woman lives. She also lives with the threat of invasion of her body space. The most extreme form of such spatial and bodily invasion is the threat of rape. (...) Women tend to project an existential barrier closed around them and discontinuous with the "over there" in order to keep the other at a distance. The woman lives her space as confined and closed around her, at least in part as projecting some small area in which she can exist as a free subject.[29]

If the scene in Rowlandson's *Narrative* stages this barrier "discontinuous with the 'over there'" of a woman's surroundings, it is also descriptive of a female sexual subjectivity on what might be

---

[28] Alden T. Vaughan and Edward W. Clark. eds., *Puritans Among the Indians: Accounts of Captivity and Redemption*, 1676–1724 (Cambridge, Massachusetts, 1981) p 42.

[29] Iris Marion Young. *Throwing Like a Girl and Other Essays in Feminist Philosophy and Social Theory* (Bloomington: Indiana University Press, 1990) p 155.

called the frontier or borderline separating woman as subject and object in relation with the cultural Other. This Other, even as subjugated by the patriarchal occupation to which she belongs, nonetheless demonstrates a sexualized violence in potential.

◆ ◆ ◆

Cabeza de Vaca's *Relación* speaks of other kinds of threats to masculine subjectivity. One can only imagine how European patterns of apparel—from the outright lavish to the utterly austere—and their attendant codes of modesty and decorum were complicated to an extreme in captivity by the forbidden intimacies between the sexes, in same-sex scenarios, and across racial or cultural lines.

In the wake of unspeakable personal and collective tragedy, and facing the continual prospect of death, what to make of all the nakedness in these narratives, the bodies of men and women in their less sublimated or baser satisfactions of primary needs? Whether by humiliation or imposed discipline—Cabeza de Vaca among the Capoques: "I had to work amid them without benefit of clothes"— nakedness looms, in one literary sense, as a clean slate, a newborn standing in the *Relación*. But it can also be read to anticipate the necessary failure of the colonizing enterprise insofar as patriarchal power over other lands and other peoples, no matter how genocidal, would never be altogether totalizing or complete.

For Cabeza de Vaca among the Mariames and Yguaces, unfamiliar sexual-social practices are made meaningful by what seems to be, for the Spanish castaway, an underlying panic of emasculation:

> They cast away their daughters at birth; the dogs eat them. They say they do this because all the nations of the region are their enemies, with whom they war ceaselessly; and that if they were to marry off their daughters, the daughters would multiply their enemies until the latter overcame and enslaved the Mariames, who thus preferred to annihilate all daughters than risk their reproduction of a single enemy.

This is also the practice of their neighbors, the Yguaces, but of no other people of that region. To marry, men buy wives from their enemies, the price of a wife being the best bow that can be got, together with two arrows or, should the suitor happen to have no bow, a net a fathom square. Couples kill their own male children and buy those of strangers. A marriage lasts no longer than suits the parties; they separate at the slightest pretext...

> The men bear no burdens. Anything of weight is borne by women and old men, the people least esteemed. They do not love their children as do the Capoques. Some among them are accustomed to sin against nature.[30]

Roberto J. González-Casanovas has suggested that Cabeza de Vaca's "description of quasi-communistic forms of social organization and praise of native simplicity and disingenuousness ultimately says more about European utopian myths on apostolic communities and chivalric codes than it does about the true sentiments and customs of the Gulf Indians."[31] But the description reveals as well the unwanted thoughts and anxieties—homoerotic availability and repulsion to do with "the sin against nature"—that troubled the male-dominant project of conquest and New World foundation.

◆ ◆ ◆

The description of punished "importunity" in the Fourth Remove is immediately followed by an overlapping passage. Rowlandson is a deft cultural observer. Inasmuch as the relation between personal narrative and impersonal description is rife with complexities and equivocations, Rowlandson's attention—for obvious reasons—is given over and over again to questions of viscera and the abject in the form (not surprisingly, given the *Narrative*'s domain) of warfare and food:

---

30   Álvar Núñez Cabeza de Vaca. *Adventures in the Unknown Interior of America*, Cyclone Covey, trans. (Albuquerque: University of New Mexico Press, 1983) p 50.

31   Roberto J. González-Casanovas. *Imperial Histories from Alfonso X to Inca Garcilaso: Revisionist Myths of Reconquest and Conquest* (Potomac, Maryland: Scripta Humanistica, 1997) p 19.

They would pick up old bones and cut them to pieces at the joints, and if they were full of worms and maggots, they would scald them over the fire to make the vermin come out and then boil them and drink up the liquor and then beat the great ends of them in a mortar and so eat them. They would eat horse's guts and ears, and all sorts of wild birds which they would catch; also bear, venison, beaver, tortoise, frogs, squirrels, dogs, skunks, rattlesnakes, yea, the very bark of trees, besides all sorts of creatures and provision which they plundered from the English.[32]

Wonder emerges after there is nothing left to forfeit. Having had her six-year-old daughter die in her arms, and having been deceived by a Wampanoag captor who tells how her son had been roasted and eaten, Rowlandson delights in amazement at her own capacity to eat the despicable:

There came an Indian to them at that time with a basket of horse liver. I asked him to give me a piece. "What," says he, "can you eat horse liver?" I told him I would try if he would give a piece, which he did, and I laid it on the coals to roast, but before it was half ready they got half of it away from me so that I was fain to take the rest and eat it as it was with the blood about my mouth, and yet a savory bit it was to me.[33]

◆ ◆ ◆

Astonishment and disdain: underlying the repeated allusion to food and other blood-drenched episodes is the anxiety of cannibalism and human sacrifice. This anxiety, at least in the case of Cabeza de Vaca's *Relación*, underscores the entire chronicle that ends in an address to the Spanish Crown: "For in the 2,000 leagues we sojourned by land and sea, including ten months ceaseless travel after escaping captivity, we found no sacrifices and no idolatry." He then counters these fears with several extraordinary passages, unique within the body of New World chronicles.

---

[32] Alden T. Vaughan and Edward W. Clark, eds. *Puritans Among the Indians: Accounts of Captivity and Redemption*, 1676–1724 (Cambridge, Massachusetts, 1981) p 69.
[33] *Ibid*, p 45.

Insomuch as Cabeza de Vaca's account oscillates between the struggle to satisfy basic needs and to overcome ineptitude, it is through a remarkable act, possibly an accident or a cultural misreading, that a conversion takes place or is so demonstrated in writing as to justify the narrative with a rhetoric of virtue. In his encounter with the Capoque and Han in the latter period of his wanderings, Cabeza de Vaca and the three other survivors undergo—either by will or imposition—a conversion as they perform the ceremony of faith healing. In agreeing to this practice, one cannot cease to wonder whether an aspect in the belief system of the Capoque and Han peoples so necessitated the coming of a stranger as to successfully heal the ailing and afflicted. Even as a scripted episode it marks the first of several syncretic thresholds through which Cabeza de Vaca will pass:

> The islanders [Capoque and Han] wanted to make physicians of us without examination or a review of diplomas. Their method of cure is to blow on the sick, the breath and the laying-on of hands supposedly casting out the infirmity. They insisted we should do this too and be of some use to them. We scoffed at their cures and at the idea we knew how to heal. But they withheld food from us until we complied. An Indian told me I knew not whereof I spoke in saying their methods had no effect. Stones and other things growing about in the fields, he said, had a virtue whereby passing a pebble along the stomach could take away pain and heal; surely extraordinary men like us embodied such powers over nature. Hunger forced us to obey, but disclaiming any responsibility for our failure or success. [...]

> Our method ... was to bless the sick, breathe upon them, recite a Pater Noster and Ave Maria and pray earnestly to God our Lord for their recovery. When we concluded with the sign of the cross, He willed that our patients should directly spread the news that they had been restored to health.[34]

The passage depicts a parallel conversion from post-chivalric conquistador, and lay or mechanical Christian, to faith healer—a miracle worker among pagans. Cabeza de Vaca had a university education and was presumably versed in the chivalric tradition and

---

[34] Álvar Núñez Cabeza de Vaca, *Adventures in the Unknown Interior of America*, Cyclone Covey, trans. (Albuquerque: University of New Mexico Press, 1983) p 54.

the Bible. Remarkable, too, is the questionable nature of a lay Christian performing what was deemed a shamanistic ritual, no matter that it may well have been disguised in the gestures of Catholicism.

Victor Turner outlined three stages in rites of passage that are relevant to questions of conversion: the moment of separation, the margin (liminal or threshold stage), and the final phase of re-aggregation.[35] In rites of passage, conversion, or other initiatory effects a person moves from one series of perceptions and vital patterns to another set altogether. Cabeza de Vaca turns a rhetorical slight-of-hand by making his consent to perform these pagan acts in a life or death decision. The subsequent culmination of faith healing and the Spaniard's transformation into a messianic figure—whose mystical idealism was either a calculated risk, or a little tactic of the habitat[36]—can be viewed as on behalf of a final cause. The great strategy of geopolitics (here, the military expedition mishandled by Narváez) transfigure Cabeza de Vaca into New World crusader for the Cross and Crown:

> They fetched me a man who, they said, had long since been shot in the shoulder through the back and that the arrowhead had lodged above the heart. He said it was very painful and kept him sick. I probed the wound and discovered the arrowhead had passed through the cartilage. With a flint knife I opened the fellow's chest until I could see that the point was sideways and would be difficult to extract. But I cut on and, at last, inserting my knife-point deep, was able to work the arrowhead out with great effort. It was huge. With a deer bone, I further demonstrated my surgical skill with two stitches while blood drenched me, and stanched the flow with hair from a hide. The villagers asked me for the arrowhead, which I gave them. The whole population came to look at it, and they sent it into the back country so the people there could see it.

---

[35] Victor W. Turner and Edward M. Bruner, eds. *Anthropology of Experience* (Urbana: Illinois University Press, 1986) p 1.

[36] Michel Foucault. "The Eye of Power," preface to J. Bentham, *Le Panoptique* (Paris: Belfond; rpt. in Colin Gordon, ed., *Power/Knowledge: Selected Interviews and Other Writings 1972–1977* (Brighton, Sussex: Harvester Press, 1980). p 149. Foucault writes: "A whole history remains to be written of spaces—which would at the same time be the history of powers (both of these terms in the plural)—from the great strategy of geopolitics to the little tactics of the habitat."

They celebrated this operation with their customary dances and festivities. Next day, I cut the stitches and the patient was well. My incision appeared only like a crease in the palm of the hand. He said he felt no pain or sensitivity there at all.

Now this cure so inflated our fame all over the region that we could control whatever the inhabitants cherished.[37]

It is this crude surgical procedure that warrants him escort from one native people to another until he and his band finally reach a Christian settlement whose officials threaten to indenture the indigenous populations that delivered him back. There, Cabeza de Vaca argues in opposition to the enslavement of Native Americans and negotiates in favor of their conversion to Christianity.[38] In his extraction of the arrowhead, one is compelled to recall the Mesoamerican practice in of human sacrifice whereby the heart of a victim was violently dislodged.[39] Moreover, because Rowlandson's eating of the horse liver evokes the consumption of something prohibited, a cannibalism of sorts, both texts are troubled by that "animality" Georges Bataille refers to as "immediacy or immanence."[40] Bataille goes on to say,

---

[37]   Álvar Núñez Cabeza de Vaca. *Adventures in the Unknown Interior of America*, Cyclone Covey, trans. (Albuquerque: University of New Mexico Press, 1983) p 59.

[38]   *Ibid*, p 98. "We are thankful to our merciful God that it should be in the days of Your Majesty's dominion that these nations might all come voluntarily to Him who created and redeemed us. We are convinced that Your Majesty is destined to do this much and that it is entirely within reason to accomplish."

[39]   Rowlandson: "[As] if they would have torn our very hearts out..." In his "True History of the Conquest of New Spain," Bernal Díaz del Castillo (1492–1581) had written:

I have already described the manner of their sacrifices. They strike open the wretched Indian's chest with flint knives and hastily tear out the palpitating heart which, with the blood, they present to the idols in whose name they have performed the sacrifice. Then they cut the arms, thighs, and head, eating the arms and thighs at their ceremonial banquets. The head they hang up on a beam, and the body of the sacrificed man is not eaten but given to the beasts of prey.

Bernal Díaz del Castillo, *The Conquest of New Spain*, trans. J. M. Cohen (Baltimore: Penguin, 1963) p 229.

[40]   Georges Bataille. *Theory of Religion*, trans. Robert Hurley (New York: Zone Books, 1989) p 23.

"The sacrificer's prior separation from the world of things is necessary for the return to intimacy, of immanence between man and the world, between the subject and the object."[41] This lapse between subject and object makes the *Narrative* and *Relación* contemporaneous with present realities of widespread mass-migration, political re-mappings, and subsequent cultural *mestizajes* added to the conditions of everyday life for different societies in uneven experiences of modernity.[42] Both texts can be viewed from the perspective as outlined by Tzvetan Todorov, when he wrote in *The Conquest of America*:

> On the level of action, of the assimilation of the other or of identification with him, Cabeza de Vaca also reached a neutral point, not because he was indifferent to the two cultures but because he had experienced them both from within—thereby, he no longer had anything but "the others" around him; without becoming an Indian, Cabeza de Vaca was no longer quite a Spaniard. His experience symbolizes and heralds that of the modern exile, which in its turn personifies a tendency characteristic of our society: a being who has lost his country without thereby acquiring another, who lives in a double exteriority.[43]

This dualism is strikingly manifest in Rowlandson's account when she catches herself in the interval that separates cultural and personal experience:

---

[41]   *Ibid.*, p 44.

[42]   Caren Kaplan. *Questions of Travel, Postmodern Theories of Displacement* (Durham: Duke University Press, 1996) p 19. Kaplan writes:

> The twentieth century can be characterized as a time when increasing numbers of people have become disengaged or dislocated from national, regional, and ethnic locations or identities. As travel, changing locations, and leaving home become
> central experiences for more and more people in modernity, the difference between the ways we travel, the reasons for our movements, and the terms of our participation in this dynamic must be historically and politically accounted for.

[43]   Tzvetan Todorov. *The Conquest of America,* trans. Richard Howard (New York: Harper and Row, 1984) p 249.

And here I cannot but remember how many times sitting in their wigwams
and musing on things past I should suddenly leap up and run out as if I had
been home, forgetting where I was and what my condition was. But when I
was without and saw nothing but wilderness and woods and a company of
barbarous heathens, my mind quickly returned to me...[44]

In exile all events are penultimate emergencies, insomuch as going
back is made impossible. Considering the Martinican modernist
Aimé Césaire, James Clifford wrote: "Perhaps there is no return for
anyone to a native land—only field notes for its reinvention."[45]

In scenes from the emergent stage of a New World theater
depicted now as idyllic utopia, now as holocaust-apocalypse,
traces left by these writings combine genocidal aggression
and victimization underscored by mutual terror, cruelty, and
amazement.[46] Relationships of uneven but mutual dispossession
emerge between *conquista* and maternity, between shipwreck and
the disintegration of a household, between the struggle for
command and the search for one's children, between anthropophagy
and child death. *Relación* and *Narrative* are joined by blood but
separated by the violent inevitabilities to which these accounts gave
way after contact and occupation. Testimonies by Cabeza de Vaca,
Mary Rowlandson, and other Europeans can be viewed as mirror-
occasions of those other custodies set into motion by colonizer and
settler alike.

◆ ◆ ◆

Survivals from the past resurface even now in the compulsion to repeat
those displaced attitudes and actions of New World relationships to
location and identity. I have in mind the writings of William Bronk.[47]

---

[44]   Alden T. Vaughan and Edward W. Clark, eds. *Puritans Among the Indians: Accounts of
Captivity and Redemption, 1676–1724* (Cambridge, Massachusetts, 1981) p 52.
[45]   James Clifford. *The Predicament of Culture: TwentiethCentury Ethnography, Literature,
and Art* (Cambridge: Harvard University Press, 1988) p 173.
[46]   Rowlandson: "in a maze and like one astonished"
[47]   There are other vanishing points here that give way to the twentieth century. I'm led to
the relationship between Hart Crane and Katherine Anne Porter in Mexico City where the

two U.S. writers were neighbors in the outlying district of Mixcoac. It's tempting to read the kind of differences established between the accounts of Cabeza de Vaca and Mary Rowlandson in the intentions and later writings of Hart Crane ("The Broken Tower" and "The Circumstance," among other poems) in light of Porter's response to Crane's life and death. Here I quote at length, as a mere suggestion of the possibilities, this letter written by Katherine Anne Porter to Mary Doherty, addressed from Basel, Switzerland, "of all places," and dated October 21, 1932:

The news of Hart's death, or rather, the manner of it, was a shock. He had told me so often he meant to kill himself, I doubted he would ever do it. He must have reached a stage of desperation beyond words to have done it. He used to frighten me half to death by threatening to cut his throat, or to jump from our roof, but even in my nervous shock, I felt he would not really, but was merely determined not to let the atmosphere around him clear for even a moment. I have had no particulars at all, no one has written one word to me on the subject, and I have not written to inquire, for the whole situation, when I left Mexico, both there and in New York, had roused my complete distrust of everyone, I felt that no matter what I said, in some quite horrible way nobody would believe or listen. The thing had been so frightful to me I could hardly believe it myself. You know how he talked and talked and slandered me, and in the uproar and confusion he created I simply felt it was useless trying to make myself heard. It was foul and outrageous, and as for me, his suicide has not changed the thing that happened. Death cancels our engagements, but it does not affect the consequences of our acts in life. And I have yet to see the end, no doubt, of what he did, while he has gone, escaped, without explaining, without once giving a sign that he realized the sin he had committed. I have several letters from him, written in sober moments after some of the worst episodes, and I wrote to him, trying to put down coldly on paper what I felt, asking him to read them over when he was tempted to repeat his insults, and to remember that I meant what I was saying, and was his friend who wished him no harm. I suppose these letters are lost, I wish I had kept copies of letters, and I have no evidence whatever that all the things he said and did against me were unfounded. And why did he? I ask myself this, and can answer only in part, and then the reasons are so tangled, so subtle, that when they are put into words they simply do not convey anything even to myself as I say them ... and they may not be the real reasons. How can I know? I know that his feelings for me were very complicated, but I do not think his feelings for me had anything to do with his behavior there. He simply came into an atmosphere different from what he had expected, he told me what he hoped for in Mexico, he had been misled by stupid, frivolous untrue accounts of homosexuality in Mexico, and to find that even there he must observe at least the fundamental rules of decent behavior, infuriated him. He would not listen to me when I told him he could not treat the Indians as he wished to. Malcolm [Cowley] and others had told him that all Indians were openly homosexual and incestuous, that their society was founded on this, he would encounter no difficulties whatever. He told me he wished to let himself go, he had come to Mexico for that, he was sick of living in two worlds. I said, it could be done, but he must at least observe one or two small rules of human relationship. He was not willing; he would not consent even to this. He was utterly debauched and lost by the time he came there. The change in him in the few months since I had parted from him, on the best terms of friendliness, was astonishing. And what he would not understand was that I sympathized with his dilemma, I hoped he might find some way of living that would relieve his mind and spirit and body of their terrible tension. I had no prejudices against his sexual habits, but I had no intentions of letting my own life be destroyed by him, simply because I felt it was not necessary that our lives come to collision in any way. It was his infuriated determination to invade my life that I resented and resisted: and if I had it to do again, I would find a way to resist it more effectually.

We used to spend long mornings on the roof talking over all the things that troubled him, and he told me then, in those rather quieter moments, that he was beginning to feel himself hardening, that his brutal acts were brutalizing him gradually, he was frightened to find that he no longer had the power to feel except by the most drastic and cruel stimulants. This physically as well as emotionally. He said he feared he had gone as far as he could in the road he had taken, and there was no way back. He confessed that his sexual feelings were now largely a matter of imagination, which drove and harried him continually, creating images of erotic frenzy and satisfactions for which he could find no counterpart in reality... These are not his words, but the substance. He said, he now found himself imagining that if he could see blood, or cause it to be shed, he might be satisfied: and he continually talked of the little fourteen-year-old carpenter's apprentice—you remember that ghastly episode—as a virgin, who might bleed when deflowered.... These things he said sober, so I will leave unsaid the things he shouted when drunken....

I did not look at all upon him as someone who must be saved and spared at the expense of everyone around him... I do not yet. But Hart was very acute in those matters and presumed outrageously on his immunity as a pathological case.... There were and are yet in the world several persons more important to me than Hart Crane ever was, and many ways of life I consider much more worth saving than his: And besides, all this talk of "saving" him—he did not want to be saved, he could not be. All that was worth touching in him he put into his poetry, and it is this I wish to remember, and to keep and foster. Not that living corpse, who wrote his poetry almost in spite of himself, and who, if he stayed in the world, would have come to worse ends....

—Katherine Anne Porter. *Letters of Katherine Anne Porter*, selected and edited and with an introduction by Isabel Bayley (New York: The Atlantic Monthly Press, 1990) pp 83–5.

His essays identify a future imperfect rehearsed in imaginative failures to disavow the hemisphere's violent underside of history. In "The Occupation of Space, Palenque," Bronk confirms a body of work that revels in a mind at odds with the arbitrary fictions of time and space. He describes the duality posited by the ancient architecture of Mesoamerica "as being here / in a long immediate present at no / distance, or somewhere else in another world, / some equivalent world, a world not reachable / from here."[48] I turn to his work in subsequent pages but for now Bronk's drifting voice transposes, as though from the past of Cabeza de Vaca and Rowlandson, into a present succession that invokes, belatedly, the contrary consciousness of New World displacement:

> If it is true of space that it is featureless and empty except as we limit its vastness and shape it by our occupation, the form of the cities we impose on it, the direction and location of the boundaries and roads, it is true also that our occupation is never quite successful. It is part of the same truth that the limits we set to space are always in some degree arbitrary, and the names we give it are given names not absolute ones. We are always in some degree still nowhere in an empty vastness. Our passionately occupied Palenques are always abandoned. We tire of the forms we impose upon space and the restricted identities we secure from them. We tire finally even of the act itself of imposition.[49]

[48]   William Bronk. "The Greeks, the Chinese, or Say the Mayans," *Life Supports: New and Collected Poems* (San Francisco: North Point Press, 1981) p 76.

[49]   William Bronk. "The Occupation of Space—Palenque," *Vectors and Smoothable Curves: Collected Essays* (San Francisco: North Point Press, 1985) p 29.

THE LOG

WHERE

IC OF

1 THIRD VOYAGE, 1498: "I WAS WRONG: THE WORLD IS NOT a sphere as has been written. Instead, it is shaped like a pear: perfectly round except for the nipple. Or like a ball from which swells a woman's breast whose nipple is ... closer to heaven, below the equator, on the Ocean sea at the end of the Orient...."[1] Columbus inscribed himself and the Old World, desires mistaken for reality, into the closer heaven he so happened upon, occasioning the events that redirected successive colonizing episodes from a former "dream of India."[2] The "East" had served as a variable, "a concept separable from any purely geographical area."[3] Columbus, as translator, misinterpreted the matter of the East into the categorically New World he was obliged to render into words, doubled thereafter

[1] "...y fallé que no era redondo en la forma que escriben; salvo que es de la forma de una pera que sea toda muy redonda, salvo allí donde tiene el pezón que allí tiene más alto, ó como quien tiene una pelota muy redonda, y en un lugar della fuese como una teta de mujer allí puesta, y que esta parte deste pezón sea la más alta é más propinca al cielo, ya sea debajo la línea equinoccial, y en esta mar Océana en el fin de Oriente...." Cristóbal Colón, *Relaciones y cartas* (Madrid: Librería de la Viuda e Hijos de Cuesta, 1892) pp 283–4.

[2] Eliot Weinberger. *Works on Paper* (New York: New Directions, 1986) p 3.

[3] Mary B. Campbell. *The Witness and the Other World: Exotic European Travel Writing, 400–1600*. (Ithaca: Cornell University Press, 1991) p 48.

into persuasions, figured as female, feral, and located at the ends of one East and at the beginning of another. The curvature of *Indies, insula, terra firma, orbis terrarum, novus mundus* spiraled out and back to situations of origin, another world, utopia, and genocidal settlement. Namely elsewhere, a place the real and imaginary are given to converge.

Increasing news of remote lands described in the first relations written as paradoxes and polemic fables in the chronicles of the Spanish missionaries, or by posterior travelers and naturalists, gave rise to the alternate myth of the noble or ignoble savage that served as colonial currency in the centuries that followed. It also prompted what Antonello Gerbi christened the dispute over the New World, insomuch as an Edenic Newfoundland became, in the eyes of the Old, "that unripe side of the earth."[4] Variously, its "inferior animal species," "impotent natives," "natural grandeur and misery," and "historic novelty" continued the tradition of recurring Western tropes of "exotic truth" and "grotesque facts"[5] employed in Enlightenment writings by naturalists like Buffon and philosophers like Hume and Voltaire, to account for effects its narrators could barely comprehend. It gave way to apologies like those of Berkeley who, in the ongoing debate, resorted to the equally popular argument about the ancient empires of Peru and Mexico as civilizations "in which there appeared a Reach of Politics, and a Degree or Art and Politeness, which no European People were ever known to have arrived at without the use of Letters or of Iron, and which some perhaps have fallen short of with both these Advantages."[6]

The dispute was often but not always founded on geographic experience of the New World; and it served the Enlightenment as a

---

[4]   John Donne. "To the Countess of Huntingdon," *The Major Works*, edited with an Introduction and Notes by John Carey (Oxford: Oxford University Press, 1990) p 67 ("That unripe side of the earth, that heavy clime / That gives us man up now, like Adam's time / Before he ate; man's shape, that would yet be....").

[5]   Mary B. Campbell. *The Witness and the Other World: Exotic European Travel Writing, 400–1600.* (Ithaca: Cornell University Press, 1991) pp 3; 47.

[6]   Antonello Gerbi. 1955. *La disputa del Nuevo Mundo: Historia de una polémica, 1750–1900.* Trans. Antonio Alatorre. (Mexico: Fondo de Cultura Económica, 1987) p 176.

cover story its authors could so tell as to disavow reflections in that "negative mirror" wherein knowledge is gained of the paltry worlds in one's actual possession.[7] A picture of Mexico in U.S. arts and writing gives way as well to transpositions of ethos and geography; to otherness and elsewhere over time.

2   New York, 1846: "Yes: Mexico must be thoroughly chastised! ... Let our arms now be carried with a spirit which shall teach the world that, while we are not forward for a quarrel, America knows how to crush, as well as how to expand!"[8] In the first days of the U.S. Invasion of Mexico, a young journalist and politician, Walt Whitman, published that battle cry in the Brooklyn *Eagle*. The dispute over the New World begins with Europe's colonial enterprise and its intensified historical self-consciousness. A U.S. imagining of Mexico begins at a time when it, too, is forging a definition of itself—expanding its southern and western borders into Mexico. By 1846, President James K. Polk had effectively engaged the nationalist and expansionist fervor that had been escalating in the American press, intent on securing the Mexican territories today comprising New Mexico and California—pushing U.S. boundaries as far west as possible. He ordered troops to the Rio Grande, into territory inhabited by Mexicans, and used the pretext of a border incident to sidestep Congress and declare war on Mexico.[9] The war enterprise obliged the signing of the Treaty of Guadalupe Hidalgo, with the resulting loss of more than half of Mexico's national territory.

Some newspapers protested, and Henry David Thoreau was imprisoned in the summer of 1846 for refusing to pay taxes employed in the war effort. But there is no denying the role played by the expanding institution of U.S. popular journalism and by "developments in American cultural history: the rise of lithography

---

[7] Italo Calvino. *Invisible Cities*, (New York: Mariner Books, 2013) p 29.

[8] Howard Zinn. *A People's History of the United States* (New York: Harper and Row, 1980) p 152.

[9] The newly independent state of Texas—"after agitation and aid from the United States"—had, of course, already seceded from Mexico in 1836 to be annexed by Congress in 1845.

and the advent of popular journalism. The Mexican War became the first event of its kind to be photographed, the first to be reported by war correspondents for mass circulation newspapers, and the first to be extensively recorded in lithographs intended for a broad audience."[10]

Those images, especially certain color engravings, some of them gathered in *Eyewitness to War: Prints and Daguerreotypes of The Mexican War*, are marked by a peculiar brand of Anglo-American romanticism that satisfied the growing desire for picturesque tourism and travel writing. It also consecrated those concepts of "rise" and "progress" and those increasing sublime feelings of nationalism in its recently christened form: Manifest Destiny. The prints survive as aesthetic precursors to what later coalesced as the dominant style of the Hudson River School. In large and small format painting, artists Frederic Church, Thomas Cole, Albert Bierstadt, and others offered "an experience in which the viewer [was] all but obliged to focus on the artist's […] technique." These works were intended to register the awe-inspiring appearance of nature, but they were also "a record of a second nature… an embodiment of a rarefied artistic sensibility" and therefore "inseparable from the dynamics of class formation"[11] Even as those works produced by earlier engravers

---

[10]   Martha A. Sandweiss, Rick Stewart, and Ben W. Huseman. *Eyewitness to War: Prints and Daguerreotypes of the Mexican War*, (Washington D.C.: Smithsonian Institution Press, 1989) p 4.

[11]   Alan Wallach. "For a Social History of the Hudson River School," *American Art*, Vol. 31, No. 2, Summer 2017. Also relevant here is Laura Hinton's assertion that "The picturesque was both empirical and fantastical. True to picturesque method, the Hudson River School landscapes …embodied this amalgam of empirical 'realism' and Romantic faith. The spectator of a typical Hudson River School canvas absorbs two contrary functions: that of the mimeticist expecting 'the world' to be contained by a 'picture', and that of the emotive fantasist seeking a more ethereal realm." Some Hudson River School painters were "artists on a mission. They intended to eternalize a wilderness that was slated for devastation. Sanford Robinson Gifford and Albert Bierstadt, in particular, were among America's first environmentalists who fought for wilderness preservation. They specifically used their Hudson River School art to combat the wilderness's appropriation under Jacksonian expansionism. They mythologized the land they depicted." Laura Hinton, "The Return of Nostalgia: A Fetishistic Spectator in Leslie Scalapino's *The Return of Painting* and the Hudson River School of Art," *Textual Practice*, 24:2, 2010, p 226.

consisted of journalistic assignments, and even though such scenes were outside the territorial limits of the United States, the natural settings of Mexico presented viewers with the desirable qualities of a regenerate sublime frontier. The elements are so rendered: the sweeping panoramic view, the luminous atmosphere and lush flora in George Wilkins Kendall's *Bombardment of Vera Cruz*; the abrupt topography of the central plateau, the maguey plants and the distant twin volcanoes Popocatépetl and Iztaccihuatl in Adolphe-Jean-Baptiste Bayot's *Molino del Rey—Attack Upon the Molino*, or his rendering of *Genl. Scott's Entrance into Mexico*, a striking depiction of the zócalo and its impressive viceregal architecture under an immense, transparent sky; or the imposing castle looming in the background of James Walker's *The Storming of Chapultepec*.[12]

More prominent than the accurate or inaccurate physical documentation is the patent fact that these prints are, almost all of them, literally occupied by the romantic "heroes" of these landscapes; that is, the U.S. forces in uniform that vie for pictorial space. The engravings visually manifest and generate public feelings akin to those published in the *New York Herald* (1847): that the "universal Yankee nation can regenerate and disenthrall the people of Mexico in a few years; and we believe it is a part of our destiny to civilize that beautiful country."[13] The U.S. Mexican War betrayed a counterpart fascination in travel accounts that disclosed another Mexico to readers in the United States. In his *Incidents of Travel in Central America, Chiapas, and Yucatan*, John Lloyd Stephens indicated the heretofore unknown expanse of the Mayan civilization in the Petén through a detailed description of its contemporary culture and ancient ruins, visually confirmed in engravings produced by his fellow explorer, the English artist Frederick Catherwood. Whether or not viewership of the prints and daguerreotypes depicting the Mexican War overlapped with that of Catherwood's published engravings, such competing images in nineteenth-century U.S. visual culture

---

[12] Some engravings were rendered by non-American mercenary artists (Bayot was French; Walker, English).

[13] Howard Zinn. *A People's History of the United States* (New York: Harper and Row, 1980) p 152.

suggest a sort of double dream; a narrative that pitted Mexico and the United States against each other as contending doubles of the New World. In one fantasy formation, Mesoamerica endowed the U.S. with an oblique form of antiquity; in another, diagnosed by Reginald Horsman,[14] it perpetuated the brutal delusion of Anglo-Saxon racial superiority.

3 Just as the advent of the daguerreotype and lithography corresponded to the North American Invasion of Mexico, the rise of the U.S. Film industry coincided with the Mexican Revolution, reflecting and altering the image surrounding Mexico's political upheaval. The figure of Pancho Villa provides a case in point.

> On 3 January 1914 [four years after the fall of dictator Porfirio Díaz and the various uprisings led simultaneously or alternately by Madero, Huerta, Carranza and Zapata] Pancho Villa signed an exclusive contract with the Mutual Film Corporation for $25,000. It was agreed that Villa would try to fight his battles in daylight and that no other film companies would be allowed on the battlefield. It was also stipulated that, if no satisfactory footage resulted from the battles, then Villa would restage them specifically for the camera....[U.S. journalists had earlier described Villa] as a criminal and a rapist, or extolled his bravery, strength and superiority, and placed him above the law.... But it was at the beginning of 1913 that the image of Villa as a providential and righteous social bandit began to take precedence over the rest. This romantic legend, which compared him to Robin Hood and Napoleon, became common currency in the United States.... To make the figure of General Villa stand out, Mutual had designed him a special uniform [convincing] him that cinema-goers would be surprised [if] the leader of the revolution did not look like a glorious guerrilla fighter. Until that moment Villa had not considered a military uniform to be of any importance. But now that he was a film star, he gave the matter due attention and allowed Mutual to have their way. Bizarrely, the general could use the uniform only in battle scenes filmed by the company, since it remained their property...[15]

---

[14] Widely considered by many institutions to be the first to critically engage with the origins of the United States and racialism. Cf. Reginald Horsman, *Race and Manifest Destiny* (Cambridge: Harvard University Press, 1982).

[15] Margarita de Orellana, *Filming Pancho: How Hollywood Shaped the Mexican Revolution* (London; New York: Verso, 2009) pp 39; 43; 53.

Mexican historian Margarita de Orellana depicts a pragmatic Villa, who sought the resources to sustain his army and found cinema as the means to this end. When offered additional money, to convert the documentary scenes into a great fictional film, he had no hesitations about cooperating with producers on the motion picture *The Life of General Villa*, going so far as to accept the starring role.[16] The feature film was to have been directed by D. W. Griffith but was finally completed by Christy Cabanne,[17] as Griffith was busy shooting *The Birth of a Nation*. The second part of the film—it had been dived into two parts—depicts the life of young Villa played by Raoul Walsh,[18] the kidnapping and murder of Villa's sister by a federal officer, his subsequent flight into the mountains, his hatred for the federal government, the beginning of his legend as a bandit, and the formation of his rebel forces, all of which led to the climax of the film, whereby Villa is finally proclaimed president of Mexico.

The end of the movie, de Orellana notes, coincided with the latent desire of a U.S. government that, in 1914, had supported Villa's forces with money and arms. She continues, "President Woodrow Wilson considered Villa the kind of leader that was necessary in Mexico at the time: a revolutionary who could stabilize social conditions,"[19] while keeping his hands off North American property. Wilson suspected, however, that Villa would eventually cease to honor foreign interests in Mexico, and the U.S. government's political reversals regarding Villa were portrayed by Hollywood in a series of subsequent films. As de Orellana points out: "The social bandit, the just man in whom the Americans placed their hopes, would become definitively the 'savage thirsty for American blood.'"[20] In a fictional film called *Liberty: A Daughter of the United States*, where

---

[16]   *Ibid.*, p 58.

[17]   William Christy Cabanne, screenwriter, film director, and silent actor who worked with actors such as Shirley Temple and Bela Lugosi. He also spent time in the Navy and made at least two films about the military, including *The Midshipman*.

[18]   D. W. Griffith cast Walsh as John Wilkes Booth in *The Birth of a Nation*.

[19]   Margarita de Orellana, *Filming Pancho: How Hollywood Shaped the Mexican Revolution* (London; New York: Verso, 2009) p 40.

[20]   *Ibid.*, p 64.

"Pancho Lopez" is a thinly-veiled Villa,

> [t]he main protagonist, Liberty, is a young American woman and clearly an allegorical character. She is continually falling into the hands of Mexican bandits, then being rescued by the Americans. Pancho Lopez will do anything to obtain the money that he needs for his revolution and will stop at nothing to oust the Americans. He is represented as a bandit greedy for American blood and money. [He begins to lead] raids into the United States and kills US soldiers, fuelled [sic] by his hatred for America, which is presented as irrational.[21]

Tellingly, these movies were produced during the failed yearlong enterprise that was the United States Punitive Expedition meant to capture Pancho Villa.[22] In addition to the various other stereotypes that Hollywood was to continually perpetuate, the "Greaser" and the "Beautiful Senorita," among others, the curious combination of Villa and Hollywood,[23] on the ambiguous borders of reality and fiction, resulted in Villa's transformation first into "exotic truth," then "grotesque fact."[24]

4 Mexico played a critical role in the occurrence of international modernism, and in the decades that followed the Revolution, it became the setting for one of the most influential cultural experiments of the early twentieth century, with a host of nationals actively forging a revision of the regional ethos: a questioning of inherited notions as to Mexico's past that would reverberate in nearly every aspect of the country's written, performing, cinematic and plastic arts. After ten years of debilitating violence, Mexico, now under the presidency of

---

[21]   *Ibid.*, p 94.

[22]   *Ibid.* Also known as the Pancho Villa Expedition or the Mexican Punitive Expedition, the United States Army's Punitive Expedition took place between March 1916 and February 1917.

[23]   Other characterizations of Pancho Villa include Pedro Lopez, also known as The Butcher, in *Lieutenant Danny, U.S.A.* In addition, animated cartoons of the period depicted Villa being captured by U.S. heroes.

[24]   This mythic, if labile, making and unmaking of Villa would later become the subject of Robert Motherwell's boisterous abstract parody entitled *Pancho Villa, Dead and Alive* (1943), one of several Mexican paintings which emerged from his summer visits to Mexico with the Chilean surrealist painter Roberto Matta.

General Álvaro Obregón, was prepared to begin a material, spiritual and even aesthetic reconstruction. After a five-year exile in the United States, during the turbulent revolutionary decade, the cultural philosopher José Vasconcelos returned to Mexico to form part of Obregón's cabinet as Minister of Education—recruiting artists and intellectuals to contribute to the goals of the "new orientations of art and culture": "Ideas in progress ranged from irrigation plans to free breakfasts in the schools to serum laboratories and baby clinics and wall newspapers and beggars' hostels and art for the people and cheap editions of Plutarch." [25]

The armed conflict and military campaigns of the battle-torn Revolution had attracted journalists like John Reed and Carleton Beals. The prospect of directly witnessing the intense activity of the post-revolutionary Renaissance, a "mystique" as it was often called among Mexicans, enticed a second host of internationals in the 1920s, 1930s, and 1940s, including artists like Sergei Eisenstein and French surrealists Antonin Artaud and André Breton, who would serve as both observers and participants in the flourishing artistic activity. The so-called mystique was more concretely a nation-building enterprise predicated on a cultural program launched by José Vasconcelos.

> Vasconcelos had returned to Mexico as rector of the National University of Mexico, and later as Minister of Public Education (1921–24). In that capacity, he gathered artists and intellectuals to contribute to the emerging revolutionary culture: a progressive agenda aimed to provide social welfare, widespread literacy, and art for the people. The muralist movement in Mexican art flourished thanks to the support of Vasconcelos who commissioned painters to cover walls of public buildings with nationalist content... [He] and the muralist painters sought to reverse the aesthetic and intellectual dependency of Mexico on foreign models by firmly grounding art and culture in native tradition. *Indigenismo*, that is, a renewed attention to Mexico's ancient civilizations and indigenous culture, linked art to the nation-building project, even as indigenous subjects could be portrayed emptied of active historical participation and meaning. Mexico was forging an image of itself by foregrounding the value of its Indian ethnicity, its ancient ruins, its manual arts, the country's long history and volcanic landscape, as well as with mythologies old and new.[26]

---

[25]   Anita Brenner. *The Wind That Swept Mexico* (Austin: University of Texas Press, 1984) p 64.

[26]   Mary Coffey and Roberto Tejada, introductory note to "The Cosmic Race" by José

The trajectories of Diego Rivera, José Clemente Orozco, and David Alfaro Siqueiros were of pivotal importance to Mexico's own artistic development, and insomuch as these artists were commissioned to undertake several mural projects in U.S., they had a demonstrable impact on visual arts produced in the United States during the 1930s. As well, this renewed interest in Mexico's autochthonous past coincided with further explorations at the various archeological sites in the central plateau and in the Yucatan peninsula, undertaken primarily by Manuel Gamio, one of the founders of modern archaeology in Mexico.[27] In short, Mexico was inventing itself, generating an array of icons and archetypes—the murals, the indigenous subsoil, the manual arts, an attention to the ruins and the abrupt landscape, as well as a pantheon of ancient and contemporary mythologies—that compelled artists in Mexico and from the United States.[28]

Vasconcelos; in Elaine O'Brien, *Modern Art in Africa, Asia, and Latin America: An Introduction to Global Modernisms* (Chichester, West Sussex: Wiley-Blackwell, 2013) pp 402–3.

[27]   For a comparative discussion of Mexican anthropologist Manuel Gamio and U.S writer Katherine Anne Porter, see José E. Limón, "Nation, Love, and Labor Lost: Katherine Anne Porter and Manuel Gamio," in *American Encounters: Greater Mexico, the United States, and the Erotics of Culture* (Boston: Beacon Press, 1998) pp 35–72.

[28]   A brief survey of the relevant scholarship includes: James Oles and Marta Ferragut. *South of the Border: Mexico in the American Imagination, 1917–1947* (Washington: Smithsonian Institution Press, 1993); Anthony Lee. *Painting on the Left: Diego Rivera, Radical Politics, and San Francisco's Public Mural* (Berkeley: University of California Press, 1999), Bruce Campbell. *Mexican Murals in Times of Crisis* (Tucson: University of Arizona Press, 2003); Renato González Mello and Diane Miliotes (eds.). *José Clemente Orozco in the United States, 1927–1934* (New York: W. W. Norton & Company, 2002); Esther Gabara. *Errant Modernism: The Ethos of Photography in Mexico and Brazil* (Durham: Duke University Press, 2008); Guisela Latorre. *Walls of Empowerment: Chicana/o Indigenist Murals of California* (Austin: University of Texas Press, 2008); Anna Indych-López. *Muralism without Walls: Rivera, Orozco, and Siqueiros in the United States, 1927–1940* (Pittsburgh: University of Pittsburgh Press 2009); Adriana Zavala. *Becoming Modern, Becoming Tradition: Women, Gender, and Representation in Mexican Art* (University Park, Pa: Pennsylvania State University Press, 2010); Mary K. Coffey. *How a Revolutionary Art Became Official Culture: Murals, Museums, and the Mexican State* (Durham: Duke University Press, 2012); Alejandro Anreus, Robin A. Greeley, and Leonard Folgarait (eds.). *Mexican Muralism: A Critical History* (Berkeley: University of California Press, 2012). eds.

5 A lasting influence Mexico exerted in the visual arts abroad was by means of its murals—especially those by Orozco, Rivera and Siqueiros—painted in the 1930s throughout several cities in the United States: Orozco's *Prometheus* at Pomona College, his work at the New School for Social Research and Dartmouth College; Rivera at the California School of Fine Arts, the Detroit Institute of the Arts, Rockefeller Center and the New Worker's School; as well as the various projects Siqueiros painted in Los Angeles.

One result was in the policy of public patronage for the arts that flourished in the United States during the 30s, via the short-lived Public Works of Art Project and the subsequent Works Project Administration. This government-sponsored movement provided employment and "spiritual stimulus" to hundreds of artists in "every state of the Union," thereby recognized "as useful and valuable members of the body politic."[29] A personal friend of Roosevelt's, the painter George Biddle wrote to the president in 1933 stating that:

> The Mexican artists have produced the greatest national school of mural painting since the Italian Renaissance. Diego Rivera tells me it was only possible because Obregón allowed Mexican artists to work at plumber's wages in order to express on the walls of the government buildings the social ideals of the Mexican revolution. The younger artists of America are conscious as they have never been of the social revolution that our country and civilization are going through; and they would be very eager to express these ideals in a permanent form if they were given the government's cooperation …. And I am convinced that our mural art … can soon result … in a vital national expression.[30]

As a consequence, artists like Arshile Gorky, Stuart Davis, and eventually Philip Guston, who had worked with Siqueiros, created works in the WPA division, following the example set by the muralist

by Erin M. Curtis, Jessica Hough, and Guisela Latorre. *¡Murales Rebeldes!: L.A. Chicana/Chicano Murals under Siege* (Los Angeles, CA: Angel City Press 2017).

[29]   Edward Bruce. "Implications of the Public Works of Art Project," *The American Magazine of Art*, Vol. 27, No. 3 (March 1934) pp 113.

[30]   George Biddle papers, 1910–1969, Reel 3621, Archives of American Art, Smithsonian Institution, Washington D.C. 26 May 2018.

agenda in Mexico.[31] Even as he disavowed the influence of his Mexican counterparts, American regionalists Thomas Hart Benton showed a studious understanding of Rivera and Orozco. Evidence of this is in the mural he painted at the New School for Social Research, *America Today*, particularly in his sculptural approach to figuration and his use of cubist perspective, as well as the flat layering and dissolution into caricature of naturalistic form. Benton's nostalgic America differs from the Mexicans' often violent visual encounter with a usable past, but both the American Scene painters and the Mexican muralists coincided in their efforts to define their respective identities through a proposed national style.

U.S. printmakers Caroline Durieux, Howard Cook, Elizabeth Catlett, Marion Greenwood, George Biddle, Fletcher Martin, John Langley Howard, Alexandre Hogue, Edgar Dorsey Taylor and Will Barnet had either lived and worked in Mexico, many at the Taller de Gráfica Popular, or directly with Orozco, Siqueiros or Rivera.[32] The particularity of Mexican muralism yielded effect as well for the New York School during the subsequent decade. At the Experimental Workshop he directed between 1935–36 in New York, David Alfaro Siqueiros demonstrated the use of Duco and other industrial paints and recommended the drip technique to generate images: among artists in attendance was Jackson Pollock whose eventual "action paintings" betray a debt to the techniques he encountered with Siqueiros.[33] So do pages from Pollock's 1938–1939 sketchbooks, the lithograph *Coal Mine-West Virginia*, and the early painting *Woman*. These works reveal aspects of the jagged mark-making, the cluster of anonymous human forms, and the imposing abstract architectural environs common in the drawings of Orozco—the stronger influence according to Pollock himself.

---

[31]   Dore Ashton. "Mexican Art of the Twentieth Century," in *Mexico: Splendors of Thirty Centuries* (New York: The Metropolitan Museum of Art, 1990) p 557.

[32]   Prints by these artists are gathered and discussed in Reba and Dave Williams, *The Mexican Muralists and Prints* (New York: The Spanish Institute, 1990).

[33]   Edward Lucie-Smith. *Art of the 1930s: The Age of Anxiety.* (New York: Rizzoli International Publications, 1985) p 13.

6 Langston Hughes, Edward Weston, Anita Brenner, and Kenneth Rexroth were among the North American writers and artists who first arrived in Mexico during the early 1920s. Hughes describing the scene in Mexico City:

> I never lived in Greenwich Village in New York, so its bohemian life—in the old days when it was bohemian—was outside my orbit. Although once I lived for a year in Montmartre in Paris, I lived there as a worker, not an artist. So the nearest thing to *la vie boheme* was my winter in Mexico when my friends were almost all writers and artists like Juan de la Cabada, María Izquierdo, Luis Cardoza y Aragón, Manuel [Álvarez] Bravo, Rufino Tamayo... Most of my friends were almost always broke, or very nearly so. But then we didn't care.[34]

The testimony sheds light on the bohemian appeal of Mexico for these and later artists.

Another attraction was the post-Revolutionary political and aesthetic agenda, particularly for a tenacious writer like Kenneth Rexroth (1905–1982) who, even in his youth, possessed a "profound sense of [...] responsibility and an awareness of the need for social change."[35] In *An Autobiographical Novel*, written by the poet in his 60s, Rexroth recalls a brief scene from his formative past when the poet visits the Mexican capital and the city of Oaxaca during the early years of the country's social reconstruction and cultural renascence. Recounting the difficulty of travel from the U.S. to Mexico in the 1920s—through El Paso, first by car, then by train, insomuch as there were "no through roads in those days from the American border to Mexico City"—Rexroth arrives to observe that, even as the "political revolution was dying down... intellectually and artistically Mexico was at the height of the wave."[36] His impressions betray the particularity of the capital's intellectual milieu, with an assessment

---

[34]   Langston Hughes. *The Collected Works of Langston Hughes, Volume 14, Autobiography: "I Wonder as I Wander."* Edited with an Introduction by Joseph McLaren (Missouri: University of Missouri Press, 2003) p 290.

[35]   Kenneth Rexroth, *An Autobiographical Novel* (Garden City, New York: Doubleday & Company, Inc., 1966) p viii.

[36]   *Ibid.*, p 344.

of his interactions with Mexico's eminent artists, the muralists Diego Rivera, José Clemente Orozco, and David Alfaro Siqueiros:

> It was all very free and open, even riotous. Nobody had become so famous as to be inaccessible. The person I liked best was Siqueiros, in those days a still completely genuine man, uncorrupted by politics. Orozco was the most impressive, but he was inaccessible, not out of snobbery but because of his lonely greatness. Rivera was simply dreadful, even then.[37]

Among the personalities that comprised Mexico City's bohemian society, a motley band of artists, intellectuals, "armed politicians, bullfighters, criminals, prostitutes, and burlesque girls,"[38] the 20-year-old Rexroth especially warms to an Austrian friend of photographer Tina Modotti, and he accompanies his new companion—a woman he never names but describes as "a tall, well-fleshed, natural pale blonde" and "one of the city's most expensive prostitutes"—to the city of Oaxaca.[39] Rexroth has few kind words in his autobiographical account

---

[37]   *Ibid.*

[38]   *Ibid.*

[39]   Rachel Adams. *Continental Divide: Remapping the Cultures of North America,* (Chicago: University of Chicago Press. 2010) p 133 "When Kenneth Rexroth recalled his visit to Mexico in his 1964 *Autobiography Novel,* he wrote, "the most spectacular person of all was a photographer, artist, model, high-class courtesan, and Mata Hari for Comintern, Tina Modotti. She was the heroine of a lurid political assassination and was what I guess is called an international beauty." Rexroth's unflattering description synthesizes the competing myths that surround Modotti, who has been claimed as a feminist heroine, a promiscuous seductress, and a hardened Stalinist. Her best-known photographs have been turned into icons that are even more familiar than the artist herself: after a bidding war with rock star Madonna, *Roses* was bought by fashion mogul Susie Tompkins, who converted it into a label for her Espirit clothing line; *Woman with Flag* inspired a 1993 sculpture by the artist Maria Grazia Collini and a well-known fashion shoot by photographer Christophe Kutner. The mythologization of Modotti and her work has obstructed a more complex understanding of her accomplishments." For a more thorough discussion of Edward Weston and Tina Modotti—their personal and professional relationship, as well as the status of their work to the history of photography and to questions of cultural difference and sexual drive in Mexico—see my *National Camera: Photography and Mexico's Image Environment*, Minneapolis: University of Minnesota Press, 2009) especially the chapter "Experiment in Related Form: Weston, Modotti, and the Aims of Desire," pp 55–94.

for the person or art of Modotti, no matter that her photographic images in those years had radicalized the aims and specificity of the medium, nor that it is Modotti to whom he owes meeting his new erotic interest. Between days and evenings spent primarily in a cheap Oaxaca hotel room with his Austrian confidante, Rexroth perceives the region to be at the "height of its revolution and practically an independent country," and in a mood of near delirious festivity: "We danced most of the nights, and when we weren't dancing we were singing and watching other people dance, and falling asleep in the dawn, exhausted with lovemaking, our heads full of guitar music. When the two weeks were over I came straight back to the States.... I have never had any desire to go back to Mexico."[40]

At odds with *An Autobiographical Novel* are Rexroth's love lyric "Oaxaca 1925" and another poem entitled "Gradualism." The wake of Mexico's 1910–1920 Revolution provided Rexroth with a context for expressing contrary desires about whether geographic and cultural locations are ever at pace with worldwide political transformation. The latter poem relates the disproportionate systems that govern physical intimacy and social change.

GRADUALISM

We slept naked
On top of the covers and woke
In the chilly dawn and crept
Between the warm sheets and made love
In the morning you said
"It snowed last night on the mountain"
High up on the blue-black diorite
Faint orange streaks of snow
In the ruddy dawn
I said
"It has been snowing for months
All over Canada and Alaska
and Minnesota and Michigan

[40]   Kenneth Rexroth. *An Autobiographical Novel* (Garden City, New York: Doubleday & Company, Inc., 1966) pp 344–5. Rexroth adds, as well in hindsight: "I loathe Mexican food which has always seemed to me only a slight improvement on Northern Ute."

> Right now wet snow is falling
> In the morning streets of Chicago
> Bit by bit they are making over the world
> Even in Mexico even for us"[41]

7   The first of Langston Hughes' several trips to Mexico was specifically to see his father who—circumventing racial prejudice he faced in the United States—had emigrated to Mexico where he eventually prospered. In addition to the artists he mentioned above, Langston Hughes associated as well with photographer Henri Cartier-Bresson, with whom he shared an apartment, and the poet Xavier Villaurrutia who wrote an important article about Hughes and translated a number of his poems. Hughes' image of an indigenous *marchanta* in "Mexican Market Woman" is the expressions of a concern similarly reflected in Edward Weston's photograph *Woman Seated on a Petate* of 1926.

MEXICAN MARKET WOMAN

> This ancient hag
> Who sits upon the ground
> Selling her scanty wares
> Day in, day round,
> Has known the high wind-swept mountains,
> And the sun has made
> Her skin so brown.[42]

The Mexican artistic revolution had rhetorically privileged Mexico's indigenous roots, and Hughes' poem tenders an identification with the brown-skinned subject of his poem, as ancient as the ground that sustains her. It also triangulates his U.S.-specific experience back into the scene so as to reflect a kinship version of what W.E.B. Dubois specified as that "sense of always looking at one's self through the eyes of others, of measuring one's soul by the tape of a world that looks on in amused contempt and pity. One ever feels his twoness—an American,

---

[41]   Kenneth Rexroth. *The Collected Shorter Poems* (New York: New Directions, 1966) p 8.

[42]   Langston Hughes. *The Collected Poems of Langston Hughes*, ed. Arnold Rampersad (New York: Vintage: Random House, 1995) p 25.

a Negro; two souls, two thoughts, two unreconciled strivings; two warring ideals in one dark body, whose dogged strength alone keeps it from being torn asunder."[43] In the briefest of imagistic lines Hughes suggests a dynamic of rootedness and diaspora wherein African-American double-consciousness is now legislator of a Mesoamerican somewhere, a timely locus of brutal historical displacements.

8 Mexico compelled Weston for very different reasons. From his home in Glendale, California, he had written Alfred Stieglitz: "Well the future will tell—I leave for Mexico City in late March to start life anew—why—I hardly know myself—but I go—I shall always work–seek–experiment …."[44] Tina Modotti, his partner in life and art, had written from Mexico to persuade him to join her, particularly now that an exhibition of his photographs had been received with excitement. Weston's work in Mexico generated portraits of artists and personalities: *Diego Rivera Smiling*, Diego's then wife *Guadalupe Marín Rivera*, the nudes of Anita Brenner, *Rose Covarrubias*, and a striking portrait of Nahui Olin (Carmen Mondragón), a poet[45] and painter

[43] W.E.B. Dubois. *The Souls of Black Folk* (New York: Washington Square Press, 1970) p 3.

[44] Edward Weston letter to Alfred Stieglitz, 21 February 1923, Box 51, Folder 1234, YCAL MSS 85, Alfred Stieglitz / Georgia O'Keeffe Archive, Beinecke Rare Book and Manuscript Library, Beinecke Digital Collections, Yale University Libraries, New Haven, CT, 26 May 2018.

[45] Nahui Olin (Carmen Mondragón). *Óptica verbal: poemas dinámicos* (Mexico City: Ediciones Mexico Moderno, 1922). For further discussion of Olin/Mondragón, see the exhibition catalog *Nahui Olin: Una mujer de los tiempos modernos* (Mexico City: Instituto Nacional de Bellas Artes, 1992). Women of this time period in Mexico, including Tina Modotti and Frida Kahlo, are too often framed in view of relationships with men. Recent critical re-evaluations have served as correctives and provided these artists/writers/critics their proper place not merely alongside these men, but on their own critical terms. As noted in *Anita Brenner: A Mind of Her Own* by Susannah Joel Glusker, "The bibliography on the lives of women artists in Mexico is expanding rapidly as consciousness of women's issues grows and the outstanding women of the twenties are recognized. Hayden Herrera's book on Frida Kahlo was among the first to popularize women artists in Mexico. The most popular women, in terms of the number of books are Frida Kahlo, Tina Modotti, Antonieta Rivas Mercado, and Nahui Olin. Frida and Tina are full-blown legends, mysterious, controversial, wild." p 58. Critical to this bibliography is Adriana Zavala's *Becoming Modern, Becoming Tradition: Women, Gender, and Representation in Mexican Art* (University Park, Pa: Pennsylvania State University Press, 2010).

in her own right, though often remembered as "the tempestuous Mexican girl raised in Paris who was the mistress of the painter Dr. Atl."[46]

Less conspicuous were Weston's still-life photographs of Mexican folk art and handcrafted objects. His resistance to picturesque aspects of the country led to a fascination with the working-class culture and vernacular art of *pulquerias* and to the formal qualities inherent in Mexican *arte popular*. Photographs like *Juguetes Mexicanos: Ragdoll and Sombrerito* (1925), *Petate Woman in Front of an Aztec Chair* (1926), and *Heaped Black Ollas in the Oaxaca Market* (1926) were meant to infuse the documentation of Mexico's manual arts with formal invention. The striking spatial illusion of another image, *Hat and Shoes* (1926), destabilizes the visual centering of the composition with a deceptive impression of flatness despite evidence of depth in the corner backdrop floor and wall. Weston wrote in his *Daybook* that "Life rhythms felt in no matter what, become symbols of the whole."[47] Handcrafted articles serve as stand-ins for the native Mexican hands and bodies whose labor gave way to Weston's view. His resulting photographs of those assembled objects honor the vernacular, the native, the local, and the indigenous; but even as they aim to encapsulate a cultural cadence, they reflect an insufficiency. They tell of the encounter with folk sources as a foreignness; a "symbol of the whole" never altogether satisfied.

Weston's pictures of *pulquerías*—a "plebian drinking shop where only pulque is consumed"[48]—circle back to Anita Brenner who had accepted a commission from the "former rector of the National University of Mexico, Dr. Alfonso Pruneda" to write "an investigation of Mexican art, placing the author in charge. The two photographers who shared this commission [were] Edward

---

46 Amy Conger. *Edward Weston in Mexico, 1923–1926.* (Albuquerque: University of New Mexico Press, 1983) p 32.

47 Edward Weston. *The Daybooks of Edward Weston*, ed. Nancy Newhall (Millerton, N.Y.: Aperture, 1973) p 154.

48 Anita Brenner. *Idols Behind Altars: Modern Mexico and its Cultural Roots* (Mineola, New York: Dover Publications, Inc., 2002) p 171.

Weston and Tina Modotti."[49] Published in 1929, *Idols Behind Altars* popularized five hundred years of Mexican art and history, aimed primarily for a U.S. audience, even as it advanced a model of cultural anthropology that sought to understand processes determined by the colonial experience. Moreover, Brenner analyzed pre-conquest materials through the lens of post-revolutionary values, modern art and pedagogy, and contemporary folk practices.

The book is rarely recognized for what is arguably its greatest merit. *Idols Behind Altars* is a modernist literary work of embedded cultural interpretation, a form whose dynamic interplay of vertiginous prose, graphic design elements, and photographs, of alternate clarity and ambivalence, made by Weston and Modotti. The writing animates the perspective of a diasporic woman who acknowledges attachments that point back to a Mexican caregiver, Nana Serapia. Brenner was born to Jewish American parents of Latvian origin in Aguascalientes, Mexico, and she witnessed first-hand the Revolution's bloody armed conflict before the age of eleven, when her family fled Mexico to take up residence in Texas. Nana Serapia's figures of speech and folk histories emboldened Brenner in her writing to respect the forms and insights of vernacular knowledge and its particular attunements to the grain of cultural storytelling. Brenner's Mexican sentences enliven scenes and historical accounts that cannot be separated from the shape of sight and sound. The metaphorical, gestural, and syntactic technique she employs in her cultural descriptions perform a refiguring of cultural objects and actors that compress vast sequences into an argument that cannot be detached from its internal structure, "the stage of linguistic semblance, an enactment of language [...] replaced by a *vocalization of the subject*."[50] The unique enactments of her prose reflect a complex capacity to translate between composite legacies and cultural temperaments:

---

[49]   *Ibid* p 7.

[50]   Michel de Certeau. "Vocal Utopias," *Representations*, No. 56, Special Issue: The New Erudition (Autumn, 1996) pp 41.

If Brenner's story is perhaps the most successful one of the women involved in the intellectual, artistic, and political life of Mexico in this period, it is in large part due to her position as a bohemian with what might be called a "hybrid identity": an American, a Mexican, and a Jew, equally at ease with the artistic and political circles in both Mexico and New York.[51]

Brenner's experiences of dispersion provided a unique vantage point into the uneven remainders surviving from the violent enforcement of Spanish colonial ceremonies and customs instituted into indigenous cultural and ritual life. One remarkable chapter of *Idols Behind Altars* is an art-historical, ethnographic, and literary account of that particularly Mexican cultural form, *pulque*—a pre-conquest beverage Brenner describes as a "milky, acrid, pungent intoxicant"[52]—at once the political economy of production and consumption, and the specific art and life practices to which the product gives way. Brenner identifies the double exploitation of peasants who harvest the sap from the maguey plant. They extract the honey thereafter brewed and fermented to produce fortunes for *criollo* aristocrats, Mexicans of European heritage who own the means of production but who dismiss the commodity as fitting only for the working classes. She reports: "'Peons are machines that run on pulque,' hacendados have often said."[53] Her understanding also allows her to appreciate the complex cultural layers contained in the vernacular form of the murals that grace the walls and facades of *pulquerías*, paintings that Weston and Modotti photographed for the publication of *Idols Behind Altars*:

> In pulquería art painter and owner collaborate with their public to produce a national property....The fusion, the Spanish-Indian image, is in the scenic panels which sometimes dethrone abstract art and use it as a frame....

51   Masha Salazkina, *In Excess: Sergei Eisenstein's Mexico* (Chicago: The University of Chicago Press, 2009) p 83. "In the course of the 1920s and 1930s, Brenner moved back and forth between New York and Mexico, operating as a general impresario and interpreter for the Mexican arts and for the Mexican Revolution in both countries. In 1927 she got in touch with Frances Flynn Paine, art agent for the Rockefellers, to do an exhibition (which took place in 1928–29 at the Art Center in New York) bringing together the largest number of works by Mexican artists to date, at the same time as she published *Idols Behind Altars*." p 82.

52   Anita Brenner. *Idols Behind Altars: Modern Mexico and its Cultural Roots* (Mineola, New York: Dover Publications, Inc., 2002) p 171.

53   *Ibid.*, p 173.

The small-town pulquería artist copies his metropolitan fellow-craftsman; but the metropolitan takes his theme and imagery from the peasant.[54]

Brenner lends critical ear and discernment to the relation between regional geography, the manual arts, and native song. She comprehends *corridos* as a mode of folk history and vernacular journalism that adopts ballad structure; and, more keenly, the marvel of subaltern resistance that is the *vacilada*, a form of word-play derision that doubles as a nihilistic philosophy of comprehensive doubt, a "caricature without moral."[55]

> The magic compact ring of voices spirals on sob and falsetto wail around the melody and tale. Mexican mood. Mood of poetry in twilight, landscape, gray, grayer, purple and black, burnt at the edges; human with a small bell, and a swathed conic hatted bundle hedged against a black doorway making a tiny musical lament. Mood of poetry in quiet dawn, when the sun stripes the sky and the bulls scratch their flanks saplings and chew clover fodder. Mood of noon, a singing screaming frying pan and a day of white light and keen black.... A blind beggar stumbling through the mob, piping on a tin whistle an *ora pro nobis*, over and over again. All the world asking lodging at everyone else's door, and a child with a hungry face selling sparkler firecrackers, "a rain of stars." Then a whoop and a crack of laughter.[56]

The *vacilada* is "a mestizo mask, fusion of bland Indian irony and Spanish picaresque baroqued by fantastic history to irresponsibility"[57] It is the brown cousin of the figure Michel Foucault described as that laughter inclined to shatter "all the familiar landmarks of my thought.... breaking up all the ordered surfaces and all the planes with which we are accustomed to tame the wild profusion of existing things...."[58] It transposes for Brenner the scope of poverty and suffering into an uprising of sensation that is the festival foreboding of elsewhere.

---

[54] *Ibid.*, pp 174; 176.

[55] *Ibid.*, p 180.

[56] *Ibid.*, p 179.

[57] *Ibid.*, p 184.

[58] Michael Foucault. *The Order of Things: An Archeology of the Human Sciences* (New York: Vintage Books, 1994) p xv.

9 ALTERNATE TAKES

9.1 Waldo Frank: "Mexico's immediate importance to all intelligent citizens of the United States [lies in the country's] "incarnate spirit of the soil" [as opposed to] "our culture in agony: the *rigor mortis* of death."[59]

9. 2 Hart Crane to Waldo Frank: "I doubt if I will ever be able to fathom the Indian really. It may be a dangerous quest, also. I'm pretty sure it is, in fact. But humanity is so unmechanized here still, so immediate and really dignified…that it is giving me an entirely fresh perspective."[60]

9.3 William Carlos William from *In the American Grain*: "No, we are not Indians but we are men of their world. The blood means nothing; the spirit, the ghost of the land moves the blood. It is we who ran to the shore naked who cried, 'Heavenly Man!' These are the inhabitants of our souls, our murdered souls that lie… agh."[61] And from "The Desert Music": "Why don't these Indians get over this nauseating / prattle about their souls and their loves and sing / us something else for a change?"[62]

9.4 Hart Crane's "The Sad Indian":

> Sad heart, the gymnast of inertia, does not count
> Hours, days—and scarcely sun and moon—
> The warp is in the woof—and his keen vision
> Spells what his tongue has had—and only that—
> How more?—but the lash, lost vantage—and the prison
> His fathers took for granted ages since—and so he looms
> Farther than his sun-shadow—farther than wings

---

[59]   Waldo Frank. "Pilgrimage to Mexico," *The New Republic*. 1 July 1931, Vol. 67 Issue 865, p 184.

[60]   Hart Crane. *The Letters of Hart Crane, 1916–1932*, ed. Brom Weber (New York: Hermitage House, 1952) p 371.

[61]   William Carlos Williams. *In the American Grain* (New York: Albert & Charles Boni, 1925) p 39.

[62]   William Carlos Williams. *The Collected Poems of William Carlos Williams, Volume II 1939–1962*, ed. Christopher J. MacGowan (New York: New Directions, 1986) p 280.

—Their shadows even—now can't carry him.
He does not know the new hum in the sky
And—backwards—is it thus the eagles fly?[63]

10 Neither Crane nor Williams are alone in their fascination and ambivalence concerning Mexico and the native Mexican. Indeed, their statements may be viewed as forming part of a tradition whereby the Indian serves as metaphor of "an incarnate spirit of the soil" in which rural Mexico was considered a "viable alternative to the individualism and competition, the concern for acquisition as an end in itself, mechanization and the specialization of labor, and the overproduction and unemployment of contemporary United States society."[64] Although it's tempting to speculate on Crane's legendary leap from the Orizaba into the Gulf of Mexico, there remains an undeniable resolve for both personal and artistic transformation in his letters and poems that emerged from his season in Mexico. He alludes to this self-fashioned exile in his poem "Purgatorio": "And are these stars—the high plateau—the scents / Of Eden—and the dangerous tree—are these / The landscape of confession—and if confession / So absolution?"[65]

If for Hughes, Williams and Crane, the Native serves an artifice to counter the reckless velocity of the U.S. technological ethos they rejected, the contrasts offered by Mexico's varied landscape provided a further source for excursions into the devotional. The volcanic mountain and its architectonic double—the Mesoamerican pyramid—assumed the quality of icon for at least two North American artists in the 1930s: the painter-poet Marsden Hartley and the photographer Laura Gilpin. Hartley's mid-career decision to work in Mexico on a Guggenheim Fellowship may well

---

[63] Hart Crane. *The Collected Poems of Hart Crane*, ed. Waldo D. Frank (New York: Liveright Publishing Corporation, 1933) p 145.

[64] Laurance P. Hulburt. *The Mexican Muralists in the United States* (Albuquerque: University of New Mexico Press, 1989) p 5. "*Pilgrimage* was the word (Waldo) Frank (had) used to describe the nature of the trips made by North American intellectuals to Mexico during the late 1920s and early 1930s, and 'devotional' the tone of the books that subsequently appeared."

[65] Hart Crane. *The Collected Poems of Hart Crane*, ed. Waldo D. Frank (New York: Liveright Publishing Corporation, 1933) p 151.

have been arbitrary, but in his work prior to Mexico, in the landscapes of his native Maine and the abstract numerical series, for example, a distinct tension attains between a "dispassionate and independent examination of structure and form"[66] and a strong underlying desire for individual emotive expression. There are indications in his letters of what might have led him to Mexico:

> [It is] a country burning with mystical grandeurs and mystical terrors. It is a country of constant geological upheavals where you feel that at any moment the earth itself might be swallowed up in its own terrifying heat, as if the vast underlying chemical purposes of nature were weary of static corrosion. [67]

Rhythmic markings and flattened shapes compose Hartley's Mexican oil paintings of 1932: *Carnelian Country*; *Earth Warming*; *Earth Cooling*; and *Popocatépetl, Spirited Morning*. They mirror a twin sense of grandeur and terror as depicted in the division of the canvas into dual fields: the blood-red earth that supports the dense cumulous sky. The oil on board *Earth Cooling* is representative of the sacrosanct attention and energetic markings that activate these works, akin to the grand hallucinatory tone used fifteen years later by Malcolm Lowry to describe the topography of *Under the Volcano*. In his novel, Lowry portrayed the landscape surrounding the volcanoes Popocatépetl and Ixtaccíhuatl as rising "clear and magnificent into the sunset." The geography is everywhere in motion: "The sun poured molten glass on the fields. The volcanoes seemed terrifying in the wild sunset... How continually, how startlingly, the landscape changed! Now the fields were full of stones: there was a row of dead trees."[68] Hartley also incorporated the Mesoamerican temples at Teotihuacan in *Cascade of Devotion* and *Tollan, Aztec Legend*, a visual statement about the superior force of time dramatized in the material survivals of a previous civilization.

---

[66]   Jeanne Hokin. "Volcanoes and Pyramids: Marsden Hartley," *Latin American Art* (Winter, 1990: 32–36) p 33.

[67]   *Ibid.*

[68]   Malcolm Lowry, *Under the Volcano* (Philadelphia and New York: J. B. Lippincott Company, 1965) pp 5; 9.

The desire to encapsulate ancient stone as permanence and continuity underscores photographs made by Laura Gilpin of the Mayan ruins and contemporary life in the Yucatan peninsula. Gilpin's life-long visual dialogue with various Native American peoples, the Navaho and Pueblo nations specifically, paralleled an interest in the ancient societies of Mesoamerica. Gilpin, writes her biographer, "wanted to see how ancient life related to contemporary life. She wanted to explore the meaning of an American past to which she and her contemporaries were linked through a common landscape, cultural artifacts and the accumulated knowledge of historical memory."[69] Her disinterest in the predominantly flat landscape of Chichén Itzá heightened her perception of monumentality and spatial relationships when photographing the ancient Mayan Toltec structures (*Temple of the Warriors from the Castillo*), arresting the formal patterns created by light, shadow and the surface quality of stone (*Sunburst, the Castillo*).

In one photograph, Gilpin captured—apparently by accident—a phenomenon that occurs at the Autumn equinox on the Castillo at Chichén Itzá: that is, the undulating shadow of a serpent down the staircase of the temple, underscoring a sign of motion that aligns with Octavio Paz's description of the stepped pyramid as "time transformed into geometry and space."[70] Overwhelmed and detained, Hartley's paintings and Gilpin's photographs foreground the pyramid as that which in Mesoamerican societies ensured continuity while submitting these structures in a resistance to time and its erosions. Similarly, the mythologies of landscape and pre-colonial served as subjects in work by George Oppen, William Bronk, Charles Olson, and Allen Ginsberg, among poets who journeyed to Mexico in the 1950s.[71]

---

[69] Martha A. Sandweiss. *Laura Gilpin: An Enduring Grace* (Fort Worth: Amon Carter Museum: 1986) p 61.

[70] Octavio Paz. *México en la obra de Octavio Paz* (3 vols.): *Vol. III*, (Mexico: Fondo de Cultura Económica 1987) p 52.

[71] Prior to this postwar nexus of U.S. writers who found in Mexico a metaphorical and narrative method, there is as well the case of Cuban midcentury poet, novelist, and essayist José Lezama Lima, whose poetry I discuss in essays that follow. In a rare excursion outside the island, Lezama Lima journeyed to Mexico by ship in 1949, arriving at the port of Veracruz and traveling from there to Cuernavaca and to the city of Taxco. Historian and critic Rafael Rojas argues that Mexico had been "a constant presence in Lezama

11 Having to flee FBI harassment for refusing to inform on the political activity of friends and associates, poet George Oppen moved to Mexico City where he lived from 1950 to 1958, making furniture as a means of living. Oppen had abandoned poetry after the 1934 publication of *Discrete Series*, and Mexico provided the poet elements that later informed his collections *The Materials* and *This in Which*. One of these concerns, the notion of habitat—both archaic and contemporary—is made explicit in "The Mayan Ground," where the sacred status of a place out of time further unsettles the terror

---

Lima's poetry, fiction, and essays. Mexico, in all its aspects, not only the Revolutionary dimension, from the *Popol Vuh* and Aztec cosmology, to the mural paintings of Orozco and Rivera, the poetry of Octavio Paz, and the novels of Carlos Fuentes, while clearly pointing back to New Spain's viceregal baroque and the pilgrimages of Fray Servando Teresa de Mier." Rafael Rojas. "México en Lezama," *La jornada semanal*, no. 787, 4 April 2010. (Author's translation).

In a letter written from Mexico to his mother in Havana, dated 18 October 1949, Lezama Lima, given to hyperbole but genuinely stunned by the sensory excitements to which the visual and sensual fields of Mexico can give way, writes:

> Dearest Mother: Bliss after bliss and green snow. I move from surprise to surprise, from much gladness to yet another gladness in which everything features like a wonder revealed. In the morning I discover the astonishing caliber of a restaurant and by afternoon, in the ecstasy of a marvel, yet another that surpasses the first. // I went to Taxco, city of silver and rose-colored stone, and for the first time I felt the emotion suited for an American Catholic to demonstrate his faith in appropriately superior form. // Here were built the only churches where the American has told the European how he is able to construct the motives and symbols of his faith. // The road to Cuernavaca and Taxco has a view of the most beautiful landscapes on display for man's eyes. // Mountains and valleys are hugged by incessant turns of the highway. // Nonetheless I miss home, and you above all. // As in the popular song I can say: my mother is ever on my mind. // My regards to Rosita and Eloísa and I recall the gusto of Baldemarra, kind and devoted. // Good Mother, pray for the best on my return travels. // A kiss on your forehead: from your son. // Joseíto.
> —José Lezama Lima, *Cartas a Eloísa y otra correspondencia* (Madrid: Verbum, 1998) p 37. (Author's translation)

Lezama Lima's travels in Mexico informed the American hemispheric poetics of his 1957 lectures that comprise *La expresión americana*. José Lezama Lima, *La expresión americana*, ed. Irlemar Chiampi (Mexico City: Fondo de Cultura Económica, 1993).

of intrusion. In reference to the Mayan books of *Chilám Balám*, the poem disavows accurate the accuracy of the calendar account so as to favor the circular return embodied by the feathered serpent Kukulkán.

THE MAYAN GROUND

... and whether they are beautiful or not there will be
no one to guard them in the days to come...

We mourned the red cardinal birds and the jeweled ornaments
And the handful of precious stones in our fields...

Poor savages
Of ghost and glitter. Merely rolling now

The tire leaves a mark
On the earth, a ridge in the ground

Crumbling at the edges
Which is terror, the unsightly

Silting sand of events—
Inside that shell, 'the speckled egg'
The poet wrote of that we try to break

Each day, the little grain,

Electron, beating,
Without cause,

Dry grain, father
Of all our fathers
Hidden in the blazing shell

Of sunlight—. Savages,

Savages, there is no mystery about them,
Given the rest of it,

They who have evolved
In it, and no one to shield them

Therefore in the days to come, in the ruts
Of the road

Or the fields, or the thin
Air of the berserk mountains—. But the god!

They said,
Moving on the waters,

The breeze on the water, feathery
Serpent,

Wind on the surface,
On the shallows

And the count of the calendar had become confused.

They said they had lost account
Of the *unrolling of the universe*

And only the people

Stir in the mornings
Coming from the houses, and the black hair

Of the women at the pump

Against the dawn
Seems beautiful. [72]

12 Arguably among the most important single poems of post-War poetry in English, Charles Olson's "The Kingfishers" anticipated the poet's arrival at Lerma, Campeche, in the winter of 1950 where he spent nearly six months investigating the design of Mayan civilization as part of a concern for that "theme [which] states that when our attentions change our culture changes."[73] Essayist Guy Davenport goes on to state:

[72]   George Oppen. *New Collected Poems*, (New York: New Directions, 2008) p 139.

[73]   Guy Davenport. *Geography of the Imagination* (Berkeley: North Point Press, 1982) p 83.

Olson uses the firm example of the Mayan cultures overgrown with jungles. The Mayan shift of attention was culturally determined: every fifty-two years they abandoned whole cities in which the temples were oriented towards the planet Venus, which edges its rising and setting around the ecliptic. The new city was literally a new way to look at a star...[74]

Though it practically defies synthesis, "The Kingfishers" is, above all, a poem whose accidents of juxtaposition vacillate between East and West; the Old World and the New; as well as the prospect of cultural revolution—including Mao in French translation. But, importantly, the poem moves between the rise of civilization from its origins ["the E on the stone": the epsilon on the omphalos stone at Delphi] and destruction, as in the Conquest of Mexico—in short, the image of a kingfisher hovering "between birth and the beginning of another fetid nest." It is the Heraclitean motion of change ["Into the same river..."] as the "discrete or continuous sequence of measurable events"[75] that constitutes history.

Visiting the nearby ruins of Chichén Itzá, Uxmal, and its surrounding sites, as well as local excavations near Lerma, Olson devoted his attention to "deciphering" the significance of Mayan hieroglyphs. In his letters to Robert Creeley, Olson registered his desire for an elsewhere in the immediate language he attributed to Mayan hieroglyphs: a "LANGUAGE AS STONE & CLAY... poems, to begin with, not yet established..."[76]—the archaic that, for George F. Butterick, doubled as Olson's "postmodern advance."[77] Olson titled a poem that sums up his call for the concrete "Abstract #1, Yucatán":

---

[74] *Ibid.*

[75] Charles Olson. "The Kingfishers," *The Collected Poems of Charles Olson: Excluding the Maximus Poems*, ed. George F. Butterick (Berkeley: University of California Press, 1997) pp 87; 90.

[76] Charles Olson, Robert Creeley, George F. Butterick, and Richard Blevins. *Charles Olson & Robert Creeley: The Complete Correspondence* (Santa Barbara: Black Sparrow Press, 1980) vol 5, p 109.

[77] George F. Butterick. "Charles Olson and the Postmodern Advance," *The Iowa Review*, Vol. 11, Issue 4 Fall 1980, p 8.

the fish in speech, or see
what, cut
in stone, starts, for
when the sea breaks, watch
watch: it is the
tongue, and

he who introduces the words (the
interlocutor) the
beginner of the word, he

you will find, he
has scales, he
gives off motion as
in the sun the wind the light, a fish
moves[78]

Allen Ginsberg's "Siesta in Xbalba," stands out as example of works composed by Beat Generation writers in their respective pilgrimages to Mexico. It orchestrates a meditation on the ruins of Uxmal, Chichén Itzá, and Palenque: a dark night of the soul in the "semblance of Eternity" and its manifestations in the anima of nature, the "illegible Scripture" of the Mayan glyphs, and a scene of animal transcendence. One deft passage—akin to a Gilpin photograph—transmits, through its reference to the ancient ruins, a dual longing for a returning elsewhere in the permanent present tense:

Yet these ruins so much
woke me to nostalgia
for the classic stations
of the earth,
the ancient continent
I have not seen
and the few years
of memory left
before the ultimate night
of war—

---

[78]   Charles Olson. *The Collected Poems of Charles Olson: Excluding the Maximus Poems* (Berkley: University of California Press, 1997) p 203.

as if these ruins were not enough,
as if man could go
no further before heaven
till he exhausted
the physical round
of his own mortality
in the obscure cities
hidden in the aging world[79]

13 In 1968, poet Jay Wright relocated to Mexico with his wife Lois Silber, and for nearly three years they made their home in Xalapa, Veracruz. Wright's attention to Mexico's history, and more broadly to New World cultural imaginations, feature in the astonishing works composed during his Mexican residence and after; double movements that drive horizons of the past as summoned in his poetic corpus to date. Published five years after his return from Mexico to the United States in 1971, Wright's 1976 book-length poem *Dimensions of History* unites diverse imaginaries of Africa and the Americas into a mythological, historical, and cross-cultural space of composition, a world system of syllabic vitality. The poem evokes a descent "by centuries, through faces of Toltec and Maya kin,"[80] radiating concentric circles that include the 1791 Haitian Revolution and its leader Henri Christophe (with an endnote reference to C.L.R. James's *The Black Jacobins*); the writer and abolitionist Frederick Douglass; the Mexican Roman Catholic priest and revolutionary leader José María Morelos who led the Mexican War of Independence; and the Spanish conquistador and colonial administrator Nuño de Guzmán, whose New World expedition failed to uncover the bounty of silver and gold he imagined awaiting him in the "Seven Cities of Cíbola," located in what is today New Mexico, Wright's birthplace. In the poem, as per the historic record, "Nuño de Guzman, governor of New Spain" and founder of the city of Culiacán, encounters Cabeza de Vaca and his companions, including the slave Esteban, or Estevan:

---

[79] Allen Ginsberg. *Reality Sandwiches 1953–1960* (San Francisco: City Lights Books, 1963) p 30.

[80] Jay Wright, *Dimensions of History* (Santa Cruz, California: Kayak Books, 1976) pp 19–20.

> Weary at Culiacán,
> he finds four sailors,
> lost in the search for the flowered
> end of things.
> Now, the friar takes the slave
> into the valley, and sends him on above.[81]

The image of Esteban twins across the centuries to evidence the brutal ironies in the "search for the flowered / end of things" that foreshadow New World histories of racial slavery. These are interlinked in the poem by a "shackled Black wrist [that] claps the clouds" and the words of Frederick Douglass: "I am your fellow man, but not your slave."[82] In Cabeza de Vaca's *Relación*, Esteban is depicted as the vanguard delegate tasked with duties of language acquisition and of serving as cultural intermediary between the Spaniards and indigenous peoples; bestowed with knowledge about the physical and human geographies of the land, although precariously subject to the antagonism that reconnaissance missions occasioned.[83] United to the phenomenon described by the title of the book's second section, "The Key that Unlocks Performance: Vision as Historical

---

[81]   *Ibid.*, p 28.

[82]   *Ibid.*, p 25.

[83]   On March 21, 1539, the Niza expedition arrived at the Río Mayo in present-day Sonora. There, Estevanico, apparently restless over the slow progress of the friar and his large party, was sent ahead as an advance scout. Separated by several days' travel from the friar and his entourage, Estevanico approached the Zuni pueblo of Hawikuh in western New Mexico where he was killed by numerous arrows fired into his body.
—*Handbook of Texas Online*, Donald E. Chipman, "Estevanico," accessed June 19, 2018.

Vera Kutzinski writes:

Estevan's death itself becomes a figure of writing, of that ambiguous acquisition of literacy that subverts historical chronology and inaugurates a new order in the form of a new set of historical and mythological allegiances....textual dwelling places of cultural exchange and transformation.
—Vera M. Kutzinski, Against the American Grain: Myth and History in William Carlos Williams, Jay Wright and Nicolas Guillén (Baltimore: Johns Hopkins University Press, 1987) p 121.

Dimension," Wright's poetic field sets Mexico into motion in an unleashing of historical times and locations that in turn give way to an oracular journey akin, for Wright at the level of lines and stanzas, to the castaway wanderings of Cabeza de Vaca and Esteban.

In a 1983 poem, "Zapata and the Egúngún Mask,"[84] Wright's poetic persona exists variously embodied and in the throes of transfiguration, now the "babe of slaves, my Yoruba shuffle and song,"[85] now the "Morelos Indian"[86] of Emiliano Zapata. The historical Mexican Revolutionary doubles as a "night body"[87] in search of the hidden figures that "trust your exile / to my strangeness."[88] This condition of self-foreignness over weeks and years make it possible to enter the day in order to begin the "sixteenth discourse on red."[89] Stanzas in Spanish feature throughout, but the boldest expression cuts the space of the opening line: "En agua divina en hoguera nací: soy mexicano"[90] [In divine water in blaze I was born: I am Mexican]. The red of blaze and "blood's ascendance"[91] include the conquest and decimation of native peoples in the destruction of "Aztec fire,"[92] the substance of Christianity in crucifixion, the Revolution's red battalions, an "April sunset in Oaxaca,"[93] and the "scarlet red sputum of Pátzcuaro,"[94] all united to the terrors of the Middle Passage and the survivals of enslaved Africans in the "black light of promise"[95] sustained by Yoruba religious practices of divination in the New World.

---

[84] Jay Wright, "Zapata and the Egúngún Mask," *Callaloo*, No. 19, Jay Wright: A Special Issue (Autumn, 1983) pp 26–38.

[85] *Ibid.*, p 27.

[86] *Ibid.*, p 37.

[87] *Ibid.*, p 38.

[88] *Ibid.*, p 27.

[89] *Ibid.*, p 29.

[90] *Ibid.*, p 26.

[91] *Ibid.*, p 27.

[92] *Ibid.*

[93] *Ibid.*, p 29.

[94] *Ibid.*, p 30.

[95] *Ibid.*, p 37.

As the poem spirals over 600 lines in the "black liquid of exchange,"[96] it demarcates a space of indwelling on the geographic borderlands between the United States and Mexico, the "Deep waters [that] will return us home / Texas   New   Mexico / Arizona..."[97]

> I am that I am
>   two steps beyond the northern line;
> I become what I am
>   two steps below it[98]

Jay Wright's poetics comes into focus along the bilingual and spiritual borderlands of Chicana feminist poet and theorist Gloria Anzaldúa— a space of individuation and resistance.

> Chicanos and other people of color suffer economically for not acculturating. This voluntary (yet forced) alienation makes for psychological conflict, a kind of dual identity—we don't identify with the Anglo-American cultural values and we don't totally identify with the Mexican cultural values. We are a synergy of two cultures with various degrees of Mexicaness or Angloness. I have so internalized the borderland conflict that sometimes I feel like one cancels out the other and we are zero, nothing, no one. *A veces no soy nada ni nadie. Pero hasta cuando no lo soy, lo soy.*[99]

Contemporary poets in the borderlands—José Montoya, Juan Felipe Herrera, Lorna Dee Cervantes, Guillermo Gómez-Peña, elena minor, Alfred Arteaga, Valerie Martínez, Marisela Norte, Sesshu Foster, Susan Briante, Rodrigo Toscano, Carmen Giménez Smith, John Michael Rivera, Rosa Alcalá, J. Michael Martinez, Harry Gamboa Jr., and Emmy Pérez, among many others—have since looked to the location of the political dividing line separating the United States and Mexico in order to critique a range of transnational inequities in the historical process, the political economy, the chronologies of culture, and the inheritance of two languages, English and Spanish. In the case of poet Rosa Alcalá—who resides in the borderland city of

---

[96]   *Ibid.*, p 38.

[97]   *Ibid.*, p 36.

[98]   *Ibid.*, p 35.

[99]   Gloria Anzaldúa. *Borderlands: The New Mestiza* (San Francisco: Spinsters/Aunt Lute, 1987) p 63.

El Paso—the method of translation serves as a model to inhabit and mediate difference. Alcalá attains this even in brief lyric moments like that of "Inflection," written from the perspective of the transnational factory economics established between Mexico and the United States: "And the dust that / confuses countries / is in your eyes, and you / blink, and you blink, / and you blink."[100] An accent-inflected articulation of the poet's name estranges her familiar sense of self and so compels the assembly-line or *maquiladora* repetition of those final syllables: an appreciation of geopolitical citizenship as being "beyond the natural borders" of our habitual locations.

14 Finally, I return to William Bronk, who—as I mentioned earlier—wrote essays and poems set in archaic cultures that rehearse a fascination with the arbitrary fictions of time and space. Whereas in previous pages I noted Bronk's affinity for the cosmological dualism of Mesoamerica, one poem in particular serves as an invocation to the duality embodied by Coatlicue and Xilonen, two goddesses from the Aztec pantheon:

TENOCHTITLAN

I did not go to Coatlicue today,
to her of the writhing skirt of serpents, skulls
suspended at her neck, clawed Mother of the Gods.
Not that it mattered: if we have learned at all
we have learned not to deny the terrible ones
their due; they have it; we are theirs to keep.
But we also learn—not knowing is it fear
or defiance teaching us—not to think
of everything always, sometimes not to think.

Xilonen, Goddess of the Young Corn, of green
and growing, grant us the solace of sweet ears
soft in the mouth; accept our truant love.
We drink to you, Xilonen, we are drunk
with deep pleasures and a deep need, drunk
with gentleness and the pleasure of gentle needs.[101]

---

100   Rosa Alcalá. *The Lust of Unsentimental Waters* (Bristol, U.K.: Shearsman Books, 2012) p 17.

101   William Bronk. *Selected Poems* (New York: New Directions, 1995) p 21.

Bronk's poem identifies an essential want that is the prime motivating factor for U.S artists and writers in the resolve of Mexico as elsewhere; a cover story for the foundational violence that unsettles U.S. literature, from Mary Rowlandson to Hart Crane and from Cabeza de Vaca to Charles Olson; the quest for exceptional cause.[102]

Bronk's poem also repeats the paradigm of a solitary self, a person "transplanted from [or to] another culture (and hence unfinished)... falling, so to speak, into experience and encountering there that ideal 'Other' in response to which he must, at the minimum, redefine himself and, at the maximum virtually recreate himself."[103] There is—not only in Bronk's poem but in much work pointing to Mexico past and present—a dual substantiation of what William Carlos Williams referred to as American Grain, the deliverance or frustration of the self in its encounter with the categorical newness of elsewhere. For the dialogue with elsewhere is a geographic exoticism, in the sense that the French poet Victor Segalen proposed at the beginning of the century, where the exotic includes "everything that lies 'outside' the sum of our current, conscious everyday events, everything that does not belong to our usual 'Mental Tonality'"[104] Segalen was right: history so telescopes, from Columbus in his closer heaven at the end of the Orient to the uncanny present, as for us to be more and more disenchanted with "the spherical world as opposed to the flat one." Segalen recalls that on a "spherical surface, to leave one point is already to begin *to draw closer to it!* The sphere is Monotony. The poles are but a fiction."[105]

15 And elsewhere is suspended someplace in between.

---

[102] Octavio Paz. *México en la obra de Octavio Paz* (3 vols.): *Vol. II*, (Mexico: Fondo de Cultura Economica 1987) p 444.

[103] Giles Gunn. *The Interpretation of Otherness: Literature, Religion, and the American Imagination*, (New York: Oxford University Press, 1979) p 191.

[104] Victor Segalen. *Essay on Exoticism: An Aesthetics of Diversity*, trans. and ed. Yaël Rachel Schlick, Foreword by Harry Hartoonian (Durham: Duke University Press, 2002) p 16.

[105] *Ibid.*, p 43.

*Contemporary poets
in the borderlands…*
*have since looked to the location
of the political dividing line
separating the United States
and Mexico*

◆

*…two languages
and the inheritance
the chronologies of culture,
the political economy,
in the historical process,
of transnational inequities
in order to critique a range*

ASSAULT ON THE QUIET CONTINENT:

THE OPPENS IN MEXICO

Kenneth Burke described the aesthetic and moral power that unembellished historical documents are able to set in motion when viewed through the frames of the literary.[1] This is possible, he argued, largely thanks to the ambivalent properties of evidence itself; in other words, the documentary record may have the potential to uncover objective fact, even as its truth remains unsettled by the authority of evidence and institutional settings that safeguard the survival of objects for the uses of history. My question is: how to account for the missing difference that makes an archive impermeable?

A fundamental frame in the life and writings of George Oppen is the fact that he and his family moved to Mexico City and lived there from 1950–1958, a narrative shot through with ambivalence for the poet during the period in question and for his commentators in the present, inasmuch as the historical record of that past is all but non-existent. Amid the papers, letters, and manuscripts that comprise the largest part of the Oppen archive are resources that provide certain keys into the life and art of the Oppen family in Mexico. Among these are George and Mary's passports,

---

[1] Kenneth Burke. "Introduction," Charles Reznikoff, *Testimony* (1934). (Objectivist Press, 1934).

birth certificate and social security cards; and Mary's oil paintings, watercolors, and other works on paper of the 1950s. Present as well are the holdings of objects made by George that serve as evidence, often missing from the future interviews and daybooks, of his reluctant relationship to the culture of Mexico and of his commitment to artistic thought and practice even as he had already entered into the much-noted period of silence in his writing.[2] The other question is this: What to say of the literary when the archive is composed not of documents but of other objects that serve as evidence?

The Materials (1962)—Oppen's reappearance in book form, an acclaimed but ever-elusive return to poetry after a 25-year lapse—opens with a poem that conveys the particularity of Oppen's lyric matter, its visual structure, and the prosody's private, conspicuously taciturn cadence. The poem, entitled "Eclogue," is one of a handful that feature overt or oblique references to Mexico, among them "Blood from the Stone," "Tourist Eye," "Coastal Strip," "Primitive," "Resort," "The Mayan Ground," and others.

ECLOGUE

The men talking
Near the room's center. They have said
More than they had intended.

Pinpointing in the uproar
Of the living room

An assault
On the quiet continent.

Beyond the window
Flesh and rock and hunger

Loose in the night sky
Hardened into soil

---

2   Mary Oppen Papers, 1913–1990. University of California, San Diego, Special Collections Library, MSS 0125, Box 4, Box 4Box Oversize FB-090, Oversize AB-002-F, Oversize FB-094.

Tilting of itself to the sun once more, small
Vegetative leaves
And stems taking place

Outside----- O small ones,
To be born![3]

"Eclogue" opens with the din of human speech, the talk of men in excess of aim, and in proximity of unspecified space, "pinpointing in the uproar / Of the living room // An assault / On the quiet continent." Here, voices tell more than was intended, the choral surge in contrast to the surrounding geography below a night sky home to "Flesh and rock and hunger," the hard and soft materials that confirm the volume's title, the stuff of place and bodily need when hunger ceases to be metaphor. The soil and vegetation and sun of days to come rehearse an indoor and outdoor spectacle of human thriving and plant life; a burgeoning equated with regeneration and the deafening germinating of life, otherwise invisible or inaudible.

Poet Michael Davidson, in the notes of the *New Collected Poems*, tells us that Oppen based his poem on Virgil's "Fourth Eclogue," which was "addressed to a newborn boy and which was understood by the medieval world to be a prophecy of Christ's coming," and that Oppen himself described "Eclogue" as his "version of a bucolic poem, a rural scene, looking out the window [where] humans [talk] of deals and triumphs as a kind of artillery bombardment against that indestructible natural world."[4] Both Oppen's politics and metaphysics are stated in this poem, as the poet often did in interviews, that the end of one's own life is by no means equivalent to the end of the world; and that we therefore share a purpose that is the transformation of an impulse, a preference, or a leaning into observation and action.[5]

---

[3]   George Oppen. *New Collected Poems*, ed. Michael Davidson (New York: New Directions, 2002) p 39.

[4]   Michael Davidson. "Introduction," *George Oppen, New Collected Poems* (New York, New Directions, 2002) p 205.

[5]   George Oppen Interviewed by David Gitin and Charles Amirkhanian, 30 March 1970, KPFA broadcast 19 April 1971.

The rural locality of the poem gives way to an upending and transvaluation of the urban domains, what another field of knowledge might call "the social production of spatiality."[6] In the immediately ensuing poem, "Image of the Machine," "every crevice of the city [is pictured as] leaking / Rubble: concrete, conduit, pipe, a crumbling / Rubble of our roots."[7] Transitions like these are consistent with the ambivalent desire in *The Materials*, and they allow Oppen to develop one of his consistent themes of contemporary urban ruin. The poetry here and in Oppen's follow-up collection, *This in Which*, is crowded with references to populace and population, intercut with images of the machine and other assaults on the "quiet continent"—the American hemisphere.

Mary Oppen's 1978 autobiography *Meaning a Life*, together with the important scholarship of Peter Nicholls on the Oppens in exile, are works that provide a critical biographic context. The nine years of political exile in Mexico coincide with and are complicated by what Oppen in later life referred to as his "rejection of poetry for twenty or twenty-five years," following the publication of his 1934 volume *Discrete* Series.[8] Few accounts of Oppen and his work can proceed without reference to it. To cite a typical example, poet and critic James Logenbach begins an essay so asserting:

> George Oppen, who wrote some of the most austerely beautiful poems of the twentieth century, is known best for not writing at all. After publishing *Discrete Series* in 1934, at the age of 26, he entered a period of silence that would not conclude until a quarter century later, when The Materials appeared in 1962.[9]

---

[6]   Edward Soja. "The City and Spatial Justice," conference paper, Spatial Justice, Nanterre, Paris, March 12–14, 2008. Soja speaks of "the urbanization of injustice, the reduction of regional inequalities, or even more broadly in the generic search for a just city and a just society."

[7]   George Oppen. *New Collected Poems*, ed. Michael Davidson (New York: New Directions, 2002) p 42.

[8]   L. S. Dembo. "'The Objectivist' Poet: George Oppen," *Contemporary Literature*, 10.2 (Spring 1969) pp 173–74.

[9]   James Logenbach. "A Test of Poetry," *Nation*, 286.5, 2008, p 29. Web. 12 March 2015.

For Rachel Blau DuPlessis, the silent temporality that haunts the space between the publication of *Discrete Series* (1934) and *The Materials* (1962), a space that contains the nine-year period in Mexico—largely viewed by the poet, in retrospect, as no more than a detour—has given way to "the mystification of that silence, an obsessive return to it."[10] Needless to say, that "silence" of a quarter century "poses some difficult questions,"[11] but equally unsettled is the location of Mexico in that silence, its relevance for Oppen's return to writing, and Oppen's lasting views on Mexico in his poems and later opinions of the place. Despite there being only one extant letter from the period between 1934–1958, critic Peter Nicholls has so organized the scarce evidence as to illuminate the question of Oppen's renewed commitment to poetry in 1958, which the poet later described as a return to the art through a "bending [of] history."[12]

What can we know? We know that George and Mary Oppen had joined the Communist Party in 1935, shortly after the publication of *Discrete Series*, and that they were active party members from 1936 to 1941. We have Oppen's word that, in terms of these political commitments, he viewed an over-identification with the role of a poet as social actor or cultural broker as dubious, even as he became aware, or was made aware, that his own work was incommensurable with the art ideology and style of the New Masses.[13] By the mid-

---

[10]   Rachel Blau DuPlessis. "Oppen from Seventy-Five to a Hundred, 1983–2000," *Jacket* 36 (2008) Web.

[11]   Peter Nicholls. "George Oppen in Exile: Mexico and Maritain (For Linda Oppen)," *Journal of American Studies*, 39 (2005) pp 1–18.

[12]   George Oppen. *The Selected Letters of George Oppen*, ed. Rachel Blau DuPlessis (Durham and London, Duke University Press, 1990) p 129.

[13]   L. S. Dembo. "'The Objectivist' Poet: George Oppen," *Contemporary Literature*, 10.2 (Spring 1969) pp 173–74. Oppen tells also that while he and Mary may not have harbored "philosophic doubts" about communism, they found the usefulness of some of the party's activities "very questionable." Looking back, he clarifies that, as opposed to "politicalizing," what called them to join the movement (party) was "to help organize the unemployed." The Oppens engaged in house to house organizing in Bedford-Stuyvesant and North Brooklyn "on the simple principle that the law would have to be changed where it interfered with relief and that settlement laws would have to be unenforceable when they involved somebody's starvation. And we were interested in

1940s, the Oppens had moved to Redondo Beach, California, where in the post-World War II population boom and housing shortage, Oppen found work in the small-scale construction business, even as he continued to head a local Party chapter. Oppen relates in future interviews what he experienced as an increasing disenchantment with Communist attitudes and his "Communist friends." He recounts a

> situation that made it impossible for us to participate anymore, even after the difficulty with our own thinking. We were under threat by the McCarthy committee and had to flee the United States. I don't think I have to tell the whole story about that. You get questioned as to who you knew and you refuse to answer and you get jailed. We did not want to get jailed; that would have been only a matter of a year—we weren't terribly important—but we had a child and it would have been a bad thing. Mexico wasn't an absolute refuge, but it made it a little more difficult to get us and we knew we needed only to make it a little difficult.[14]

In her memoir as well, Mary tells of the disintegration of their Southern California arcadia as visits from the FBI became more frequent and the questions more "nagging and persistent."[15] It was clear, she writes, "from their questions, that they had a dossier with information about us far back into our lives."[16] On June 11, 1950, the Oppens departed by car for Mexico with their 10-year old daughter Linda, and Mary's memoir tells of the exotic "old colonial house"

---

rioting, as a matter of fact—rioting under political discipline. Disorder, disorder—to make it impossible to allow people to starve. It also involved the hunger march on Washington as well as local undertakings." Oppen related also: "The situation of the old left was the theory of socialist realism, etcetera, etcetera. It didn't seem worth arguing; it would have been impossible to argue, it didn't seem to me to be of utmost importance at the time. We stayed carefully away from cultural commissions, and people who wrote poetry for the New Masses and so on." George Oppen Interviewed by David Gitin and Charles Amirkhanian, 30 March 1970, KPFA broadcast 19 April 1971.

[14]   L. S. Dembo. "'The Objectivist' Poet: George Oppen," *Contemporary Literature*, 10.2 (Spring 1969) p 175.

[15]   Mary Oppen. *Meaning A Life: An Autobiography* (Santa Barbara: Black Sparrow Press, 1978) p 193.

[16]   *Ibid.*

they rented in the San Ángel district; of the schooling they provided
Linda, and of the several occasions on which they were subject to
police surveillance. Little is said, though, of the social circle in which
they moved; "we were friendly with many of the Hollywood exiles,"[17]
Mary notes. "[B]ut she doesn't elaborate—and there is no real sense,"
Peter Nicholls remarks, "of beauty and strangeness of the then
unpolluted city that so impressed other US émigrés and visitors."[18]

Mary Oppen's memoir, just under 200 pages, devotes in total
"a mere eight pages to their entire period of exile."[19] Her feelings
of displacement and isolation are equated with the "bourgeois life"
they viewed as their only option. "Because to live as the lower classes
live in Mexico," she wrote, "is a life fraught with danger due to lack
of hygiene in such a poverty-stricken, undeveloped country."[20]
Appropriate to their lifestyle, George and Mary took art classes at
La Esmeralda Escuela de Pintura y Escultura (woodcarving and
painting, respectively), and George "became a partner in a furniture-
making business."[21] Mary wrote:

> We were not expatriates by choice, and we were unrelenting in *withholding
> ourselves* from becoming exiles forever. We wanted more than anything
> to return home to the United States. To be artists in these conditions
> was impossible to us. We needed to be freely in our own country, to have
> time to assimilate the violent years before turning them into thought
> and poetry.[22]

When asked about his involvement with Mexican culture,
given the extent of their time there, Oppen once made reference

---

[17]   *Ibid*, p 199.

[18]   Peter Nicholls. "George Oppen in Exile: Mexico and Maritain (For Linda Oppen),"
Journal of American Studies, 39 (2005) p 5.

[19]   *Ibid*.

[20]   Mary Oppen. *Meaning A Life: An Autobiography* (Santa Barbara: Black Sparrow Press,
1978) p 200.

[21]   Peter Nicholls. "George Oppen in Exile: Mexico and Maritain (For Linda Oppen),"
Journal of American Studies, 39 (2005) p 6.

[22]   Mary Oppen. *Meaning A Life: An Autobiography* (Santa Barbara: Black Sparrow Press,
1978) p 200 [emphasis added].

to some interaction, but of efforts pursued "unsuccessfully." In 1969, he offered the following, "I think every American's experience is unsuccessful in this regard. I could tell very nice stories about Mexico, but I also have a lot of negative feelings I don't even want to state. The fact is that it's not a very good place for Americans to be." The interviewer presses the point:

Q. What bothered you in particular?

A. I really will be attacking Mexico if I get into that, and there's no particular reason. But it had to do with my sense of being a craftsman, for whatever it's worth, and my sense of not being an executive. In Mexico[,] foreigners are not permitted to produce objects, and the law is rigorously enforced. I set up a small business, which was not easy. One becomes accustomed to paying bribes everywhere and with the greatest possible tact and skill—a situation of infinite corruption, to begin to tell it, a society, a culture really trapped and not the fault of the people. They are trapped by their culture, by the relation of men and women, by the absolute corruption of government, by the habits of bureaucracy, the habits of people. One is forced to change class very sharply in Mexico; if one is a foreigner, one has to be an upper-bourgeois citizen, as a matter of law or necessity. None of these things was easy for us; they were by no means easy.

Q. What kind of a business did you manage to set up?

A. I made—"made" in the upper-bourgeois sense—furniture. I never touched a tool. I set up with a Mexican partner, a very wonderful man and a very fine craftsman.

Q. Was there any specific reason for your coming back in 1958?

A. Just that we could; the McCarthy thing was over. We only went to Mexico in the first place because we couldn't get passports. We weren't illegally in Mexico but we were helplessly there, and we paid an infinite series of bribes.[23]

---

[23]   L. S. Dembo. "'The Objectivist' Poet: George Oppen," *Contemporary Literature*, 10.2 (Spring 1969) pp 176–7.

At stake for the Oppens was not only the corruption of the Mexican government and its bureaucratic apparatus, but also what R.G. Collingwood called the corruption of consciousness. To the degree that Octavio Paz described the fraudulence of the Mexican public administration as a remainder of the colonial condition, wherein private individuals dispose "of the public trust as though it were proper to them,"[24] U.S. American poet Muriel Rukeyser appealed to Collingwood's account of the corruption of consciousness in her 1949 book *The Life of Poetry* as being

> forms of weakness—the ruling-out of emotion, overspecialization, aversion to the disclosure of oneself to oneself, the repressive codes, neurotic embarrassment and coldness, contempt for others, criticism by projection propped up with lies—[...] a cascade of penalties which cause suffering in those who feel them and in those on whom, in turn, their weakness is vented. They are all forms of what Collingwood names the corruption of consciousness.[25]

And Rebecca Schreiber, in *Cold War Exiles in Mexico*, provides evidence of actual FBI collusion with Mexican intelligence and of the Dirección Federal de Seguridad, the Mexican secret police, which "monitored left wing Americans and Mexicans."[26]

Prior to their 1950s exile, in the summer of 1934, the Oppens had visited Mexico with two friends from Berkeley and had seen "the ideas of socialism applied in a poverty-stricken nation.... We admired Cárdenas, the President of Mexico, and we observed that Mexico was coming to a new life." Mary Oppen goes on to name Rivera, Orozco, and Siqueiros as "political artists whose murals covered walls of government, schools and public courtyards,"[27] thus conveying a specified awareness of the cultural sphere. But upon their

---

[24] Octavio Paz. *El ogro filantrópico: historia y política (1971–1978)* (Madrid: Seix Barral 1979) p 53 [Author's translation].

[25] Muriel Rukeyser. *The Life of Poetry*, (Paris: Current Books, 1949) p 48.

[26] Rebecca Mina Schreiber. *Cold War Exiles in Mexico: U.S. Dissidents and the Culture of Critical Resistance* (Minneapolis: University of Minnesota Press, 2008) p 15.

[27] Mary Oppen. *Meaning A Life: An Autobiography* (Santa Barbara: Black Sparrow Press, 1978) p 19.

return to Mexico they found the country undergoing development and the kind of modernization historians describe insofar as "United States Corporations such as Proctor and Gamble, General Motors [and others had become] familiar presences, prompting Mexican nationalists to wonder whether the program of the Revolution had become reversed."[28]

♦ ♦ ♦

Central to my purpose then are a series of photographs[29] serving as evidence of the furniture Oppen made—"'made' in the upper-bourgeois sense" of never touching a tool for which he later expressed disdain or resignation. Here we see retail items he produced with his Mexican business partner, the "very fine craftsman" George fails to name in the interview above, but whom Mary identifies in her autobiography, by first name only, as Carlos. These photographs provide a glimpse into Mexico City in the 1950s, imparting information about a particular clientele, the interior design and lifestyle aspirations of a certain Mexico City middle-class, and about the household commodity forms that Oppen produced as a decade-long means of living.

Made of thickly grained wood with an unfinished surface, a cradle built with high legs and rocking supports features a protective hood carved in streamlined curves perched over the box-like encasement with lines so free of ornament as to resemble a tiny coffin. Partially shielded from the sun, the object is photographed in an exterior courtyard or balcony garden lined with terra cotta tiles, presumably the client's home. The composition encapsulates a striking contrast between the cradle's empty recess and the surrounding exuberance of tree foliage and potted plants. In another photograph, a kitchen interior—on a particularly hefty mass with ridged edges and a shallow carved-out depression—there nestles a gourd bowl. The

---

28   Mark T. R. Gilderhus., "United States-Mexican Relations since 1910: A Survey," *Twentieth-Century Mexico*, ed. W. Dirk Raat and William H. Beezley (Lincoln: University of Nebraska Press, 1986).

29   University of California, San Diego Library, Special Collections, MSS 0125, Flatbox 109, folder 2.

low side table, a slab of wood carved into an organic Brutalist shape balances on four tiny slender legs, and it stands apart from the other furnishings, less unique items conforming to a standardized taste for French provincial country-kitchen components, a breakfast table and a cupboard, whose shelves are lined with Mexican ceramic ware, possibly from Tonalá, Jalisco.

In yet another photograph, a client's chessboard set energizes Oppen's rectangular table whose surface, together with polished timber-like legs and ground-level stretcher frame, all converge into a hard-geometric unity. In another interior still, two bar stools accentuate a formal economy of line in the sleek tapered legs as set against the more rudimentary finish displayed on the front wood panels of a home dining-room bar. Another style of table appears in two photographs. Visible on one—staged with an ashtray and an austere table-lamp—is a dark varnish or laminate top. The table's skirt undergirding serves also as a kind of stretcher with a fretted design element close to each leg, a mid-century ornament that gestured to Mexican antiquity. In the other snapshot, duplicates of the same model serve as large living-room side tables in a residence whose architectural plan employed the volcanic rock of central Mexico popularized, among others, by mid-century architects like Juan O'Gorman, as in his residence outside Mexico City (1953–1956, demolished in 1969) and Luis Barragán in his Jardines del Pedregal residential project begun in 1945. In Barragán's view, the aesthetic severity of Mexico Valley's volcanic landscape, its angular weight and irregular fragility, could be so tamed in the home interior as to suggest "a partnership in the Kingdom of Nature [as opposed to] the aggressive tendencies of contemporary life."[30]

There are other examples—a lounge-style cantilevered wooden chair with high, sloped back, and sweeping curved armrests—that survive as evidence of the kind of household items whose manufacture Oppen supervised. Linda Oppen Mourelatos, George and Mary's daughter, relates that most of the furniture was made to client's order, even as many of the elements in the photographs,

---

[30] Luis Barragán. "Una poética del espacio," *Artes de México 23* (1994) p 28.

the chess set above for example, "would have been the customer's own."[31] In Mexico, many mid-century middle-class interiors were a variegated declension of the International Style[32] in architecture and design, joined to a critical brand of regional modernism in design that defied the former's rationalist aesthetic and functionalist affinities, its regularity of composition and austerity of form, with pre-conquest materials and motifs, colonial manual art or decorative artifacts, folk paintings, and other hand-made crafts, and with unique objects, both domestic and foreign, found at flea markets and antique shops, like those that comprise La Lagunilla in Mexico City. This design for living can be linked to different artists, architects, and designers as idiosyncratic as Jesús Reyes Ferreira, or Luis Barragán, Mario Pani, and Mathias Goeritz. They championed an assemblage aesthetic whose aim was a broader cultural poetics that sought a cohesive "integration" of the arts. [33] This phenomenon had as much to do with the realm of fine arts, as it did with commercial enterprises. Privileged art-world and middle-class designs for living formed part of a broader economic program involving foreign investment initiatives and increased industrialization of society; and with these the need for new office buildings and housing projects like the Centro Urbano "Presidente Juárez" designed by Mario Pani and Enrique del Moral with exterior murals by Cárlos Mérida.[34] In keeping with aesthetic tendencies and bourgeois aspiration and taste, Oppen appears to have enjoyed a steady client base, especially as related to concurrent social developments taking place in Mexico.[35]

---

[31] "Most of the furniture listed was made on order. The chess set would have been the customer's own // The rocking chair and the lounge chairs were prototypes and stayed at home. None of the carvings sound like portraits of anybody in family, tho' George did make one of Mary," Linda Oppen, electronic communication 4 October 2015.

[32] *Modern Architecture, International Exhibition*: New York, Feb 10 to March 23, 1932, Museum of Modern Art (catalog), New York, 1932.

[33] Mathias Goeritz. "La integración plástica en el C.U. Presidente Juárez." *Arquitectura* (Mexico City: December 1952) 8; Documents of Twentieth-Century Latin American and Latino Art: A Digital Archive and Publications Project, ICAA-735979.

[34] *Ibid.*

[35] About the Organization of American States charter, Eduardo Galeano writes: "Latin

A June 1959 article in the U.S. American monthly *Harper's Magazine* connects Oppen's small-scale furniture business to another phenomenon that defined the 1950s in Mexico. In an ironizing historical allusion, author Daniel James refers to the not-so-distant past to describe an uprising "without bloodshed or headlines" as the "Sears, Roebuck Mexican revolution," a process "peaceful, gradual, and profound in its effects."[36] In its aim to conquer new markets in Mexico and Latin America, the impact of this quintessentially U.S. enterprise proved "more significant than anything accomplished by any big-name official mission we have sent south in recent years."[37] In the wake of World War II, hemispheric security initiatives, like the Organization of American States, redefined the geopolitical, economic, and cultural alliances between the United States and Latin America, episodes of cultural and political expediency that Claire Fox narrates with remarkable depth in her book *Making Art Panamerican*. Cold War defense strategies, arts programming, and the increasing focus on the region as an object of interest had repercussions for both north and south; debates about Pan-Americanism and Latin Americanism formed a "power-knowledge nexus...which facilitated the growth of the U.S. commercial empire in Latin America."[38] In connection to this, the *Harper's* feature viewed the foreign investment narrative of Sears, Roebucks and Company[39] in Mexico as an unwitting entrepreneurial effort of social advancement.

American enterprises continue in control of already established and less sophisticated industries and techniques, while private investment from the United States—and probably from other industrialized countries also—rapidly increases its participation in certain dynamic industries, which require a relatively high technical level of development," Eduardo Galeano. *Open Veins of Latin America: Five Centuries of the Pillage of a Continent*, trans. Cedric Belfrage (New York: Monthly Review Press, 1997) p 206.

[36] Daniel James. "Sears, Roebuck's Mexican Revolution," *Harper's Monthly* (June 1959) p 65.

[37] *Ibid.*

[38] Claire F. Fox *Making Art Panamerican: Cultural Policy and the Cold War* (Minneapolis: University of Minnesota Press, 2013) p 6. Fox relates as well: "Though hemispheric security was a priority of the United States in the new organization [OAS], for many Latin American political leaders, the incentive to form a regional alliance went beyond a desire to gain access to international arenas and an entrenched fear of communism; it was also perceived as a means to check U.S. expansionism." (p 92).

[39] Later shortened to "Sears" solely and referred throughout this essay thusly.

Daniel James recounted the Mexican government's efforts to attract foreign industries with tax exemptions and incentives, and of the highly publicized 1947 opening of Sears in Mexico City, the first of subsequent headquarters throughout Latin America, 55 stores and 13 sales offices also in "Brazil, Colombia, Costa Rica, Cuba, El Salvador, Mexico, Panama, Peru, and Venezuela."[40] The economic upsurge had led to an increase in money—wages and cash flow that provided salaried Mexicans with purchasing power. But the success of Sears had to do as well with "merchandise practices."[41] Unlike its national competitors, Sears seized the opportunity to welcome the lower to midlevel functionary and upwardly mobile office worker, replacing the class-conscious practices of its national competitors (Palacio de Hierro, Casa Armand, and Francia Marítima) that catered chiefly to the higher-income groups or "carriage trade," with more commercially democratic attitudes. At the national chains in Mexico, according to *Harper's*, "goods and prices were hidden," "quality was not guaranteed, and variety was limited."[42] Sears, by contrast, offered clearly marked labels, product reliability, and fixed prices, such that

> when Sears discovered that its novel practices were attracting people of all classes, it concluded that it would pay to supply them with goods made in Mexico and bring prices [further] down.... Some items, like refrigerators, which are still manufactured in relatively small quantities in Mexico, fetch higher prices than in the United States; but generally the merchandise sold by Sears de México is priced well within the pocketbooks of a majority of the Mexican urban population.[43]

Sears stimulated economic growth, the article claimed, by doing business with a "total of 2000 independent Mexican suppliers, large and small," stimulating a "modern consumer-goods industry," and, more generally, Mexico's commercial production. Key to the formation of the Mexican middle class were "durables"—"household furnishings and appliances [that had] become available in mass

---

[40] Daniel James. "Sears, Roebuck's Mexican Revolution," *Harper's Monthly* (June 1959) p 66.
[41] *Ibid.*
[42] *Ibid.*
[43] *Ibid*, p. 67.

quantities for the first time." Products made locally in Mexico, even while "popularizing American styling," gave way as well to a middle-class re-appreciation of "indigenous crafts like ceramics." Also, even as "basic industries like steel boasted great modern plants" with Mexico at the leading edge in terms of Latin America's "capital-goods production, articles for retail trade were still made either in private dwellings by hand or in tiny 'factories' with one or two machines."[44]

This series of forces so coalesced as to make it difficult, from a historical perspective, to view Oppen and his furniture business as untethered to U.S. American commercial interests in Mexico; to the taste formation of Mexico City's aspiring classes in light of Sears and its merchandise strategy; or to the increased mass production of items heretofore consigned to the manual skills of the workshop. Oppen's poems from *The Materials* are contingent on such a confluence of factors, structures of feeling, and cross-cultural involvements. In his 1934 *Discrete Series*, Oppen had enlivened a stark succession of sense experiences from the impact of industrialization on everyday life. In that serial poem—in its own way modular in terms of design construction—Oppen had exposed the contradictions made visible in Depression-era New York City by linking material dispossession to action as exclusionary as the closing doors of a missed elevator, the spectacle of automotive show rooms and movie signs, or—despite the "prudery" of its market brand name—the erotic sheen of a corner drugstore Frigidaire. Now the lapsed writer and incidental craftsman in Mexico was primed to appreciate the values of technique in the hand-made; a cultural issue compromised by the intensified manufacture of assorted commodities and durables for the Mexican middle class. In retrospect, Oppen admitted a reluctance to identifying with the economic class that not only composed his client base, but to which, for all intents and purposes, he belonged in spite of himself. Mexico intensified for him an ambiguity never entirely resolved as per his "sense of being a craftsman, for whatever it's worth, and [his] sense of not being an executive" in light of the actual "upper-bourgeois" confines of his *habitus* in Mexico. Oppen's

---

[44] *Ibid.*

self-identification in terms of class was in conflict with the rapidly changing status of craft and craftsmanship within the expansion of Americanized retail industries like Sears where mechanized means of production detached and dehumanized the kind of practical knowledge attainable at the interface of head and hand in its contact with the materials.

Which leads us to Oppen's woodcarvings. As Mary relates in her memoir, she and George enrolled in art classes at the Escuela Nacional de Pintura, Escultura y Grabado "La Esmeralda." From that engagement and training there survive, in the holdings at UCSD, dozens of works by Mary in various media—from acrylic on paper to stitching on burlap—and evidence of 15 woodcarvings made by George, 6 documented in black and white photographs, and 7 actual objects. The largest of these extant works is "Bust of a Woman" (13" x 30" wide). In this unstained wood rendering, the sitter's hair appears pulled back or worn very short. Her upper body dwarfs the mountain range below, as though the cropped perspective were slanted from an unspecified elevation. The sanding and polishing in the areas of the face show care to achieve anatomical precision and a severity of expression, particularly around the lips. The composition attains its particular psychological force by means of the prolonged wing-like push-cut carving marks that so lead from the left- and especially the right-hand edges to the pull-cut work around the head as to produce the illusion of the figure hovering independent of her surroundings. An unattributed photograph of Mary included in the publication of *Meaning a Life*, made in 1957, was the likely source for Oppen's interpretation.

Excluding this work, Linda Oppen remarks that the carvings "were made from photos Mary took during her interest in camera work," primarily people or places with no "particular back story...."[45] Another woodcarving depicts, under the bough of a tree that tantalizes with its one hanging fruit, an unidentified couple (Couple, 13" x 16"). The woman on the left sits with hands folded at her lap, beside the man whose gaze is cast directly at the viewer while he

---

45   Linda Oppen, electronic communication, 15 October 2015.

clutches in his arms an object. Is it a model version of the crafts to which Oppen often alluded, as in his brief poem "Carpenter's Boat" a less overtly Mexico-related poem on the later pages of *This in Which*.

CARPENTER'S BOAT

The new wood as old as carpentry
Rounding the far buoy, wild
Steel fighting in the sea, carpenter,
Carpenter,
Carpenter and other things, the monstrous welded seams
Plunge and drip in the seas; carpenter,
Carpenter, how wild the planet is.[46]

In another woodcarving that depicts male and female figures dwarfed by the imposing trunk and energetic angular boughs of a tree, there loom, in the distance, contoured traces of an urban skyline (Two figures beside tree, 22.5" x 27"). This woodcarving serves as a double to the dialectic pull between "Eclogue" and "Image of the Machine," the two poems that inaugurate Oppen's 1962 return to publication in *The Materials*. In his later working papers and "daybooks," Oppen wrote, in all caps: "OUR MACHINERY AND CONSTRUCTIONS REPLACE THE MYTHS AND INSTITUTIONS OF TRIBAL MAN IN FORMING A PSYCHIC PROTECTION AGAINST THE CHAOS OF THE NATURAL WORLD."[47] There is a connective thread as well in Oppen's Mexico poems: ambivalent references to the "tribal" and "savage" that can be read, as related to the pre-industrial myth Claude Levi-Strauss had in mind in "La pensée sauvage." That is, not as a limiting primitivist description, but as a form of "untamed thought," a hidden grammar of diverse behaviors, a function that the mental processes of cultures, like those of Mexico, positioned other to that of a 20th century American poet.[48] Vincent

---

[46] George Oppen. *New Collected Poems*, (New York: New Directions, 2008) p 128.

[47] George Oppen. "Philosophy of the Astonished," (Selections from the Working Papers Ed. Rachel Blau du Plessis), *Sulfur* (27) (Fall 1990) p 214.

[48] Vincent Debaene. *Far Afield: French Anthropology Between Science and Literature*, trans. Justin Izzo, Chicago (University of Chicago Press, 2014).

Debaene writes:

> *The Savage Mind* bequeathed to the discipline the idea that observable
> differences in the sensible world can serve as sources for a logic of the
> concrete, enabling it to "tinker" [bricoler] with meanings, without the
> need to postulate a mental, collective, or individual subject that imposes
> its formal constraints on the content.[49]

In Oppen's poetics, the automated thought consistent with the
arrival of the machine threatened to corrupt or degrade the synthetic
thought of the craftsman.

In this sense a stylized figure of Death ("Death," 8" x 7") a work
possibly left unfinished, suggests Oppen's potential familiarity
with the pictorial tradition of the calavera popularized by Mexican
printmaker José Guadalupe Posada. Others, like the "Industrial
Scene with Workers" (18" x 22.5") indicate the labor motif that
typified the work of Mexican muralists, a subject that resonated
especially in the "Courtyard of Work," a 1923 mural cycle Diego Rivera
executed at the Ministry of Education, under the direction of José
Vasconcelos.[50] Another woodcarving of a male head ("Head," 12" x
17") is unique in that it visibly features Oppen's signature. Depicted
is the mutual distress of figure and foreground, the male sitter
pressed against the surrounding chaos of frames and beams. In a
letter George wrote in 1958 to his daughter Linda—George and Mary
were preparing to visit her in New York where she was now enrolled
as a student at Sarah Lawrence—Oppen mentions several of the
woodcarvings in reply to his daughter's request for one. He describes
them by subject, the "small one of a carpenter," an "adolescent with
books under his arm," and a work featuring a tree. His reference to
"the Carlos" is the woodcarving portrait he produced of the Mexican
craftsman who worked as his partner in the furniture business:

---

[49]   Vincent Debaene, "Levi-Strauss: What Legacy?" *Rethinking Claude Lévi- Strauss*
(1908–2009) ed. Robert Doran, (New Haven: Yale University Press, 2013) p16.
[50]   The one unfinished Oppen woodcarving in this set is a preparatory sketch for what
was to be a landscape (Landscape, 20" x 9.5").

I mean I don't like the artist to be abstract—all the art I really remember
is like Williams, Reznikoff, Rembrandt—you know who and where and
what the artist is // and what picture of mine (how very nice of you to
ask) shall I bring....The adolescent with books under his arm is the best
carved but what a subject!! The small one of a carpenter? The one who sort
of builds himself into a trap – the stained wood. The tree is too big – the
Carlos too big. Probably the carpenter, no? Sad tho he is. Or which do you
want....[51]

George and Mary were not the first or only U.S. Americans
to attend art school in Mexico. In the early 1950s, artists Elizabeth
Catlett and Margaret Taylor Goss Burroughs[52] trained at the
very same Escuela Nacional de Pintura, Escultura y Grabado "La
Esmeralda" that George and Mary attended—one wonders, did they
ever meet? Founded as an art school intended to train especially
workers and campesinos, "La Esmeralda" had boasted among its
faculty during the 1940s renowned makers including Diego Rivera,
Francisco Zúñiga, Frida Kahlo, Carlos Orozco Romero, Federico
Cantú, Luis Ortiz Monasterio, María Izquierdo and Agustín Lazo.
Located at the time on the Callejón de la Esmeralda, now Calle San
Fernando, the art school premises also placed Oppen well within
walking distance of the murals at the National Preparatory School
and the Ministry of Culture, thus in contact with the objects, if not
the debates, around Mexican modernity in its post-Revolutionary
forms.

Around the time George and Mary attended "La Esmeralda,"
faculty artist Francisco Zúñiga published a broadside, "Esmeralda:
Órgano Independiente," with the purpose of provoking a debate
on the perceived "decline" or "decadence" of the art school in which
the "pocos de talento que luchan ... son de condición humilde" ("the
talented few who struggle [aspire].... are of modest upbringing")
in the face of the many from the privileged classes whom Zúñiga
described as "señoritos pedantes," loosely translated to mean

---

[51]   George Oppen. *The Selected Letters of George Oppen*, ed. Rachel Blau DuPlessis
(Durham and London: Duke University Press, 1990) p 11.

[52]   Rebecca Mina Schreiber. *Cold War Exiles in Mexico: U.S. Dissidents and the Culture of
Critical Resistance* (Minneapolis: University of Minnesota Press, 2008) pp 23, 35.

something like "the pampered and pedantic." The question Zúñiga raised was whether art schools like "La Esmeralda" contributed to the tradition of Mexican fine arts or to the vernacular or popular arts? He notes, "the only thing we produce is a high percentage of art aficionados and privileged pedants. The majority of students lack enthusiasm, the requisite condition for youth... [all of which gave way to the kind of artist who remains] ignorant of the elements [proper to their artistic] vocabulary."[53] This conversation was connected to other debates during the 1950s as well, Esther Acevedo reminds us, in the "ongoing discussion between realistic art and abstract art" in which many students did not "see the importance of technical training."[54] Suggested too in Zúñiga's broadside was the ill-fitting nexus of careerism in the cultural bureaucracy, and art as a kind of internal tourism for the pampered sectors of Mexico.

◆ ◆ ◆

It was in *The Materials* (1961) and poems like "Tourist Eye" that Oppen addressed the leisure time of tourism:

> One might look everywhere
>
> As tourists do, the halls and stairways
> For something bequeathed
>
> From time, some mark
> In these most worn places

---

[53]   Francisco Zúñiga."La decadencia de las escuelas de arte," *Esmeralda: Órgano independiente*, no.1 (Mexico City: September 1954) p 1. "Lo único que estamos creando es un alto porcentaje de aficionados al arte y de señoritos pedantes. La mayoría del estudiantado carece de entusiasmo, condición indispensable de los jóvenes.... (el artista que) desconoce los elementos de su lenguaje." Documents of 20th-Century Latin American and Latino Art: A Digital Archive and Publications Project, ICAA-812445.

[54]   Esther Acevedo. "Annotations" to Francisco Zúñiga, "La decadencia de las escuelas de arte," *Esmeralda: Órgano independiente*, no.1 (Mexico City: September 1954) p 1; Documents of 20th-Century Latin American and Latino Art: A Digital Archive and Publications Project, ICAA-812445.

Where chance moves among the crowd
Unearned and separate[55]

How to stage or rehearse, then, the internal and external
contradictions of the reluctant foreigner whose presence in Mexico
can be viewed as that of the stranger whose undecidability serves
as a kind of corruption to cultural unity.[56] What I have in mind is to
create a speculative space of encounter between George Oppen and
the work of other foreigners at the time in Mexico, like the painter,
architect, and art educator Mathias Goeritz. In the recent exhibition
and attendant catalog *Defying Stability, Artistic Processes in Mexico,
1952–1967* (Desafío a la estabilidad, procesos artísticos en México
1952–1967), Israel Rodríguez addresses the discourse around the
problem of representation in 1950s Mexico, an issue "that pervaded
the intellectual and artistic debate at the time. The didacticism of
post revolutionary art [had] made realism its manifestation par
excellence,"[57] even as realism was no longer sustainable with the
widening acceptance of abstraction as meaningful form. Rita Eder
provides an account of the arrival to Mexico of German-born artist
Mathias Goeritz, with his wife photographer and model Marianne
Gast, by way of Spain and Guadalajara.

   In the early 1950s, Architect Ignacio Díaz Morales and art
historian Ida Rodríguez Prampolini invited Goeritz to join the faculty
in the new School of Architecture. He accepted, even as he eventually
moved to Mexico City where he founded the Museo Experimental
El Eco in September 1953, which he likened to a sort of "Mexican
BAUHAUS."[58] In 1952, Mathias Goeritz wrote: "Regarding my own

[55]   George Oppen. *New Collected Poems*, (New York: New Directions, 2008) pp 64–5.

[56]   Zygmunt Bauman. "Modernity and Ambivalence," *Theory, Culture & Society* Vol. 7
(London: 1990) p 155.

[57]   Israel Rodríguez. "Imaginaries: Introduction," *Defying Stability: Artistic Processes
in Mexico 1952–1967*, ed. Rita Eder, translation, Elisa Schmelkes (Mexico City, Mexico:
Universidad Nacional Autónoma de México, 2014) p 117.

[58]   Andrea Giunta. *Goeritz/Romero Brest, Correspondencias* (Buenos Aires: Facultad de
Filosofía y Letras-Universidad de Buenos Aires/Instituto de Teoría e Historia del Arte Julio
E. Payró, 2000), cited in Rita Eder, "Two Aspects of the Total Work of Art: Experimentation
and Performativity," *Defying Stability: Artistic Processes in Mexico 1952–1967*, ed. Rita Eder,

work, I yearn for that which is externally 'representative'—which some no longer recognize in it, but still exists—to lose significance, and become an interior expression of the human."[59] In this, Goeritz was linked to Oppen's own struggle with the possibility of expression, even as life forms that defy representation except in the "design for living" they prompt on the space of the page: "We do not sit outside of reality, think abstract thoughts of setting ourselves problems about reality which is somehow visible to us.... On the contrary, life has led us into the subject matter itself (final phrase derived from Hegel)."[60] Goeritz's method was abstract even as his desire was for "that which is externally 'representative,'" though some viewers would remain incapable of recognizing it as such. Israel Rodríguez submits that, following Goeritz, a "new generation almost completely gave into nonfigurative art, joining an international process that had been taking place since the beginning of the century, and that had always occupied a marginal position in Mexico."[61]

Commissioned for the wall of a study room of the Biblioteca "Lino Picaseño" in the Facultad de Arquitectura UNAM, Mathias Goeritz recreated a "Plastic Poem," (1953) similar to one that had existed in the experimental arts space that was his conception and of which he was founder, the Centro Escultórico del Eco (Museo Experimental Eco). The mural consists of a plaster support painted to serve as bright yellow background, onto which the artists applied in low relief a series of ciphers made of plywood, lacquered in black matte paint. Goeritz viewed the work as being divided into three groups: the topmost Sculptural Poem, followed by a so-called

---

translation, Elisa Schmelkes (Mexico City, Mexico, Universidad Nacional Autónoma de México, 2014) p 71.

[59]   Israel Rodríguez. "Imaginaries: Introduction," *Defying Stability: Artistic Processes in Mexico 1952–1967*, ed. Rita Eder, translation, Elisa Schmelkes (Mexico City, Mexico: Universidad Nacional Autónoma de México, 2014) p 117.

[60]   George Oppen. "Selections from George Oppen's 'Daybook'" ed. Dennis Young, *The Iowa Review*, Vol. 18, No. 3 (Fall, 1988) p 4.

[61]   Israel Rodríguez. "Imaginaries: Introduction," *Defying Stability: Artistic Processes in Mexico 1952–1967*, ed. Rita Eder, trans. Elisa Schmelkes (Mexico City, Mexico: Universidad Nacional Autónoma de México, 2014) p 117.

Pictorial Poem, and below that a Sentimental or Emotional Poem.[62] Hovering close to the left of the pictorial plane, the verses consist of two quatrains and a final concluding line or envoi. The yellow surface visually pulses as an unfamiliar environment for the inscrutable lexicon meant to convey what appear to be three distinct languages, each with its corresponding script. The work was in keeping with some of the earliest examples of concrete poetry that began to appear in Europe and Brazil between 1952 and 1953 but before a Concrete Poetry movement had been internationally consolidated. The mural assemblage can be read at the interstice between writing and image systems, and it conveys, for example, elements of poetic prosody in the form of visible "slant" or perfect end rhymes in the first two quatrains.

The first quatrain appears written in runic figures stylized in heavy boldface, evoking divinatory symbols or runes like those found etched into small pieces of bone in the letter of the ancient Germanic alphabet, that, through use and transmission, was linked to the Roman alphabet, a linguistic correlative to Goeritz's own expatriate and exiled condition as a German-speaking subject in his new Hispanophone environment. The second quatrain appears as though it were an amalgamation—possibly of Arabic the alphasyllabary script of India and Nepal (Devenagari, used in Hindi and Sanskrit)—whose curvature and undulations see to undergo a transmutation in the now angular, now flattened, ascendants of the characters. The final line of the poem is abstracted more radically into what appears to be a purely pictographic language, like those of Mesoamerican writing systems of Nahuatl, Mixtec, and others. Adam Herring describes Maya writing as lines that "represented the presence of antiquity" even as they embodied a vital discourse of performance and performative deixis,"[63] the indexical function of a word or expression whose meaning is dependent on the context. Situated in the Facultad de Arquitectura, "Plastic Poem" prompts the

---

[62] Concepción Christlieb Robles. *Biblioteca 'Lino Picaseño' de la Facultad de Arquitectura*, (paper), Web, p 5.

[63] Adam Herring. *Art and Writing in Maya Cities, A.D. 600–800: A Poetics of Line* (Cambridge: Cambridge University Press, 2005) p 106.

viewer to inhabit speech as its own form of estranging environment. Similarly, language—the English language—had become for Oppen the consistent reminder of his precarious status as a tourist. This was no metaphor. The Oppens had been roundly denied U.S. passports and had resided in Mexico for eight years on periodically renewable but contingent tourist visas.[64] Here the analogies multiply, inasmuch as for Oppen, linguistic estrangement as a kind of tourism further conflated into the vague connections that, as did Sears in Mexico, linked craftsmanship to a new consumerism.

To read George Oppen's *The Materials* through the lens of Mathias Goeritz's "Plastic Poem" is to collapse "the externally 'representative'"—namely the exile condition of Oppen in the historic moment of 1950s Mexico, under conditions that made it difficult for him to recognize things in terms of what they are in themselves but rather in exchangeable terms of an "interior expression," related to the furniture Oppen made for the Mexican middle-classes, another kind of appearance, the commodity form. The differing cultural displacements of Oppen's "Tourist Eye" and Goeritz's "Plastic Poem," speak of a condition that, even as it widens the sphere of experience, foreignizes habit. Consequent to the material and urban de-centerings of Mexico City, Oppen and Goeritz were obliged to contend with the estranging experience of foreignness that cannot know identical relation as that which American pragmatist John Dewey (no stranger to Mexico himself) called the "categories of continuity"[65]— that is, the sway between prosthetic effect and internalized particular, between inclination, tendency or impulse, and environment.

A final display of estrangement clarifies the enigma of Oppen's much noted "rust in copper dream" and the standard account of it in *Meaning a Life*. Mary refers to disturbances that link what she qualified as "the violent years" of Mexico, the couple's evident social and cultural isolation from their surroundings, the relentless "withholding ourselves from becoming exiles forever," the distance from a "politics of experience," the upscale inclination of their class

64 Rebecca Mina Schreiber. *Cold War Exiles in Mexico: U.S. Dissidents and the Culture of Critical Resistance* (Minneapolis: University of Minnesota Press, 2008) p 17.

65 John Dewey. *Experience and Education* (New York: Simon & Schuster, 1997) p 33.

status in Mexico and the reckoning it compelled as to their "previous stage of 'proletarianization.'"[66] These factors led Mary to a seek out the assistance of a Mexican psychiatrist, "who had recently returned from study in the United States," and was thus fluent in English. A "young and intelligent" doctor, she continues, "[he] had advanced ideas of women's freedom"—a feminist!—but goes unnamed in the historical record. I quote at length:

> The psychiatrist asked to see George [who recounted a dream that] he and his sister were going through his father's papers after his father's death. In a file marked 'miscellaneous' was a paper entitled 'How to Prevent Rust in Copper.' George thought, 'My old man was a little frivolous perhaps, but he certainly knew that copper does not rust.' He shook the bed with his laughter, but I did not find the dream funny... But George tells of driving on Avenida Insurgentes in Mexico City, weaving the truck from side to side, laughing at the dream of rust in copper that he was going to discuss with the psychiatrist. When he sobered and drew up to the curb, he said to himself, 'I'll kill myself driving this way,' and drove the rest of the way carefully. When he told the doctor the dream, laughing again at its ridiculousness, the doctor stopped him. // 'You were dreaming that you don't want to rust, he said. On the way home George stopped and bought a pad of paper and some pencils and started to write *The Materials*.[67]

Under periodic surveillance from the Mexican secret police; subject to bribery that enabled him to maintain his business activities in Mexico; having never acquired even rudimentary language skills in Spanish; cut off for ten years within a world whose sphere was confined to the household, the furniture workshop, and the occasional art-school class—it comes as no surprise that Oppen experienced life in Mexico as "tourists do," looking everywhere "For something bequeathed // From time, some mark / In these most worn places // Where chance moves among the crowd // Unearned and separate...."[68]

---

[66]   Mary Oppen. *Meaning A Life: An Autobiography* (Santa Barbara: Black Sparrow Press, 1978) p 200.

[67]   *Ibid*, pp 201–2.

[68]   George Oppen. *New Collected Poems*, (New York: New Directions, 2008) pp 64–66.

Even as copper does not rust, its metal properties are no less vulnerable to the oxidization that produces verdigris, or patina, a corruption of the surface, a coating that disguises the displacement at play in the dreamwork, if for instance, one supposes it was the sustainability of wood and not of copper at risk of corruption. In the noted passages of *Capital* on the commodity form, Karl Marx wrote of the materials secretly altered though labor. In his example the properties of wood are "altered by making a table out of it," and that the table rearranges consequently "into something transcendent." Marx continues: "It not only stands with its feet on the ground but, in relation to all the other commodities, it stands on its head, and evolves out of its wooden brain grotesque ideas far more wonderful than 'table-turning' ever was."[69] By means of "table turning," Oppen in Mexico had been given to the illusion of the singular, immune to the surrounding ethos, sensual life, and labor force; to the material conditions and human relations—of Carlos, the craftsman, with Oppen in the workshop—that made possible the means for his family-providing. The philosopher Sara Kofman, remarking on the "black magic" of Marx, wrote that ideas, as "products of the mind," are akin to "commodities, products of the human hand," insofar as they "give the illusion of being autonomous once cut off from the processes of their own genesis."[70] For the carpenter "who sort of [built] himself into a trap," the "rust in copper dream" did not manifest so much that Oppen feared rusting, but that he had been unable to recognize the material properties of a language craft that until then only woodcarvings and furniture, made in Mexico, had been able to elucidate in disguise. Rust in copper was the cover story for a set of analogies that connected material potential, craftsmanship, the indwelling of language, and art as a kind of internal tourism when it is "'made' in the upper-bourgeois sense" for the comfortable sectors of Mexico. Rust in copper was the patina that had enveloped a material commitment to art in the idea of livelihood. For Oppen, it was an idea

---

[69] Karl Marx. *Capital: A Critique of Political Economy*, trans. Samuel Moore and Edward Aveling (New York: The Modern Library, 1906) p 82

[70] Sarah Kofman. *Camera Obscura: Of Ideology* (Ithaca, New York: Cornell University Press, 1999) pp 8–9.

that so confused accommodation, household, and hideaway as to be unable to view "Beyond the window" where there is "Flesh and rock and hunger" that could inaugurate in language an "assault / On the quiet continent."

Despite his lifelong ambivalence about the years spent in Mexico, Oppen eventually wrote work so indebted to its urban particularities, its cultural processes, and its people, "A crowd, a population, those / Born, those not yet dead, the moment's / Populace, sea-borne and violent."[71] The genesis of *The Materials* cannot be cut off from the Mexican dream that so unclouded his vision as to replace a manifest image of himself as carpenter with the inconvenient image of himself as a poet and so return to what Ezra Pound saw in the author of *Discrete Series*, able to make "expression [...] coterminous with [...] content."[72]

In 1958, the year the Oppens began the process that led to their return to the United States, Hannah Arendt published *The Human Condition*. She wrote: "To live together in the world means essentially that a world of things is between those who have it in common, as a table is located between those who sit around it; the world, like every in-between, relates and separates men at the same time."[73] How to Prevent Rust in Copper? George may have had in mind to answer that question when—on pads of paper and the pencils he purchased in Mexico City—he sat down to write in *The Materials*—this:

> Together, and among the others,
> The bequeathed pavements, the inherited lit streets:
> Among them we were lucky—strangest word. [74]

---

71   George Oppen. *New Collected Poems*, (New York: New Directions, 2008) p 43.

72   Ezra Pound. "Preface," *Discrete Series*, George Oppen, *New Collected Poems*, (New York: New Directions, 2008) p 3.

73   Hannah Arendt. *The Human Condition* (Chicago: University of Chicago Press, 1958) p 52. She adds: "The public realm, as the common world, gathers us together and yet prevents our falling over each other, so to speak. What makes mass society so difficult to bear is not the number of people involved, or at least not primarily, but the fact that the world between them has lost its power to gather them together, to relate and to separate them."

74   George Oppen. "Blood from the Stone," *New Collected Poems*, (New York: New Directions, 2008) p 53.

TRANS
LATING

THE COUNTER CONQUEST

"THE IMAGE IS THE SECRET CAUSE OF HISTORY," wrote mid-century modernist José Lezama Lima (Havana, 1910–1976) in an essay theorizing the *imago*, and the enterprise of image making. In fact, he went so far as to claim that the very

> hypothesis of the image is possibility.... But the image must side with death, must endure the opening of the ark as superlative enigma and fascination, that is, in the fullness of embodiment, so that possibility may achieve meaning and surge into historical timeliness.[1]

In this respect, Lezama Lima fashioned a poetics of the paradox where contraries are drawn to coexist in procreative motion. His comprehensive method—a categorical "poetic system"—is structured by means of a wager on the generative yielding power of the image, the severed status in which language and the visible world are cleft as "a continuity that questions / and a rift in response."[2] There is, in his work, a shifting continuum between the high Gongorism of the Spanish golden-age baroque and his own

---

[1]   José Lezama Lima. "26 de julio: Imagen y posibilidad," in *Imagen y posibilidad* (Havana: Editorial Letras Cubanas, 1981) p 19 [Author's translation].

[2]   José Lezama Lima. "Dissonance," *José Lezama Lima: Selections*, (California: University of California Press) p 86 [Author's translation].

brand of Caribbean surrealism—where vocabulary, syntax, image, and metaphor are rendered both luxuriant and warped, or largely cut off from their source in Iberian tradition. A literary figure that might serve to describe the poly-eroticism of Lezama Lima's ability to create stasis-into-motion-and-back is the anacoluthon, that ellipsis by which a poetic statement begins with a series of initial assumptions and concludes otherwise with an altogether shifted set of modified terms, only to begin again by hovering at the edge of an indeterminate gap opened in the present tense.

Following Lezama Lima's *Death of Narcissus* [Muerte de Narciso]—a mid-length poem published in 1937—*Enemy Rumor* [Enemigo rumor] (1941) was his first sizable collection. In that book, Lezama Lima established a formal breadth and a set of tonic residues that point simultaneously to Garcilaso de la Vega, Francisco de Quevedo, Comte de Lautréamont, Paul Valéry, and Rainer Maria Rilke. The book progresses from the mode of pastoral invitation[3] to increasingly broader and less familiar landscapes, but not without a neo-classical interlude of "infidel sonnets," including those to the Virgin Mary: Lezama Lima was a life-long Catholic, no matter how *sui generis*. In extended lines that are gushes of respiration (he was also asthmatic), the poems perform a concealment behind appearances, a task accomplished by bringing an image to the extreme foreground of the poetic frame[4] to recede again into vista perspective wherein organic life and inert matter erupt in all-over animation and effervescence. Hardly a lesser copy of an original phenomenon, the image for Lezama Lima insinuates itself as a pleasure-producing, potentially destructive quantity that subsists side-by-side with what is valued, and often privileged, as its physical analogue.

---

[3]   See Nathaniel Tarn's elegant rendering of "An Obscure Meadow Lure Me" [Una oscura pradera me convida] in *Con Cuba: An Anthology of Cuban Poetry of the Last Sixty Years*, trans Elinor Randall et al, ed Nathaniel Tarn (London: Cape Goliard, 1969).

[4]   Carmen Ruiz Barrionuevo. "'Enemigo rumor', de José Lezama Lima" in *Coloquio Internacional sobre la obra de Jose Lezama Lima: Poesia*, ed. Cristina Vizcaino (Madrid: Editorial Fundamentos, 1984) p 172.

According to Lezama Lima,

> Poetry itself becomes a substance so real, so devouring, that we find it in all presences. And this is not a floating, not the poetry of Impressionist light, but rather the production of a body that constitutes an enemy, and it watches us from that vantage point. But each step in that animosity provokes a stele or an ineffable communication."[5]

Both "Insular Night: Invisible Gardens" and "A Bridge, A Remarkable Bridge," the two major poems with which *Enemy Rumor* concludes, are products of this agonistic force, seen as fertile and never-ending—insofar as production triumphs over the supposed last word of material demise. In the former work, this is staged as the logic of optics and light; in the latter, as the engineering that not only makes possible social exchange, but that also links the rendered world to everyday life. These works offer contemporary poetic praxis, with its not infrequent condescension toward the cultural currency of the senses, a lesson in the values of astonishment. And the image of dewdrops [*rocío*] appears on such numerous occasions, it would be remiss not to foreground its hidden sonic markers of affirmation [*sí*], conjunction [*y*], or potentiality and difference [*o* | *y* | *o*]—an entire world of relation as such a diminutive sign is able to contain, and like the bead of moisture that is its signified, reflective of Lezama Lima's colossal canvases.

In translating his work, I've sought to maintain the idiosyncrasy of Lezama Lima's Spanish—the repeated parataxis, the luxuriant baroque cadences and register, the anacoluthic statement-making and shifts—as they might be rendered in the poetic availabilities of the contemporary U.S. American avant-garde. These compatible attributes are an attempt to reconfigure a specific mode of verbal manufacture but as addressed within a radically different cultural and aesthetic context, with its particular poetic legacy and formal bylaws. In this, they aim to read one version of postmodernism

---

[5]   José Lezama Lima in a letter to the poet Cintio Vitier. Quoted in Carmen Ruiz Barrionuevo. "'Enemigo rumor', de José Lezama Lima" in *Coloquio Internacional sobre la obra de Jose Lezama Lima: Poesia*, ed Cristina Vizcaino (Madrid: Editorial Fundamentos, 1984) p 172.

within its own specific circumstance but also as compared to advanced poetic design practiced elsewhere, in order to establish, in the words of Lezama Lima himself, "a form in its becoming" within a "landscape [that] turns to a meaning, an interpretation or a sheer hermeneutic"[6]—that is, a translation's historic vision.

Although his reputation in English still rests almost entirely on his novel *Paradiso*,[7] the sheer range of work produced by this Cuban modernist/postmodernist has yet to be rendered into English.[8] His *Obras completas* include over five-hundred pages of collected poetry and certainly twice as many pages of essays and assorted prose. Written from 1971 to 1976, and posthumously published in 1978, *Fragmentos a su imán*, from which I've translated the poems I discuss in what follows, is a work that reveals a series of final inflections in Lezama Lima's lifelong "poetic system." Without the unabashed symbolist swirl or constraining elegance of previous work, but armed with the unstoppable onrush akin to his long poem *Dador*, for instance, *Fragmentos* features a more audibly strident cadence and mode as the poems stage a three-ring circus of images telescoped into immanent high-minded slap-stick:

> The comedic fat-lady
> and wormy lover
> fumbling with the lock
> on a window—affected speech
> as they pull their hair.
> ("They Slip Through the Night")[9]

---

[6] José Lezama Lima. "Mitos y cansancio clásico," *La expresión americana,* ed. Irlemar Chiampi (Mexico City: Fondo de Cultura Económica), 1993, p 49; also, José Lezama Lima, *El reino de la imagen,* ed. Julio Ortega (Caracas: Biblioteca Ayacucho, 1981) p 369 [Author's translation].

[7] José Lezama Lima. *Paradiso*, trans. Gregory Rabassa (New York: Farrar, Straus and Giroux, 1974).

[8] Until the publication of *José Lezama Lima: Selections*, edited and with an introduction by Ernesto Livón-Grosman (California: University of California Press, 2005) there were notable exceptions: the superb translations by James Irby of "Ten Prose Poems," *Sulfur* (3) 1982, 40–51; and his translation of several stunning essays, such as the pivotal "Confluences," *Sulfur* (25) Fall 1989, pp 155–174.

[9] José Lezama Lima. "They Slip Through the Night," trans. Roberto Tejada, in *José*

Or they enact stop-action still-lifes about to implode:

> Inside the bottle,
> one-third of a year in a damp cave,
> a skeleton, a mill, a wedding:
> the prison baroque.
> ("The Neck")[10]

In *Fragmentos a su imán*, the subject is often the poetic process, a form of dissonance that scrutinizes language "effacing itself and plunging forward / with the laughable eyes of a lobster."[11] The writing in *Fragmentos* teems with images of isolated enclosure and resignation: a veritable "prison baroque."[12] *Fragmentos a su imán* might well be translated—and in keeping with the provisional world of Lezama

---

Lezama Lima: Selections, edited and with an introduction by Ernesto Livón-Grosman (California: University of California Press, 2005) p 84.

[10] *Ibid.*, p 82.

[11] *Ibid.*, p 86.

[12] For all intents and purposes, after 1959, and despite the success of *Paradiso*, Lezama Lima's writing remained unabashedly disregarded by an oblivious cultural apparatus, and the writer essentially lived in self-imposed confinement during the latter years of his life. The early to mid-1970s saw a renewed but nonetheless ambivalent official interest in Lezama Lima. For Cuba's Generación de los ochenta, Lezama Lima wielded a certain mystique due in large part to certain scandalous receptions of his novel Paradiso, and to the implications and aftermath of the Padilla Affair. In its wake Lezama Lima was at best ignored or held in check by the cultural apparatus; at worst he was censored and denied visas to travel. "The story, of course, is by now well known. The board of the Unión de Escritores y Artistas Cubanos (UNEAC: Lezama Lima was a member of that board) awarded Padilla's collection of poems, *Fuera del juego* [*Outside the Game*], the Julián del Casal prize for literature. When, however, certain Padilla poems were deemed critical of the Revolution, UNEAC's executive committee found it necessary to pen a letter that condemned Padilla's 'subversive' activity. All of this would eventually lead, directly and indirectly, to the jailing of Padilla, to an international outcry (especially among leftist intellectuals who had placed their faith in the Revolution) and, finally, to Padilla's famous mea culpa: a lengthy confession, delivered by Padilla in front of a meeting of Cuban intellectuals and officials (Lezama Lima was not present), in which Padilla denounced not only his own 'anti-Revolutionary' activities, but also those of many artists." Brett Levinson, *Secondary Moderns: Mimesis, History, and Revolution in Lezama Lima's "American Expression,"* (Lewisburg, Pennsylvania: Bucknell University Press, 1996) p 178

Lima; that is, tentatively—as *The Fragments Drawn by Charm*. The poems here are often generated by a sense that matter and meaning are incessantly performing apocalyptic rehearsals of "a genesial, copulative relatedness,"[13] an all- encompassing, cyclonic conjunction or totalizing ejaculative surge where "Everything everywhere [is] looming."[14] As is clear to readers of *Paradiso*'s infamous Chapter VIII, Lezama Lima was obsessed with the phallic illusoriness of monumental scale and excess.[15]

That excess was moderated by deprivation. To recall, Lezama Lima was asthmatic, and his symptoms possibly grew even more pronounced with age, and with the increased austerity in the decades following the 1959 Revolution, when medications became increasingly more difficult to obtain. It comes as no wonder that earlier in 1938 he had already defined poetry as a "photograph of breathing."[16] It is in this sense that the fits and starts of imaginal sequence come to formally rhyme here with the repeated references to actual respiration. In his poetics of the paradox, whereby conflicting opposites momentarily coexist in procreative stand-off, Lezama Lima sought, as suggested by Rubén Ríos Ávila, to make of his respiratory system a syncopated microcosm for the solar system and by extension, for universal knowledge.[17]

In what follows, I outline a provisional framework for the broader theoretical task of analyzing the range of problems and predicaments inherent to rendering Lezama Lima into English without forfeiting the idiosyncrasy of the original. I turn to works on the theory of translation, including Walter Benjamin's oft-cited "The

---

[13]   José Lezama Lima. "They Slip Through the Night," *José Lezama Lima: Selections*, (California: University of California Press) p 106.

[14]   José Lezama Lima. "Octavio Paz," trans. Roberto Tejada, *Sulfur* (38) Spring 1996, p 111.

[15]   Emilio Bejel, *Gay Cuban Nation* (Chicago: The University of Chicago Press, 2001) "When Lezama Lima published *Paradiso* in 1966, it sparked a controversy that prompted government officials to temporarily block its distribution (ostensibly because of the book's explicit homosexual scenes)" p 115.

[16]   José Lezama Lima. "Del aprovechamiento poético (1938)" in *Analecta del reloj* (Havana: Orígenes, 1953) p 257.

[17]   Rubén Ríos Ávila. *"La imagen como sistema"* in *Coloquio internacional sobre la obra de José Lezama Lima: Poesía* (Madrid: Editiorial Fundamentos, 1984) p 131.

Task of the Translator," and more recent contributions in continental philosophy like those of Gilles Deleuze and Jacques Derrida. But more to the point of this essay, I discuss one of the most celebrated and influential poems from *The Fragments Drawn by Charm*, "El pabellón del vacío" [Pavilion of Nothingness] for it contains Lezama Lima's own theory of translation. In the process, I wonder whether appraisals of poetic works can be historically refigured when read in relation to artistic practice in parallel cultural contexts. I ask what might be gained by reading one version of modernism within its own context and compared to other sites of advanced artistic production, and by whose standards will avant-garde practice in parallel traditions be judged? Can a comparative analysis of twentieth-century art and writing produced in this hemisphere belie distinct paradigms of degree and kind, while also pointing toward a new model between the Americas?

◆ ◆ ◆

I return to the assertion that Lezama Lima's entire poetic system is structured by means of a wager on the generative yielding power of the image; of language and material reality cleft as "a continuity that questions / and a rift in response." In his lifelong corpus, but especially in *The Fragments Drawn by Charm*, physical bodies attain substance and find centering by way of mirror-play—often ambiguously sexed and sexualized as subjects.[18] In "The Embrace,"

---

[18] To appreciate the sexual articulation in Lezama Lima's writing is to "consider homosexual desire as a drive for an image which is at once always the same and always different, always the same and always the other. In this process, [Lezama Lima excludes] any feminine manifestation except for the maternal, and [reveals] instead the threatening and excessive presence of Nothing, of *Nada*, perhaps death itself, as in the story of Narcissus." Damiano Benvegnù, "Images of Narcissus: Figuring Identity in José Lezama Lima and Pier Paolo Pasolini," *Comparative Literature Studies*, Vol. 52, No. 4 (2015) p 823. A biographical note is applicable. Following the death of his mother, and as per her dying wishes, Lezama Lima enters into matrimony with María Luisa Bautista, his personal secretary. See Julio Ortega "Vida y obra de José Lezama Lima" in *José Lezama Lima, El reino de la imagen*, ed. Julio Ortega (Caracas: Biblioteca Ayacucho, 1981) p 576. "1964: El 12 de setiembre muere su madre y el poeta sufre una honda depresión. Se casa

Lezama Lima blurs distinctions between self and other only to propel the difference into motion again, now emboldened with generative and destructive force, with the "unknown breath / of otherness" that reflective likenesses allow:

> The two bodies
> elapse after smashing the intervening
> mirror, each body renders
> the one it faces, beginning
> to perspire like mirrors.
> They know there's a moment
> when a shadow will pinch them,
> something like dew, unstoppable as smoke.
> The unknown breath
> of otherness, of the sky bending and blinking, that eggshell
> very slowly cracking.
> ["The Embrace"][19]

In two of the longer philosophical poems of The Fragments, Lezama Lima continually articulates a mobile theory of the image, a constant concern in his work. In "Nacimiento del día" [Birth of Day] he writes: "The body hid inside the house of images / and later it reappeared identical and similar / to a stellar fragment, it returned."[20] It is this duality of "identical and similar," this simultaneity of likeness and representation, that allows for the alternate term that powers Lezama Lima's poetic discourse:

> The mirror with its silent central
> vortex of groped water,
> unites images again with their body.
> It's the first trembling answer.
> Where did the mirror come from,
> that aerolite hurled by man?
> How did the crystal that breaks into air
> without corrupting it, grow dark inside
> detaining the image?

---

con María Luisa Bautista, su secretaria, siguiendo el consejo de su madre."

[19]   José Lezama Lima. "The Embrace," trans. Roberto Tejada, José Lezama Lima: Selections, (California: University of California Press) p 18.

[20]   Translation by Roberto Tejada.

There, advancing, nothing is detained
only nothingness fixedly sways.
["The Gods"][21]

♦ ♦ ♦

This nothingness detained but that "fixedly sways" is one of Lezama Lima's descriptions of the simulacrum—that is, and more in keeping with his poetic system, the *imago*. Gilles Deleuze, in "The Simulacrum and Ancient Philosophy," provides a thorough blueprint to the project of "reversing Platonism."[22] To transpose "the Platonic motivation" necessitates a disavowal of those divisions between essence and appearance, between the intelligible and the sensible, between idea and image, between the original and the copy, and between the model and the simulacrum; to renounce a structuring of the world based on resemblances. If Plato divides the domain of images-idols in two—into copies-icons and simulacra-phantoms—he does so "because they are endowed with resemblance. But resemblance should not be understood as an external relation. It goes less from one thing to another than from one thing to an Idea, since it is an idea which comprehends the relations and proportions constitutive of the internal essence."[23] For Deleuze, the simulacrum is not a copy of a copy: *simulacrum and copy form two parts of a single term; they are internal to each other.* Delueze states that "The copy is an image endowed with resemblance, the simulacrum is an image without resemblance."[24] The underside of resemblance, of the similar, or of identity, is the disparity or difference that generates or sustains the simulacrum. Insomuch as a term can never be selfsame or identical to itself, "The simulacrum is built upon a disparity or upon a difference. It internalizes dissimilarity.... If the simulacrum has a model, it is another model, a model of the Other (*l'Autre*) from which there flows an internalized dissemblance."[25]

---

[21]   *Ibid.*

[22]   Gilles Deleuze. *The Logic of Sense* (New York: Columbia University Press, 1990) p 253.

[23]   *Ibid.*, p 257.

[24]   *Ibid.*, p 258.

[25]   *Ibid.*

The simulacrum includes the differential perspective; and the observer who submits to the simulacrum, is transformed and deformed by such a viewpoint. In short, there is in the simulacrum a becoming-mad, or a becoming unlimited, as in the *Philibus* where "more and less are always going a point further," a becoming always other, a becoming subversive of the depths, able to evade the equal, the limit, the Same, or the Similar: always more and less at once, but never equal.[26] This applies to Lezama Lima and the *Fragments Drawn by Charm*. Insomuch as the Platonic copy is the Similar, and Aristotle's aim is to establish representation as well-founded, limited, and finite, then Lezama Lima's project of poetic-visual representation— the *imago*—is upset by a discrepancy or contradiction. Insomuch as copies engage difference from the standpoint of a previous similitude or identity, and to the degree that simulacra oblige us to think similitude and identity as the product of a deep disparity or difference, then simulation can be viewed as Nietzsche's eternal return in that this movement constitutes the only Same—the same of that which differs; it allows for only one resemblance—"the resemblance of the unmatched."[27] In this respect, the modern project—a modernity with which Lezama Lima identified, and into which he inscribed his own poetic system—is defined by power of the simulacrum: "Artifice and simulacrum are opposed at the heart of modernity, at the point where modernity settles all of its accounts, as two modes of destruction: the two nihilisms."[28]

♦ ♦ ♦

As mentioned above, Lezama Lima's poetry in *Fragmentos a su imán* resonates with the Platonic-Deleuzian question of the identical and the similar—indeed the problem of representation and the simulacrum. In the poem "Birth of Day," Lezama Lima relates that: "The body hid inside the house of images / and later it reappeared

---

[26] *Ibid.*

[27] *Ibid.*, p 265.

[28] *Ibid.*

identical and similar /to a stellar fragment, it returned."[29] This simultaneity of likeness and representation, of fixity and movement, are the terms that set into motion a theory of translation underlying the closing poem in *The Fragments Drawn by Charm*, which I have translated as "Pavilion of Nothingness."

Following Walter Benjamin in "The Task of the Translator," one challenge facing the translator of "El pabellón del vacío" and *Fragmentos a su imán* is set into motion at the tenuous dividing line between the rendering of subject matter and the transmission of essence or effect. According to Benjamin, the successful translation creates a tension or dynamic sustained "up in the air"[30] and in a synthesis: "Translation is so far removed from being the sterile equation of two dead languages that of all literary forms it is the one charged with the special mission of watching over the maturing process of the original and the birth pangs of its own."[31]

These theoretical tensions and effects are performed in Lezama Lima's poem "Pavilion of Nothingness" along with a number of other concerns related to the logic of translation. The poem stages its drama by way of the double or second self, to elaborate a theory of absence or want and a theory of productive desire. For this, it relies on the image of the *tokonoma*, or that niche or recess in Japanese architecture, usually in the living room of a residence, often housing a *kakemono*, an ornamental pictorial or calligraphic scroll. The poem hinges on the tension between text and image, and between the terms "tokonoma" and "vacío" [nothingness, void, recess, hollow]. This effect is paralleled in the strange interval between the poem's voice and its surrogate persona in the form of the poem—a self-discontinuous with its subjectivity. This is the subject matter of "Pabellón del vacío," even as lines further address the aims of art making, localize a theory of translation, and perform a species of counter-conquest. Here, I quote

---

29   José Lezama Lima. "The Birth of Day," trans. Roberto Tejada, *White Wall Review* 36 (2012): pp 13–19.

30   Walter Benjamin. *Illuminations: Essays and Reflections*, trans. Harry Zohn. (New York: Schocken Books, 1969.) p 215.

31   Walter Benjamin. "The Task of the Translator" in *Illuminations: Essays and Reflections*, (New York: Schocken Books, 1969) p 73.

the poem in its entirety:

PAVILION OF NOTHINGNESS

I join the screw
posing questions in
the wall, a lackluster sound
color covered with a blanket.
But I falter and momentarily
blind, I can barely feel myself.
All at once, I call to mind,
with my fingernails I tunnel
a tokonoma in the wall.
I need a tiny hollow,
it's there I go diminishing
to reappear anew,
to touch myself and set my forehead in its place.
A tiny hollow in the wall.

Multiplier of weariness
the café I'm sitting in,
the insistent daiquiri
returning like a face of no use
for death, for springtime.
With my hands I trace the length
of a lapel that feels cold to me.
I wait for no one and I insist
on someone's pressing arrival.
All at once, with my fingernail
I draw a tiny crevice on the table.
There it is, the tokonoma, the hollow,
I'm in company unrivaled,
a corner conversation in Alexandria.
We're together in a round
of skaters through the Prado.
He was a child who inhaled
all the tenacious dew from the sky,
even then with the hollow, like a cat
that circles the whole body
with a silence full of flickerings.

Within reach of what surrounds us,
 and close to our body,
the stubborn notion that says our soul
and its enwrapping fit
inside a tiny hollow in the wall
or on tissue paper scratched with a fingernail.
I'm diminishing
I'm a point that disappears and returns
and I fit full-length inside the tokonoma.
I make myself invisible
and on the verso I recover my body
swimming at the beach,
encircled by bachelors of art with banners of snow,
mathematicians and baseball players
describing sapodilla ice cream.
The hollow is smaller than a deck of cards
and it can be as big as the sky,
but we can shape it with our fingernail
along the brim of a coffee cup
or in the sky that falls beside our shoulder.

The beginning is united with the tokonoma,
in the hollow a kangaroo can hide
without forfeit of its bounding joy.
The apparition of a cave is
mysterious and begins to disentangle its dreadful.
To hide there is to tremble,
the hunter's horns resound
in the frozen forest.
But the hollow is soothing,
we can lure it with a thread
and usher it in to insignificance.
I scrape the wall with a fingernail,
slivers of lime crumble down
as though they were shards
from the celestial tortoise shell.
Is the barrenness in the hollow
the first and final path?
I fall asleep, in the tokonoma
the other still walking is the one I evaporate.
1 April & 1976 [Author's translation]

Readers familiar with the Spanish original will observe how the word "vacío," which forms part of the title as well the body of the text, makes different appearances in the English translation: as "nothingness" in the title of the poem, and as "hollow" throughout the body of the text. As the poet's persona "falters" in the opening stanza, in an attempt to find enclosure within the material reality of surrounding space, he "calls to mind" the notion of the void or nothingness and "tunnels / a tokonoma in the wall." In the following stanza, the tokonoma is again recalled as an irrepressible capacity to contain and surge forth. The body itself is likened to the tokonoma in that it is comprises both surface and undersurface:

> I'm diminishing
> I'm a point that disappears and returns
> and I fit full-length inside the tokonoma.
> I make myself invisible
> and on the verso I recover my body
> swimming at the beach,
> encircled by bachelors of art with banners of snow,
> mathematicians and baseball players
> describing sapodilla ice cream.

I translate "vacío" in the title as "nothingness" to establish the movement Lezama Lima describes in another poem ["The Gods"] as a detained and detaining image in whose advancing "only nothingness fixedly sways." The play between "nothingness" and "hollow" is an attempt to give fuller resonance to Lezama Lima's own theory of the image that blurs that dividing line between the similar and the same, between self and other ("The other still walking is the one I evaporate") and between the original and translation. In the view of Jacques Derrida (*The Ear of the Other*):

> The original is not a plenitude, which would come to be translated by accident. The original is in the situation of demand, that is, of a lack or exile. The original is indebted a priori to the translation. Its survival is a demand and a desire for translation, somewhat like the Babelian demand: Translate me. Babel is a man, or rather a male god, a god that is not full since he is full of resentment, jealousy, and so on. He calls out, he desires,

he lacks, he calls for the complement or the supplement or, as Benjamin says, for that which will come along to enrich him. Translation does not come along in addition, like an accident added to a full substance; rather it is what the original text demands—and not simply the signatory of the original text but the text itself.[32]

♦ ♦ ♦

"The image is the secret cause of history," wrote Lezama Lima. The claim further evokes Homer's Odysseus and his descent into the underworld in search of his shadow-mother who, after several withdrawals and elisions, urges her son to remain no longer in that somber valley but to return without delay to the light. "The force of encounter ...ascends toward the timely, occupies that space where light strikes its enemies and dispossesses the medusa of its infinite features."[33]

Lezama Lima's "Pavilion of Nothingness" and *The Fragments Drawn by Charm* reject the irresolvable contradiction that constitutes "the impossible." Lezama Lima preferred to think of the "difficult" [*lo difícil*] as the hard kernel constitutive of the poetic imagination, and of poems as the "contradiction of contradictions"[34] ["Dissonance"], a self-effacement whose task is to propel or redirect. Translation, as both a poetics and a politics, is the art of uneasy possibilities—at the level of design and constituent subjects. Lezama Lima began his astounding essays gathered in *La expresión americana* as follows:

> Only the difficult is stimulating; only resistance that defies us can incite, maintain and span our potential for knowledge—but what, in fact, constitutes the difficult? Is it plainly that which is submerged in the maternal waters of the obscure? The original conception devoid of causality, antithesis or logos? It is form in its becoming by which a landscape turns to a meaning, an interpretation or a sheer hermeneutic,

---

[32] Jacques Derrida. *The Ear of the Other* (Lincoln: University of Nebraska Press, 1988) pp 152–3 [Emphasis added].

[33] José Lezama Lima. "26 de julio: Imagen y posibilidad," *Imagen y posibilidad* (Havana: Editorial Letras Cubanas, 1981) p 19.

[34] José Lezama Lima. "Dissonance," trans. Roberto Tejada, *Sulfur* (38) Spring 1996, 117–118.

so as to point to a reconstruction marking its effect or disuse in a definitive way, its ordering force or muffled echo—in a word, its historic vision.[35]

Like the modalities of the identical and the different that are so crucial to Lezama Lima's understanding of the image, "El pabellón del vacío" contains directives for the poem's rendering into another language. The two Lezama Limas—the poem's persona and the eventually evaporated "other still walking"—make voluptuous the spellbound qualities and quantities that, in any given historic moment, may be deemed the shortcoming of one's vernacular, or the productive excess of the other's.[36] In the barrenness of an interpretive hollow, in the metaphoric interplay of counter-conquest and utopia, a baroque image of the body, "the first and final path," emerges at last in excess of itself.

---

[35]   José Lezama Lima. *La expresión americana* (Havana: Editorial Letras Cubanas, 1993) p 7 [Author's translation].

[36]   Walter Benjamin. "The Task of the Translator" in *Illuminations: Essays and Reflections*, (New York: Schocken Books, 1969) p 72.

Can a comparative
analysis of twentieth-century
art and writing
produced in
this hemisphere

♦

belie distinct paradigms
of degree and kind,
while also pointing toward
a new model
between the Americas?

IS

OF THOSE ALIGNED WITH AT LEAST ONE visible column of the U.S. American avant-garde, more than a few writers have been so obedient to formal mandate and the certainties of development as to discount the likelihood that those imperatives, as with every hazard of orthodoxy, are narrowly if any longer defiant of our state of affairs. There's a discernable commitment to modernist idolatry and, along with it, the symptomatic hubris of an avant-garde baffled by the news that, actually, other modes of critical practice and meaning- making thrive in excess of any centralizing desire. So ensuing dismissals and misrecognitions by the avant-garde's upper administration are yet another belated cover story for U.S. American attitudes of exception, with a paternalism generally assigned, even as a partial admittance, to developing regions deemed in need of modernization. This bad faith is in keeping with what Zygmunt Bauman has called, in his view of our devotion to the credit card, "addictive" modernity,[1] and it appears not without a diminishing. Most detrimental in terms of poetry, this closure or essentialism of the medium and typically its domestic circulations, beget an obscuring of the citizen in favor of the consumer. Having found increased welcome in once-restricted spaces—universities, professional organizations, mass circulation

---

[1] Zygmunt Bauman. "Life on Credit," *Soundings* (London, England), 41:1, 63.

periodicals, special collection archives—the poetic avant-garde has proliferated over the last thirty years owing to an ever-expanding producer-consumer base, no longer sustainable as a unified creative class.

♦ ♦ ♦

In one important sense, modernism cast a spell to fix the future at an endpoint in our relationship with the present as a process beholden to the past. Sweeping transformations today in the wake of global finance capital, intensified displacement, greater high-speed communication networks, and reverberating effects of these experiences on labor and value, have all but eroded the developmental time frame of modernism and its understanding of scale. To be sure, this ongoing historic process has yielded increasingly site-specific environments of impact and evaluation; and in these locations it has modified concrete and potential economies of imagined cultural status. If the modernist project and capitalism continue to associate as a shared repertoire of aspirations, certain cheerful inflections of avant-garde practice today appear so untroubled as to largely ape or disregard the symptoms of these deep-seated social transformations— and the role of the United States in that process. This omission speaks of a modernism complicit with "the long line of capitalist accumulation methods [that have] eventually exhausted its potential: once more capitalism, in the course of its expansion, has eaten up the milieu indispensable for its survival."[2] In this scenario, modernist methods for producing critical antagonism are readily subsumed as just another carefree aesthetic consumer choice. Why not? If the crisis of the avant-garde is commensurate with the global downturn, with the perverse logic of credit boom and bust, then admission into the cultural marketplace is jeopardized by the expanding numbers thought to guarantee the cultural benefit of a few. In brazen pursuit of immediate gratification, how many advocates of formal innovation risk losing sight of modernism's critical reason for being?

---

[2]   *Ibid*, 56.

♦ ♦ ♦

There is a vast range of poetic practices that so work in tandem with other forms of knowledge as to provide contradictory pleasures that also hazard a diagnostic. This writing conveys the culture concept as a system of attitudes and instruction, human sensuous activity, the broadest environments of life as activations in the public sphere by means of a daydreaming embodied as intervals of contemplation and sense experience. If we measure the depth of Nietzsche's claim that a word is only "a copy in sound of a nerve stimulus" and concept the "residue of a metaphor,"[3] the political ante of the language arts so escalates as to be more than an "internal relations" model for artistic change. This urgency compels us not only to redirect our assigned social scripts, but to set higher ambitions as to what can be said, in keeping with Stephen Greenblatt, about the "systemic organization of ordinary life and consciousness [...], the pattern of boundary making and breaking, [and] the oscillation between demarcated objects and monological totality..."—that is, a cultural poetics.[4]

♦ ♦ ♦

Inasmuch as I've lost faith in the sustainability of an avant-garde as a definable formation, especially in an expanding media environment of over-production and calculated obsolescence, I want writing to re-imagine citizenship today in terms that include a voluptuousness of the self and its overcast contingencies. I seek to reconcile two expansive propositions that in many ways are incompatible. U.S. American minimalism, grounded in the media specificity of its objects and materiality of form, endures because it is well equipped to expose artistic autonomy with the methods of mechanized labor and thereby to reanimate the relationship of art and industry. A

---

[3]   Friedrich Nietzsche. "On Truth and Lies in a Non-Moral Sense" in *Philosophy and Truth; Selections from Nietzsche's Notebooks of the Early 1870s*, Atlantic Highlands, N.J.: Humanities Press, 1979, pp 81; 85.

[4]   Stephen Greenblatt. "Towards a Poetics of Culture" in *The New Historicism*, ed. H. Aram Veeser, (New York, Routledge, 1989) p 8.

Latin American neo-baroque, the extension of historic surrealism, enacts a pageantry of excess and seduction as public engagement, in interplays of violence and sensuality, with a view to the social field not as system of fixed values, but as an irreverent open-ended archive of meaning.

◆ ◆ ◆

In previous pages, I suggested that Cuban modernist José Lezama Lima identified difficulty as a motivating feature—not in terms of mere representation or strictly formal effects. He viewed difficulty with optimism as enabling of the interpretive project, a defiance given to incite the potential for knowledge as the "ordering force" of "historic vision."[5] In this respect, difficulty requires thoughtfulness and the unique understanding attained in the joyful labor of making things. Metaphoric language is difficult to the extent that our relationship to generosity, in the broadest sense, is likewise a problem. Psychoanalyst Adam Phillips and historian Barbara Taylor compel this question of closure and availability by asking why there exists a social anxiety around kindness when it plainly produces pleasure. They submit this is because kindness, a style of obedience to the life of others, involves, like metaphor, a loss of boundaries.[6] Dissolution, then, of the strictly formal imperative invites a more difficult reckoning with our investment in the medium as message.

◆ ◆ ◆

There is room for an ethos of carefulness in our era of increased mechanized labor, post-production, and outsourcing. Even as digital storage and retrieval can facilitate rhetorical possibilities and methodological scale, user interface imposes limitations also and calls for more nuanced technological imaginations to punctuate the

---

[5] José Lezama Lima. *Imagen y posibilidad*, edited with a prologue and notes by Ciro Bianchi Ross (Havana: Editorial Letras Cubanas, 1981) p 19 [Author's translation].

[6] Adam Phillips and Barbara Taylor. *On Kindness* (New York: Farrar, Straus and Giroux, 2009).

proliferating cacophony of statistics, unwanted thoughts, accidental associations, and renewed colonialities of power on the global network. Richard Sennett directly links the shifting relations of labor and workplace to manufacture. "If craftsmanship, with its vibrant tradition of ... mastery of a particular skill, doesn't constitute merit," then with every incentive for innovation favored over verifiable aptitude "...you are constantly, as it were, walking away from your own commitments."[7] My desire is for careful energizing words to structure the astonishment that is our accountability to language, foresight, and gesture; when metaphoric language in the mediated world can so beckon into action—into experience and knowledge—as to prompt the unforeseen. Constitutive of social space and cultural selfhood, the syllabic realism of metaphor obliges an urgent kind of carefulness that emboldens the critical imagination to alter our picture of the present and the shape of things in a future tense. It aspires to what George Oppen envisioned when, in "A Language of New York,"[8] he found in the antagonisms of history the premise for hope.

> Possible
> To use
> Words provided one treat them
> As enemies.
> Not enemies--Ghosts
> Which have run mad
> In the subways
> And of course the institutions
> And the banks. If one captures them
> One by one proceeding
>
> Carefully they will restore
> I hope to meaning
> And to sense.

7   Richard Sennett. "What Do We Mean by Talent?" *The Political Quarterly*, Vol. 77, Issue Supplement, s1, pp 163–167, June 2006 [Italics added].

8   George Oppen, "A Language of New York," *New Collected Poems* (New York: New Directions, 2008) p 116.

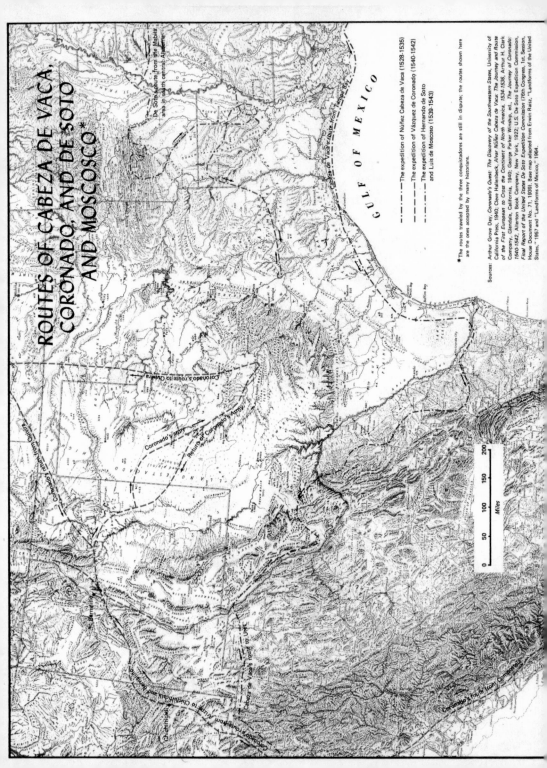

ROUTES OF CABEZA DE VACA, CORONADO, AND DE SOTO AND MOSCOSCO*

De Soto's route from the Mabila area in south central Alabama

GULF OF MEXICO

------- The expedition of Núñez Cabeza de Vaca (1528-1535)
——·—— The expedition of Vázquez de Coronado (1540-1542)
-------- The expedition of Hernando de Soto (1539-1543) and Luis de Moscoso

*The routes traveled by the three conquistadores are still in dispute; the routes shown here are the ones accepted by many historians.

Sources: Arthur Grove Day, *Coronado's Quest: The Discovery of the Southwestern States*, University of California Press, 1940; Cleve Hallenbeck, *Alvar Núñez Cabeza de Vaca: The Journey and Route of the First European to Cross the Continent of North America, 1534-1536*, Arthur H. Clark Company, Glendale, California, 1940; George Parker Winship, ed., *The Journey of Coronado, 1540-1542*, Allerton Book Company, New York, 1922; U.S. De Soto Expedition Commission, *Final Report of the United States De Soto Expedition Commission* (76th Congress, 1st. Session, House Document No. 71, 1939). Base map adapted from Erwin Raisz, "Landforms of the United States," 1957 and "Landforms of Mexico," 1964.

Cabeza de Vaca's route from Texas

Coronado's route to Quivira

Coronado's Army

Return of Coronado's Army

Coronado's route from Compostela

Coronado's route from Culiacán

Chichimecas

Coronado's route from Compostela

Cabeza de Vaca's route to Uek

Compostela

Guachichil and Zacateco

Miles
0   50   100   150   200

THE STORMING OF CHAPULTEPEC SEPT: 13TH 1847.

LOS
ACILA
Ovalado
ENTRE-FUERTE
DE EL BUEN TONO, S.A.
Por la Yunta De Silao....
Como Se lla- ma la Piesa Panchito
Enti me Vengo Pensando

ANGOS
DORES

A. ACEVEDO
ERICH 08

2ª Calle de
Jaime Nunó

A mi me pelas
los dientes soy
Chango Vacilador

A poco tu ser la
Fuentes Changa
Prieta y Ablador

El era Tony
Fuentes pero es
muy Cumplidor

THE ZONE
ZONE IS
IS IMMA
IMMAN
CE THE Z

ON AN APPOINTED AFTERNOON IN HAVANA, three young aspiring poets from the *Generación de los ochenta* Reina María Rodríguez, Andrés Reynaldo, and Osvaldo Sánchez, to whom the following owes acknowledgment—found themselves adrift in the sweltering streets and passages of old downtown Havana. Impulse gave way to banter about paying an unexpected call to a certain venerable poet, and in the rapid-fire give and take, Rodríguez and Reynaldo impetuously darted up the street to knock at the residence famously situated on Trocadero 162. The hasty novices were met at the door by José Lezama Lima himself, who was neither expecting visitors, nor unaccustomed to this kind of intrusion. The duo unabashedly announced themselves as writers; that they were there to meet the esteemed maestro. The elder man of letters, bedraggled—tank T-shirt snug around his corpulent body, tucked into his khaki trousers; cigar firmly brandished in hand—asked them what they had read of his writings. Insofar as Lezama Lima's work was all but unavailable and scarcely distributed at the time—a veritable out-of-print suppression—they sheepishly replied that they hadn't had the opportunity to read him much. "So, if you haven't read me, why have you bothered to come? What do you take me for—the Capitol Building?" he grumbled and wasted no time in bidding the minions farewell with a slam of the door, as if to punctuate the crusty objection to his negligible status as a national monument.

♦ ♦ ♦

The infamous Padilla affair, during which poet Heberto Padilla submitted to a public repudiation of alleged counterrevolutionary cultural workers,[1] Lezama Lima among them, had a lasting impact on the poet and his work. Officials denied his requests for travel visas and the cultural apparatus prevented his work from appearing in book publication. These actions against him gave Lezama Lima a certain aura that captivated those who came to be known as the *Generación de los ochenta* (the 1980s Generation), a nexus of writers, artists, and intellectuals that had flourished within the social standpoint of the Revolution and achieved visibility during the 1980s. Poet and critic Osvaldo Sánchez, in a sidelong reference to Ernesto "Ché" Guevara and his essay "Socialism and Man in Cuba," addressed the defining conditions this generation strove to defy:

---

[1]   Kristen Dykstra writes: "In 1971, Padilla was arrested and charged with conspiring against the Revolution. After his release, on the night of April 17, 1971, Padilla delivered a 'self criticism,' an exaggerated proclamation of guilt. Padilla's performance of denouncing his previous activities and counterrevolutionary behavior took place before an audience of party officials and fellow UNEAC members [Unión de Escritores y Artistas Cubanos]; ...it had far-reaching repercussions, serving to polarize the Latin American intellectual community as to the role of politics in artistic production, and variations on this debated continued for the rest of the century." Kristen Dykstra, "Afterward: The Only Moment I will Witness," in Reina María Rodríguez's *Violet Island and Other Poems*," trans. Kristin Dykstra and Nancy Gates Madsen (Copenhagen & Los Angeles: Green Integer, 2004). Dykstra is the superb translator of other volumes by Reina María Rodriguez, including *Other Letters to Milena* (Tuscaloosa: The University of Alabama Press, 2014)], as well as of collections by other vital poets from Cuba, including: Omar Pérez, *Did You Hear about the Fighting Cat?* (Exeter: Shearsman Books, 2010); Omar Pérez, *Something of the Sacred: A Book in Two Parts* (New York: Factory School, 2007); Angel Escobar Varela, *Breach of Trust* (Tuscaloosa: The University of Alabama Press, 2015); Juan Carlos Flores, *The Counterpunch (and Other Horizontal Poems)* (Tuscaloosa: The University of Alabama Press, 2016); Marcelo Morales, *The World as Presence* (Tuscaloosa: The University of Alabama Press, 2016). For an additional discussion of Heberto Padilla, see Emilio Bejel, *Gay Cuban Nation* (Chicago: The University of Chicago Press, 2001) p 116.

[T]hese 'children of the Utopia' discovered that it wasn't particularly stimulating to be the 'docile wage-workers of official thought.' So it was that in the early 1980s, the State began to feel increasingly threatened by the critical discontent and the political distrust shared by the youngest members of the intelligentsia, whose obsession with turning Cuba's social reality into a truly liberating enterprise was to disclose, eventually, all the moral atrophy and the ideological contradictions of a system based on simulacra, manipulation, and inefficiency.[2]

The dissatisfied included Reina María Rodríguez and other poets of the *Generación de los ochenta* who enlivened the figure and function of the simulacrum with techniques comparable to those advanced at the time in the visual culture produced by Cuban painters, sculptors, multimedia and performance artists. Insofar as the sum of these actions signaled a series of antagonisms directed at the official state apparatus, at austere political and sexual attitudes that governed daily life, and at other persistent remainders from Cuba's "grey years" (1971–1976), the poetry of the 1980s participated also in a general revision specific to the written medium. By the 1980s, the stale rhetoric of conversationalism, then the dominant mode of poetic discourse, was seen as a vacant endeavor: one that belabored the limits of sincerity with self-certain depictions of complex moral and social realities.

Examples of work by Reina María Rodríguez and other poets of the *Generación de los ochenta* reveal poetic forms of address that served to counter the belated discourse of a previous generation and its claim to linguistic transparency. Rodríguez and others so made audible the lapses and excess of language in the unruly modulations of lyric drive as to contest preordained speech effects, personhoods, and political locations.

◆ ◆ ◆

Roberto Fernández Retamar and other poets of the largely male *Generación del Caimán Barbudo*—Raúl Rivero, Luis Rogelio Nogueras, and Guillermo Rodríguez Rivera, among others—were much less

---

[2] Osvaldo Sánchez. "Utopia Under the Volcano: The Cuban Avant-Garde in Mexico," trans. Roberto Tejada, *Sulfur* (32) Spring 1993, p 308.

reliant on the image, as they had been on the rhetoric of a coherent self and the strategies of the catalogue and pamphlet, weighted with tendentious parallelisms and statement; "that avalanche of words," according to Sánchez, "accredited by a militancy of facile prattle, and by an everyday reality reduced to vapid chronicle."[3] Luis Rogelio Nogueras, in a poem entitled "Loss of the Love Poem Called 'Mist'" exemplified some of the characteristics of a style assumed to value the canonical themes of poetry, while establishing an unaffected relationship to craft, emotional sincerity, and intimate association with the implied reader:

> Yesterday I wrote a magnificent poem
> sadly
> I lost it somewhere
> and now I can't remember it
> but it was great
> it said more or less
> that I was in love
> it said it, of course, in another way—
> it was really good—
> but she was in love with another guy
> and then there was a really beautiful part about
> the trees the wind and then
> it said something about death it didn't
> say death, of course, it said
> dark claw or something like that
> then there were some extraordinary lines
> and toward the end
> it told how I walked
> through an empty street
> convinced that life would begin again
> on some corner
> of course it didn't say it that pretentiously
> it was a good poem
> sad loss
> sad memory[4]
> [Translated by Mark Weiss]

---

3   Osvaldo Sánchez. "Los hijos de la utopía" *Blancomovil*, No. 49, June/July 1991, p 4 [Author's translation].

4   Mark Weiss, *The Whole Island: Six Decades of Cuban Poetry, a Bilingual Anthology* (Berkeley: University of California Press, 2009) pp 343–5

Sánchez and other poet-critics identified Cuba's gradual paradigm shift as the uneven distributions of intellectual and cultural effects in Latin America. In the collapse of modernity's master narratives, systems of value that locate the self in society underwent a comprehensive reevaluation of the communication media and other sites of representation; and poetic language reflected the dubiousness of sociocultural accounts invested in the teleology of utopia. A cognitive shift could be traced to increased social disaffection with the emancipatory promises of the Marxist-Leninist state; with the lack of equity and inclusion in the political process and cultural expressions; with the self as a knowable function, or hypothesized only as a tangle of unwanted thoughts and drives; and all the while media discourses further fused the symbolic order to the real. In this, Jean Baudrillard had identified the transfigured impact of mass communication technologies on social relations and global events:

> Simulation is no longer that of a territory, a referential being or a substance. It is the generation of models of a real without origin or reality: a hyperreal. [...] Conversely, simulation starts from the utopia of the principle of equivalence, from the radical negation of the sign as value, from the sign as reversion and death sentence of every reference.[5]

Baudrillard had made no claim for the simulacrum as an isolated emergence. He located the figures of simulation as alternate currents that refer to concrete historic antecedents: "Behind the baroque of images hides the grey eminence of politics."[6] Baudrillard's argument enlisted metaphors of a first-order reflection devolving into a second-order masking and distortion, and again into an absolute third-order elision. The process that had originated in the "murderous capacity of images" in counterpoint to "a dialectical capacity of representations

[5]   Jean Baudrillard. *Jean Baudrillard: Selected Writings*, edited and with an introduction by Mark Poster (Stanford, California: Stanford University Press, 1988) p 166; see also Jean Baudrillard, *Simulations* (New York City: Semiotext(e), Inc, 1983. Texts by Baudrillard and other French poststructuralist cultural theorist circulated in the original language—consistent with the simulacrum—from hand to hand in photocopied form.

[6]   Jean Baudrillard. *Jean Baudrillard: Selected Writings*, edited and with an introduction by Mark Poster (Stanford, California: Stanford University Press, 1988) p 170.

as a visible and intelligible mediation of the real," gave way to a world where abstractions were no longer the domain "of the map, the double, the mirror, or the concept." Rather now the map "precedes the territory."[7]

Baudrillard's associative reasoning—with its appeals to utopia as being tantamount to "an uninterrupted circuit without reference or circumference"[8]—ought to have struck a particular chord among Cuba's critical mass:

> ...simulation starts from the Utopia of this principle of equivalence, from the radical negation of the sign as value, from the sign as reversion and death sentence of every reference. Whereas representation tries to absorb simulation by interpreting it as false representation, simulation envelops the whole edifice of representation as itself a simulacrum.[9]

Poets from Cuba's *Generación de los ochenta* successfully deployed the literal and figurative function of simulacra. They endured the risk of direct reference by also deploying open-ended statements about the formal "transparency" of conversationalism and the supposed "transparency" of the State. In so doing, despite Cuba's insularity and seeming cultural closure, there was a porousness and a receptivity on the part of revolutionary culture—an insular peculiarity earlier identified and championed by Lezama Lima—that allowed the ideas of major postmodern thinkers to reach Cuba, in editions brought back from Europe, translations edited in Mexico and Spain, circulating from hand to hand, or through conversational exchange at sites of alternative knowledge like the improvisational community that Reina María Rodríguez hosted on the *azotea* rooftop of her downtown Havana home.[10]

---

[7]   *Ibid.*, p 166.

[8]   *Ibid.*, p 170.

[9]   *Ibid.*, p 170.

[10]   Kristin Dykstra, "Afterward: The Only Moment I will Witness," in *Violet Island and Other Poems*, trans. Kristin Dykstra and Nancy Gates Madsen (Copenhagen & Los Angeles: Green Integer, 2004) pp 190–1; 193.

In this shift from the modern to the postmodern, subjectivity was viewed as an effect of language (Barthes), a product of institutions (Foucault) or a result of the unconscious and its endless chain of desire (Freud and Lacan). As Ben A. Heller notes:

> These young poets have embraced the assimilative poetics of Lezama as no other group previously, producing a poetry startling for the density and richness of allusions. Opening up to Lezama was an opening up to world culture, which was a strong statement at a time when official Cuban culture was stagnating, bound to an ideology that was undergoing a spectacular collapse in the international arena. For these young poets, to be cosmopolitan has also meant to read literary theory, the works of Foucault, Barthes, Derrida, de Man, Lacan, and Žižek—readings that have contextualized for them the crisis of the unitary subject....[11]

While her writing represents one kind of struggle and innovation, her home represents another. The *azotea* has served as a space for readings and discussions in the time-honored tradition of *tertulias*, gatherings both social and intellectual; at the same time, it is a place for performing a strangely visible resistance to the revolutionary embrace of local culture... For Rodríguez herself, the ultimate ideal for the rooftop was to produce work that would level hierarchies of all kinds. This ideal had at least two reasons for being important to her. It mirrored her aesthetic interests, her interest in language and transgression. It also conflated domestic and intellectual spaces, challenging gender divisions.

See also Marta Hernández Salván, *Minima Cuba: Heretical Poetics and Power in Post-Soviet Cuba* (New York: SUNY Press, 2015) p 97

[Reina María Rodríguez's Azotea] became a bastion of intellectual independence where intellectuals discussed texts that often questioned orthodox Marxism and the national canon of Cuban literature. Rodriguez was instrumental in creating what critics have called the "cultural center of Havana" during the late eighties and nineties.... In homage to Virginia Woolf and the Bloomsbury group, Rodriguez organized readings every Thursday and gathered large groups of young writers at her house for readings, discussions and lectures.... During its decade of existence, the Azotea established a reputation on and off the island. Poets of that period remember it as a space of comfort that shielded intellectuals from the most difficult material conditions of the so-called Special Period.

[11]   Ben A. Heller. *Assimilation/Generation/Resurrection: Contrapuntal Readings in the Poetry of José Lezama Lima* (Lewisburg, PA: Bucknell University Press, 1997) p 160.

For Cuba this meant, according to critic Madeline Cámara, that in order to reconstitute any valid sense of subjectivity, artists and intellectuals had "to break down the 'traps of faith' hidden in the books used by the educational system at all levels, including propaganda and everything written in support of official discourse;" the result being "a kind of hermeneutics of suspicion that attempts to delve deeper than the simple chains of cause and effect that dominant ideology imposes on insular teleology."[12]

Reina María Rodríguez employs various figures of postmodernity to great effect in a poem from her collection *En la arena de Padua*[13] [On the Sands of Padua], a turning point in her poetics. Though not published until 1992, the poems that comprise the series were written from the mid to late 1980s. Her previous three volumes—*La gente de mi barrio* [The People in My Neighborhood, 1976], *Cuando una mujer no duerme*[14] [When a Woman Can't Sleep, 1980] and *Para un cordero blanco*[15] [For a White Lamb, 1984]—were still relatively steeped in the elegiac tones of an organized, "recognizable" self as per the conventions of conversationalism. In "The Zone," Rodríguez metaphorically inscribes herself in the surrogate locus of poetic praxis. There, she manages at once to suggest an individual and political reality on the verge of outbreak or explosion. The "zone of immanence" is a surface of unstable appearances but also a *way out* of indwelling; there, diminutive deliverance of the everyday obtains a refocusing:

---

[12] Madeline Cámara. "Third Option: Beyond the Border," *Bridges to Cuba / Puentes a Cuba*, ed. Ruth Behar (Ann Arbor: University of Michigan Press, 1995) p 223. Despite the aesthetic proximity to Lezama Lima, *Generación de los ochenta* poets never fully deployed or exploited the strategies and effects at the level of language as did a slightly more senior generation of writers throughout Latin America; poets primarily from the Southern Cone and Mexico, like those gathered in *Medusario: Muestra de poesía latinoamericana*, eds. Roberto Echavarren, José Kozer, and Jacobo Sefamí (Mexico City: Fondo de Cultura Económica, 1996). In addition to the editors, other poets in the anthology include Eduardo Milán (Uruguay-Mexico), Tamara Kamenszain (Argentina-Mexico), Néstor Perlongher (Argentina), and Coral Bracho (Mexico), among others.

[13] Reina María Rodríguez. *En la arena de Padua* (Havana: Ediciones Union, 1992).

[14] Reina María Rodríguez. *Cuando una mujer no duerme* (Havana: UNEAC, 1982).

[15] Reina María Rodríguez. *Para un cordero blanco: poesía* (Havana: Casa de las Américas, 1984).

THE ZONE
Tarkovsky

I'm here in the magnetic field
the dense zone where
the grass trembles
bending toward you.

I found my way inside
thanks to the white drawing of the animal
I owned in that other death.
the oracles never come to pass except in silence
when the magnetic
needle of the aftermath oscillates beyond us
uncertain   we've walked under cold rain.
deactivated bombs
in the happiness room
and ephemeral flowers
over fish devoured by fame.
each form has donned its apparel
and now they resemble what they are:
a simulacrum.
but the zone is immanence
and coming back from the place coming back into focus
the release of each hour[16]
[Translated by Roberto Tejada]

In *En la arena de Padua*, Rodríguez begins testing the limits of what an image can contain and, by contrast, the degree to which image-making can expose. In response to both Lezama Lima's gendering of mirrors as reproductive, Rodríguez's poetic persona speeds the lulling pace of conversationalism to breaking point. She sets the delirium of excess into motion in one poem that combines the resolve to assert sexual difference into the realm of exposition, with a nod to the body horror and modern gothic of Roman Polanski's *Rosemary's Baby*—a filmic gesture akin to the science-fiction mise en scène of Andrei Tarkovsky's *Stalker* in "The Zone." In the process she makes claims about the female body, and writing itself, as weird zones of

---

16   Reina María Rodríguez. "Two Poems," trans. Roberto Tejada, *Mandorla: Nueva escritura de las Américas / New Writing from the Americas*, no. 4, 1995, pp 186–7.

indetermination:

... I know that everything was very fast and that I was looking inside with a tall, round mirror, which served as a rear-view mirror, and I know I lost myself definitively that time, I was weakening from staying always on the wrong side in the mirror, clinging to my Herman Hesse book by my fingernails. I feel my face falling asleep, it makes me shudder and cramp and I sense that my legs are also cramped, strained, that I have my face and my feet planted in that mirror, and I'm searching ... where is the devil? and the navel that used to be small, an illusion in the center of my belly, is pushing outward, pulling inward, he's responding to me.

... there he'll be born out of your tenderness and your wickedness, where the devil is always engrossed with the power of the solitude and the births. I cried out, I opened my eyes wide and looked at the clock: it's not the black clock from our ceremony, it will never be the black clock of eternity, but it's not the accidental clock either, the ephemeral one. I've seen myself in the faces of the clock, fuller, more normal, in the time behind the embrace, where everyone is running off to look at the real time, while I'm pushing, struggling, I writhe to find that other time without hour hands ... just for the insane. but it's not your fault, or theirs, it's the fault of the devil who will also be born from my only navel, from its cavity, from its impatience without a reflection in any unilluminated mirror, in a smashed mirror with burning edges, where I can decapitate myself without desire, or look at myself with a hardened expression, less liquid, less fragile, learning those things about the devil like all of the other women.[17] [Translated by Kristin A. Dykstra]

Somewhere in between these two limits, Rodríguez points over and over again to a lifelessness, a weariness, a standstill, a lassitude. In torques that explore how subjectivity is rendered operative by language-trace, another poem, "Paradise. Storefront. Monte Street," enunciates—presumably at a drowsy, half-barren *tiendita* or five-and-dime—a ghost economy caught between a form of stadium triumphalism and the manic droning of the everyday.

> nothing specific definable: nothing costly
> the point being not to die not to see
> a boredom that once pertained to light

---

[17]   Reina María Rodríguez. *La detención del tiempo / Time's Arrest*, trans. Kristin Dykstra (New York: Factory School. 2005) pp 32–33.

stains here and there
no one knows what of.
spent timeworn   nothing costly
waiting for a buyer to come: useless garment
my left breast out from under my blouse
there's a whetstone.
the rats watch us, distrust us, watch us
their reddish eyes behind a cardboard box.
items that meant something once
simulation. ovation.
the melody is mediocre a music blending
        droning
to complaints from the fan[18]
[Translated by Roberto Tejada]

♦ ♦ ♦

This droning doubles back to Baudrillard's simulacrum as read in relation to Lezama Lima's theory of the image. For Lezama Lima, language and material reality are separated as "a continuity that questions / and a rift in response,"[19] as creative oscillations between the "identical and similar," between likeness and representation, an interval that gives way to "fullness of embodiment, so that possibility may achieve meaning and surge into historical timeliness."[20]

Some of Rodríguez's contemporaries enliven this third-term imaging in thick descriptions or encoded critiques about the "moral atrophy"[21] and ideological contradictions of contemporary Cuban reality. Others deploy the literal and figurative uses of the simulacrum to make broader statements, as I've mentioned, about the formal clarity of conversationalism as the window that alleges to provide a subject its view of the social arena and the state's reality

---

[18]   Reina María Rodríguez. "Two Poems," trans. Roberto Tejada, *Mandorla: Nueva escritura de las Américas / New Writing from the Americas*, no. 4, 1995, pp 187–8.

[19]   José Lezama Lima. "Dissonance," *José Lezama Lima: Selections*, (California: University of California Press) p 86 [Author's translation].

[20]   José Lezama Lima. "26 de julio: Imagen y posibilidad," in *Imagen y posibilidad* (Havana: Editorial Letras Cubanas, 1981) p 19 [Author's translation].

[21]   Osvaldo Sánchez. "Utopia Under the Volcano: The Cuban Avant-Garde in Mexico,"

principle. One prominent figure is that of a failed utopia, regardless of ideological guise. In "Un hombre sin élite" ["A Man Without an Elite"] from his collection *Algo de lo sagrado* (1982–1988), Omar Pérez (1964) investigates how the revolutionary subject (or New Man) had been reduced to an effect of official institutions (or, in his words, "functional seasons") oblivious to the pending storm of social relations, be it in the old despotic bourgeoisie or the new state bureaucracy.

A MAN WITHOUT AN ELITE

A swelling, a subject drunk on functional seasons
a vertigo that trembles the branches of trees,
that's the conclusion of a vagrancy
along the smoldering side of a paradise devoid of intimates
a paradise that offers no other certification
except for a storm of ashes and white hands.
No one knows the exact taste of a face
no one knows and the puffing of cheeks
will spoil any lavish reincarnation,
two faces or a hundred are easy to love

but a single face is unattainable, a fistful of earth.
The blood of those shedding their otter pelts
emphasizes the zealotry of a sun
weakening without the force of its solar spots,
lacking skill, the elites, who corrupt everything,
crack the edge of the stars
on the notch of someone's back, imperfect and unpunished.[22]
[Translated by Roberto Tejada]

In contrast with Reina María Rodríguez and others who have deployed the motif of detonation, Marilyn Bobes explores the dilemma of silence by way of censorship and erasure. Neo-baroque in reference and procedure, this poem stems from a project begun in the 1990s in which the sonnet forms of the Spanish golden-age

trans. Roberto Tejada, *Sulfur* (32) Spring 1993, p 308.

[22]   Omar Pérez. *Algo de lo sagrado: Something of the Sacred: A Book in Two Parts*, trans. Kristin Dykstra and Roberto Tejada (New York: Factory School, 2007) pp 46–47.

poet Francisco de Quevedo are submitted to the surveillance and expurgations of an outside inspector, the poet herself:

DANGERS OF SPEAKING AND STAYING QUIET:
LANGUAGE OF SILENCE
by Marilyn Bobes

Since it is fierce
ifI say
what excuse
if I stay quiet, who will be able to

But without speaking to you
      sight   semblance
in the silence
they say

and whoever makes them happen
and whoever orders silences, understands them[23]
[Translated by Ruth Behar]

As with Lezama Lima, the open, the fluid, the multiple, and the figurative sense of sexuality and its differences were explored, albeit diffidently, by certain representatives of Cuba's *Generación de los ochenta*.

In this context—that is, political space where social surveillance and sexual paranoia so fuse together as to confuse—Baudrillard's "death sentence of every reference" submits further foreboding. Suggestive of this "unlikely repression" is an untitled poem by Osvaldo Sánchez from his 1982 collection *Matar al último venado* [Slaughter the Last Deer]:

carnation frost in flames
 a wound of boyhood and of memory

let me deliver unsheathed your boreal edge

---

[23] Marilyn Bobes, "Dangers of Speaking and Staying Quiet. Language of Silence," trans. Ruth Behar, *Bridges to Cuba / Puentes a Cuba*, ed. Ruth Behar (Ann Arbor, University of Michigan Press, 1995) p 197.

unabashed of your gunpowder if it detonates and
I'm injured

carnation a whicker

  a sparrow   poisoned mouth upward
  and wet in my hand mouth numb and
  bruised in its dream

tiny communist salvation to tower with
you
inexorable lush sword
over our most unlikely repressions[24]
[Translated by Roberto Tejada]

Cuba's *Generación de los ochenta* had taken to task a prior call for a social poetics and rather put into practice César Vallejo's definition of a poetics of the political. Vallejo wrote that "the political receptivity of the artist is produced, preferably and in its superlative authenticity, by creating concerns and a nebulous politics that are far vaster than any catechism or collection of express ideas, and therefore with a clarity greater than any questionnaire listing the unease or periodic ideals of a nationalist or universalist policy."[25]

If poetry is political when produced in relation to a community whose shared patterns of value and conviction are implicitly affirmed or visibly contradicted—or, better still, when expression discovers those other patterns a society fails to recognize; and if lyric discourse emerges when the predicament of subjectivity itself becomes the object of inquiry, then the poetics and politics of Reina María Rodríguez and other participants in the *Generación de los*

---

24   Osvaldo Sánchez. *Matar al último venado* (Havana: Unión de Escritores y Artistas de Cuba, 1982) p 44.

25   César Vallejo. "Los artistas ante la política," in *Desde Europa: Crónicas y artículos (1923–1938)*, edited with notes by Jorge Puccinelli (Lima: Ediciones Fuente de Cultura Peruana, 1987) p 254 ("La sensibilidad política del artista se produce, de preferencia y en su máxima autenticidad, creando inquietudes y nebulosas políticas, más vastas que cualquier catecismo o colección de ideas expresas, y por lo mismo, limitadas, de un momento político cualquiera, y más puras que cualquier cuestionario de preocupaciones o ideales periódicos de política nacionalista o universalista.").

ochenta point out the simulation, instability, and the social structure in gradual halt or on the verge, deploying "the magnetic needle of the aftermath" to show "the smoldering side of a paradise"—that is, the dissonant exchange-value of the lyric subject in relation to the counterfeit promises of utopia.

STRATEGICDISLOCATIONSOFIDENTITYSTRATEGICDISLOCATIONSOFSTRATEGICDISLOCATIONSOFIDENTITY

To the development and increased complexity of poetry by Latinx writers in matters of literary alignment, geographic location, cultural heritage, historical viewpoint, and the varieties of social and sexual life, there remain underlying questions of poetic identity and media format. Aesthetic differences commonly dissolve around attitudes concerned with the natural status of poetic language and the implied location of its occurrence. To the degree that poets develop their craft external to the framework of some literary community or another, likewise has poetic activity thrived outside the places historically consigned to provide the genre its authority. To complicate the difference between maker and words made— a challenge crucial to any contemporary writing defined by a critical standpoint—we can pursue a storyline that accounts for Latinx poetries as through the lens of exceptions to the imagined norm.

Talk-piece writer-performer David Antin reminds us that from the mid 1960s to the early 1970s, conceptual artist Vito Acconci initially belonged to a "loose network of experimental writers"[1] before abandoning poetry for the art world. Acconci's example is the reminder, too, of a largely unexplored archive of word environments

---

[1]   David Antin. "Words into type: David Antin on Vito Acconci" *Artforum International*, vol.44 no.7 March 2006, p 51.

that sometimes fail to pass as poetry, to the degree that these works take shape in locations largely eccentric to the field as commonly perceived. Insofar as a genealogy for experimental writing by poets of Latinx descent has become increasingly visible, the telling ought not to exclude a variety of poetic practices more broadly understood. To recall, one foundational text for Chicanx-Latinx letters, José Montoya's "El Louie"[2] was crafted by a multimedia practitioner who early bridged the division between word and image through his interconnected identities as a printmaker, poster artist, and as member of the Royal Chicano Air Force art collective. Composing the visual plane of José Montoya's *Calendario '77* is a September 1977 calendar page, with abbreviations for each day of the week in Spanish, initials of the Royal Chicano Air Force (R.C.F.C.), a sharp yellow ground incorporating deep red and blue volumes, and a front-page section of the *Los Angeles Herald Examiner* dated June 1, 1943, with headlines that betray public media expressions of white supremacy, telescoping from WWII to the present, in anti-Asian and anti-Mexican-American racism: "WAR [PLANES]...Kill 400 Japs..." and "Zoot-Suiter Hordes Invade Los Angeles." The print's formal and thematic reporting points back to the bebop phrases that inflect the bilingual vitality of the poetic voice, and the aspirational style of the deceased and lamented anti-hero, in Montoya's 1970 elegy "El Louie":

> Louie hit on the idea in
> those days for tailor-made
> drapes, unique idea—porque
> Fowler no era nada como
> Los, o'l E.P.T. Fresno's
> westside was as close as
> we ever got to the big time,
> But we had Louie and the
> Palomar, el boogie, los
> mambos y cuatro suspiros
> del alma[3]

---

2   José Montoya. "El Louie," *Rascatripas* 2 (Oakland, California, 1970) n.p.; reprinted in Luis Valdez and Stan Steiner, *Aztlán: An Anthology of Mexican American Literature* (New York: Vintage Books, 1972) pp 333–337.

3   *Ibid.*

Montoya's visual and poetic practice together form a critical association that coaxes participants into the circumstance of art's legibility by upsetting the customary categories of knowledge; by underlining the dubious stability of particular containers—museum, person, printed matter in the public sphere; and by reiterating the situational personality of meaning.

Relevant to Latinx poetries are the writings, actions, and site-specific work of conceptual artists that have continued the line of inquiry prompted by Duchamp and subsequent artist collectives like Fluxus and Art & Language. To speak only of those based in California, that tradition telescopes back to include the pioneering example of ASCO[4] in the 1970s and 1980s, as well as to more recent collaborations

---

[4]   ASCO, sometimes written Asco (*asco*, Spanish for nausea), was a Chicanx artist collective from East Los Angeles, active in the 1970s and 1980s. Art historian C. Ondine Chavoya has contextualized the work of Asco as "a collaborative creative corps" whose original members

> Harry Gamboa Jr., Gronk, Willie Herrón, and Patssi Valdez, engaged in performance, public art, and conceptual multimedia art. The artists merged activism with performance in response to this turbulent social and political period in Los Angeles and within the larger international context of alternative youth cultures and radical politics of the late 1960s and early 1970s. // Asco created art by any means necessary, often using their bodies and guerilla, or hit-and-run, tactics.... Manifesting their ideas in the public arena of the streets, the artists recognized the power of public representation and documentation and expertly learned to circumvent traditional institutions by creating alternative methods of access and distribution. Their work critically satirized and challenged the conventions of modernists 'high' art as well as though of 'ethnic' or community-based art. The connotations of their self-adopted name, Asco, testifies to the initial effect of the group."
> —C. Ondine Chavoya, "Internal Exiles: The Interventionist Public and Performance Art of Asco," *Space, Site, Intervention: Situating Installation Art*, ed. Erika Suderburg (University of Minnesota Press: 2000) p 189.

Increasingly, scholars have focused on what Robb Hernández identifies as the "unseen facets of queer marginality" that activated Asco's performance methods. Robb Hernández, "Drawing Offensive/Offensive Drawing: Toward a Theory of Mariconógraphy, *MELUS*, Volume 39, Number 2, Summer 2014, p 125. In this sense Leticia Alvarado writes:

> Asco conjured affective communities through an embrace of a decidedly queer abject aesthetic. Its members deployed a familiar *rasquachismo*, partnered

between author Sesshu Foster and artist/photographer Arturo Ernesto Romo-Santillano.[5] Often uniting both the documentary and theoretical impulse, these are tactics that deploy linguistic enactments whose bearing on poetic address is hardly incidental.

Beyond his involvement with ASCO, Harry Gamboa Jr, in his parallel identities as a maker who employs the media of photography, performance, video, installation, and poetic writing, has produced a range of work that remains critical to an understanding not only of Chicano art and its history, but also to a more accurate depiction of the avant-garde as per the wake of minimalism in the United States. Conceivably because his identity as a visual artist often eclipses his poetic practice, Gamboa Jr.'s writings are rarely discussed in the context of present-day Latinx poetry. Moreover, his work consistently discredits accepted categories, creating innovative alternatives to reveal a history otherwise rendered invisible by dominant cultural institutions and media industries. By turns dryly humorous, eerily dreamlike, and always surprising, Gamboa Jr.'s art practice is a critique of new urban life forms represented by Los Angeles in the last decades of the millennium when the city came into its own as an idiosyncratic cultural nexus.

Referring at once to the city's seismological instability and its demographic transformations, Gamboa Jr. describes Los Angeles as "constantly shaking, constantly moving,"[6] as environmental and social landscapes in recurrent flux. In interviews and lectures, he remarks how L.A neighborhoods transfigure in terms of cultural, economic, or racial composition; how freeways were built to carve up and designate particular areas, and how control and surveillance

---

with the glittery veneer of the alternative punk scene. This rendered their daily bodily presentations and public street actions an affront to the heteronormative, patriarchal ideal upheld by the Chicano nationalist project focused on representation and defended by the inhabitants of East Los Angeles.
—Leticia Alvarado, "Asco's *Asco* and the Queer Affective Resonance of Abjection," *Aztlán: A Journal of Chicano Studies* 40:2 Fall 2015, pp 64–65.

[5]   Sesshu Foster, "Interview with Juan Fish (Supposedly); photographs by Arturo Ernesto Romo-Santillano," *Mandorla: New Writing from the Americas*, no 12, 2009, pp 11–22.

[6]   Harry Gamboa Jr, conversation with author, 20 April 2017, University of Houston, Houston, Texas.

gave way to the historical social isolation of East L.A. Even as the city experienced civil uprisings in the 1960s, until the 1970 Chicano Moratorium in East L.A., that part of the city had remained largely off the city's self-imagined grid. The urban infrastructure provided limited arteries—among them, the recently removed 6th Street Bridge—facilitating access to East L.A.[7]

Harry Gamboa Jr.'s writings, in conjunction with and independent of ASCO, mirror the "freeway-map ontology of Southern California"[8] identified by cultural historian Mike Davis when he showed that "while established Black and Chicano neighborhoods were losing several thousand [housing] units a year to freeway construction, non-Anglos were able to purchase only 3.3 per cent of the new housing stock constructed during the 1950s boom."[9] Gamboa Jr.'s poetry voices the resulting segregation, social alienations, and the "car-culture phenomenologies" [10] of urban life dictated by the automotive and aerospace industries across multiple locations of Los Angeles, as well as the "mental geographies [that] betray class prejudice"[11] in the Southern and Baja California borderlands.[12] His poem "Opposing Fast Lanes" builds on the momentum of "inequality / That approaches at lethal speeds" when:

> Someone from the other side
> Dares
> Breaches the wall
> Slams head-on
> Disintegrates
> Beneath relentlessly spinning wheels
> Crushed beyond recognition

---

[7]   *Ibid.*

[8]   Mike Davis, *City of Quartz: Excavating the Future in Los Angeles* (New York: Vintage Books, 1992) pp 66–7.

[9]   *Ibid.*, p 168.

[10]   *Ibid.*, pp 66–7.

[11]   *Ibid.*, p 375.

[12]   For more on the cultural significance of Chicanx art in East L.A., see the ELA Guide (www.elaguide.org), curated by Sesshu Foster, Arturo Ernesto Romo-Santillano, and other collaborators.

No better for the wear and tear
Life moves at 70 mph
I glance out to the unknown
Faces
That whizz by
They
On their fast lane
Going backwards to continue
Their story
The brief encounters with each face
Highlight the dangers of
Cultural collision
I fail to merge into obscurity[13]

"Opposing Fast Lanes" serves as a fable about the liabilities of cultural encounter for subjects "from the other side" in an accelerated cityscape established by narrow definitions of belonging. In language resembling "delayed, detonated bombs,"[14] Gamboa Jr. stages the collision of voices particular to the Boyle Heights vicinity and the collusion of language with "the theatricality of everyday life in East Los Angeles."[15] Motivated by a drive to figure "everyone" and "everywhere / disguised as / Nothing," the poet's brand of Boyle Heights surrealism or barrio baroque aims often to expand the proprietary nature of the self. Especially telling is the aptly titled "Deleted to Meet You," whose persona is in possession of "Five forged passports / Rubber-stamped to death":

[...]

I had been
Everyone/everywhere disguised as
Nothing
Rumors surfaced in
Guadalajara/Berlin/Montebello
Credited me

---

13   Harry Gamboa Jr, *Urban Exile* (Minnesota: University of Minnesota Press, 1998) pp 534–5.

14   C. Ondine Chavoya and Harry Gamboa Jr., "Social Unwest: An Interview with Harry Gamboa Jr," *Wide Angle* 20:3 (1998) p 68.

15   *Ibid.*

With
The bombing of suicide bridges
The discoverer of latent lovers
The assassination of a border guard
[...]
It must be comforting to count
The worms crawling out
My brittle face
An opaque landscape of anonymity
Distorted by the certainty of
Infinity
The dissolution of identity
Is what you'll write
On the blank postcard
That was my
Life [16]

With its ever-shifting and therefore uncontainable speaker—at once credited with bombing, discovery, and assassination—Gamboa Jr.'s poem stages the forms by which representation is inclined to determine social identities, while jointly permitting the poetic self to be an actor in the making of history. This agency in the processes of history and representation further attains in Gamboa Jr.'s understanding of the stage:

I used to do theater more or less anywhere, but it became too dependent on performers showing up, and it became too dependent on people memorizing lines. So I adapted my style of doing theater, where I didn't really need actors or rehearsal time; you just had to be there on the day of the show. For two or three plays I gave the performers the text while the audience was already seated, and the curtain was down. We'd do a run-through, lift up the curtains, and hope for the best. Some turned out very well, others were disastrous—but for me it was the most fun."[17]

Enactment and self-fashioning similarly inform Gamboa Jr.'s photographic series *Chicano Male Unbonded*; his resolve to configure

---

[16]   Harry Gamboa Jr, *Urban Exile* (Minnesota: University of Minnesota Press, 1998) pp 525–526.

[17]   "A Matter of Record: An Interview by Roberto Tejada with Harry Gamboa Jr.," Spot (Houston: Houston Center for Photography) Fall, 2017, p 21.

an anatomy of Chicanx masculinities and to establish an archive of its particular iterations regardless of the sitter's gender presentation or object choice. Employing a visual schema in which each portrait aims to defy type and foreground exception, in 1994 Gamboa Jr. asked poet and performer Roberto Bedoya to pose for a photograph. At the time, Bedoya[18] had already participated in various art communities, among them the San Francisco writers associated with the New Narrative.[19] He had been the first person of color to serve as director of the avant-garde multimedia arts center Los Angeles Contemporary Exhibitions (LACE), submitting his resignation after seven months due to "philosophical differences"[20] with board members resistant to his vision of equity and inclusion. At the time Gamboa Jr. made this portrait, Bedoya was now a producer of cultural programming for The Getty Research Institute for the History of Art and the Humanities.

Gamboa Jr. was inspired to create this portrait by a performance piece Bedoya had created with fellow artist Daniel Joseph Martinez at the Santa Monica Museum of Art. Lampooning NPR's syndicated *Car Talk* radio format, the two artists sat on stage behind a desk piled high with art books immortalizing the Western canon, while the audience was encouraged to submit objects for appraisal or to otherwise pose questions to the ersatz authorities. The parody

---

[18] For an example of Bedoya's writing from this period, see Roberto Bedoya, "'Scene One,' from *Decoto*," *Writers Who Love Too Much: New Narrative Writing 1977–1997*, eds. Kevin Killian and Dodie Bellamy (New York: Nightboat Books, 2017) pp 180–9.

[19] "The writers associated with New Narrative arguably reflect the culmination of San Francisco's history of experimental poetry and social activism....In terms of form, New Narrative can often be thought of as a "fellow traveler" of the Language poets, as exemplified by the non-linear verbal gymnastics of Dodie Bellamy's *Letters of Mina Harker* and the reduction and redaction techniques in her later *Cunt Norton*, which uses as its source text the patriarchal canon of the 1975 *Norton Anthology of Poetry*. Unlike Language poetry, at any rate, New Narrative draws on a queer tradition that foregrounds the affect and sexuality." Kaplan Page Harris. "Bay Area Poetics,1944–1981," *A History of California Literature*, ed. Blake Allmendinger. (Cambridge University Press: 2015) p 258.

[20] Jan Breslauer. "The Forces Behind Bedoya's Resignation." *Los Angeles Times* Dec 27 1990, p F6. See also Shauna Snow, "Roberto Bedoya: A New Face at LACE—and a New Direction," *Los Angeles Times,* May 17 1990, p OCF4.

derided the exclusionary art world establishment by conflating aesthetics with mechanics, and expertise with entertainment. Bedoya's trickster *rasquache* attitude[21] led him to improvise an outfit for the performance in "a kind of punk queer Cantinflas drag."[22]

Improvisation and the playfully unscripted animate the *Chicano Male Unbonded* series. Almost all the images are photographed at night, almost always in a kind of space deemed potentially dangerous, suggested by location and available light sources, and using high-speed film. Gamboa Jr. has remarked:

> I can make anyone look dangerous, but the setting is contingent on the way the light is distributed. There tends to be a single light source that dominates, and then a subtle diffusion. And because I used a wide-angle lens, there's an implied vanishing point—both physical and psychological. With such a wide-angle lens, if the subject isn't properly centered the body becomes distorted."[23]

In this study of many-sided masculinities, compositional elements—

[21] Chicano theorist Tomás Ybarra-Frausto linked a "rough and tumble performance style" to the "delight and refinement" found in what is more generally deemed banal, lowly, or uncouth. As the "good taste of bad taste," Ybarra-Frausto further mobilized the meanings of *rasquache*: "the aesthetic sensibility of los de abajo, of the underdog," an attitude embodied and exercised by working-class Mexicans and Mexican Americans, "rooted in resourcefulness and adaptability, yet mindful of stance and style." Tomás Ybarra-Frausto, "Rasquachismo: A Chicano Sensibility," *Chicano Art: Resistance and Affirmation, 1965–1985*, eds. Richard Griswold del Castillo, Teresa McKenna, and Yvonne Yarbro-Bejarano (Los Angeles: Wight Art Gallery, University of California, 1991) pp 156; 155; 159. Chicana artist and theorist Amalia Mesa-Bains offered a feminist critique of the hetero-patriarchal assumptions of early Chicano art formations when she redefined the activist art practice of rasquachismo "as a survivalist irreverence." (Amalia Mesa-Bains, "Domesticana: The Sensibility of Chicana Rasquache," *Distant Relations: A Dialogue among Chicano, Irish, and Mexican Artists* (Santa Monica, California, 1995) p 158.

[22] Roberto Bedoya, telephone communication with author, 17 June 2018. For more on rasquachismo, Cantiflas and queer cinema, see: B. Ruby Rich. "Queering the Social Landscape." *New Queer Cinema: The Director's Cut* (Durham, NC: Duke University Press Books, 2013) pp 167–182. For more on ASCO and drag, see: Rudi Bleys. "Queer Visions of Latino/a Exile." *Images of Ambiente: Homotextuality and Latin American Art, 1810–Today* (London and New York: Continuum, 2000) pp 171–226.

[23] "A Matter of Record: An Interview by Roberto Tejada with Harry Gamboa Jr.," Spot (Houston: Houston Center for Photography) Fall, 2017, p 21.

the upright figure in disfigured surroundings—are meant to mirror the desire, fear, and loathing common to representations of Chicanx subjects in the media: "The whole thing is warped, and the whole notion of being a Chicano male on the street is warped, basically, on account of social conditions. It's the notion of man alone, repeated over and over again...I look for ephemeral things that in some way denote dignity."[24] The personas portrayed in Gamboa Jr's *Chicano Male Unbonded* exude defiance in the face of antagonism akin to the personas of "Deleted to Meet You" and other poems. In opposition to forms of certainty over the "opaque landscape of anonymity," Gamboa Jr.'s writings and camera works remind us that our social and writerly identities are apt to coincide, but more likely to endure as mutually dissolving ostensible selfhoods.[25]

---

[24] *Ibid.*

[25] For a discussion that links the work of Harry Gamboa Jr. and ASCO to other contemporary practices like those of the Mongrel Coalition Against Gringpo, see Carmen Giménez Smith, "Make America Mongrel Again," *Harriet*, The Poetry Foundation, April 19th, 2018.

By turns dryly humorous,
eerily dreamlike,
and always surprising,
Gamboa Jr.'s art practice
is a critique
of new urban life forms
represented by Los Angeles

♦

in the last decades
of the millennium
when the city
came into its own as an
idiosyncratic
cultural nexus.

ELIÁN THROUGH LOOKIN GLASS

THE IMAGE IS THE SECRET CAUSE
OF HISTORY—JOSÉ LEZAMA LIMA

GH THE
G GLASS

THE POINTS ARE SCARCELY WORTH REITERATING. Even as it unfolded in real time, and from what can be culled in virtual retrospect, the story of Elián González happened as an entanglement of actual event, media spectacle, and social audience. On television breaking news, in countless daily papers and weekly magazines, over the internet, as material for late-night entertainment or daytime talk show, the chain of events that transpired in light of the boy "delivered by dolphins from the sea" became something of a volatile public topic, and something also of a national debacle whose complexities grew in compelling or tedious narrative proportions, depending on one's own particular threshold for monomania.

By now the facts are common knowledge, the stuff of contemporary legend.

Following Thanksgiving Day, a month before the year 2000 celebrations, a five-year-old boy was spotted and rescued off the South Florida coast, the survivor of a raft that had departed from Cuba with the boy and eleven adult men and women—including Elián's mother, who perished, like so many anonymous others before her and today across the globe, in the failed effort to stake one daily reality over another. Stunned by the situation, INS officials in Miami placed the recovered boy in the care of his great-uncle Lázaro and

21-year-old cousin Marisleysis, Elián's self-styled surrogate mother-to-be. No sooner had the heroics of Elián's survival been hailed as nothing short of a miracle, a symbolic triumph for Miami's anti-Castro exile community, when custody claims arrived from Cuba, made by the boy's father, Juan Miguel González, and by Fidel Castro himself, placing Elián in the middle of a family feud whose resonant wagers involved the political arena at large.

Therein followed a five-month dramatic tangle between family protagonists, the U.S. legal system, and the press, concerning extant immigration laws as per the extraordinary nature of the case, interpretations of the Cuban Adjustment Act and INS protocol, family demands and indictments: a succession of court rulings, appeals, and negotiation stalemates. Claims were fired left and right not only by Castro and U.S. Attorney General Janet Reno, but also by lawyers, commentators, and other authorities of the day, not to mention the likes of presidential hopeful Al Gore. Replete with both spontaneous and orchestrated rallies held in Miami and Havana, the story commanded a remarkable attention span and an undeniable emotional range that passed, indistinguishably at times, from genuine personal grief, awe, outrage, bureaucratic chill, the inadvertently laughable, collective hysteria, and threatening demonstrations of violence—all captured under the omnipresent eye of the camera.

Before the sensational Easter weekend events—and despite the amount of verbosity in the form of articles, interviews, and editorials—the story of Elián González had been syncopated into the form of a video sequence that was the standard crib or prelude to the daily update. For those unable to catch *Good Morning America* and the Diane Sawyer interview, for those who missed that episode of *60 Minutes* or *Nightline*, for the majority who tuned in only at random or intermittently, or who obtained their news online, the lead-in, with its doubtless variations, was constituted by and large as follows: A glassy-eyed, nearly lifeless Elián, bundled in an army green blanket, as he is carried away on a stretcher. Cut to: Elián on a jungle gym, alone at play or with a family member or friend, now wearing blue jeans and T-shirt in the backyard of his Miami relatives' home. Cut to:

Demonstrators outside the chain-link fence of the modest González home, flags and placards abounding (ELIÁN LIVES IN AMERICA NOW; KEEP ELIÁN FREE). Closer frame of: Elián, led by the hand of great-uncle Lázaro, greeting supporters as they dangle rosary beads out for the boy to touch. Cut to: Elián greeting the cameras and visitors, an uncertain smile on his face, and arms waving half-hesitantly above his head. Cut to: A beaming and triumphant Lázaro González, who swaggers hand in hand with Elián down a Miami street, the boy dressed in a white short-sleeve shirt and navy-blue corduroys. A vexed Juan Miguel now making an inscrutable waving gesture with his arm at the door of his temporary U.S. residence. Final shot of: Elián again, in play clothes, at his swing set.

The above news montage was often interjected with talking head-shots of Gregory Craig, Kendall Coffey, or Janet Reno, whose counterpoint established a visual rhetoric of hieratic presence, suggesting the big and small of a cool political sphere above, and the impassioned infantile reality of family drama and childhood charge below. (Similarly, think also of the April 17 *Time* magazine cover depicting a colossal Juan Miguel towering over a diminutive Elián waving the American flag.) The message of the repeated sequence insinuated that harmony had been restored after the determinant calamity, for which the boy now stood as a child messiah in answer to some unstated prayer, with a new order now under threat of disruption. The sheer optimism of the images betrayed the overt sympathy, often affirmed by popular opinion as reported by the press, for Elián to be returned to his father—the optic intimations of the camera at radical odds with the editorial.

The infamous "Elián video" is another case in point. Produced by the Miami relatives and delivered to the Spanish-language network Univisión in purported response to the Washington arrival of Juan Miguel and the grandmothers, the snippets of footage shown on the major networks and in real video on various websites depicted Elián sitting cross-legged on a bed as he gesticulated his transparently rehearsed account before the camcorder. Wearing a red T-shirt, gold chains, and striped shorts, his face a primer of emphatic expressions, Elián alternately raised and then lowered his index fingers in double downward plummet, with accented stress on consecutive terms of the phrase "Papá, ¡yo no quiero ir a Cuba!" It was called "unsettling," "obscene," "creepy," and "one of the world's scariest videos," not least because Elián managed perhaps to embody the bantam tyrant dormant in each one of us. It verged on the sinister, even as many commentators failed to pinpoint why. Elián had already become a phantom image of himself; had already, possibly much earlier but never more clearly than in this footage, slipped through the looking glass of childhood as it is represented in the era of simulation; he had heroically, if only for reasons of endurance—and in what concerns most things Cuban—risen to the performative occasion, upsetting pious adult notions as to the so-called psychology of the under-aged. In yet another contradiction that failed to go unnoticed by the media in the thick of its show time, Janet Reno—possibly in very reference to the Elián home-video performance—advised citizens and viewers to turn off the TV. But days later she waxed, "One of the beauties of television is that it shows exactly what the facts are."[1]

This change of heart was doubtless in reference to what came next. Like all good copy, the story had long been sustained with the rhetoric of unpredictability, if only by default or as though to mirror the legal process itself.[2] This Eleventh Circuit Court ruling—

---

[1] "At a news conference in Washington, Reno was asked whether the photograph had raised the question of excessive force. "One of the beauties of television is that it shows exactly what the facts are," Reno said. "And as I understand it, if you look at it carefully, it shows that the gun was pointed to the side, and that th [sic] finger was not on the trigger."

She defended the use of force, saying that there could have been guns in the crowd, or in the house, and the priority was the safety of Elian and the federal agents.

"The safety of all was paramount. And when law enforcement goes into a situation like that, it must go in prepared for the unexpected," the attorney general said." "Was the Gun Pointed At Elian?" (*CBSNEWS.COM*, 2000).

[2] "The true legal merits of this case will be finally decided in the future...we need to think more and hard about this case, for which no sure and clear answers shine out today."—As screen-quoted on *TalkBack Live*, CNN, April 21, 2000. To view transcripts of not only this episode of *TalkBack Live* but other episodes dealing with this case, visit: http://www.cnn.com/TRANSCRIPTS/tl.html.

which had compelled Elián to remain in the U.S. during the asylum appeals process—equally fueled mounting tensions that led Reno to her ultimate April 22 decision, on a weekend pregnant with the successive anniversaries of Waco, Oklahoma City, and Columbine: the forcible retrieval of Elián by INS officers from his "Little Havana" residence in a dramatic and much-debated predawn raid.

What followed was a din of real-time coverage, including repeated footage of INS officer Betty Mills, in her strenuous wince of adrenaline and expediency, as she clutched a terrified Elián close to her, sweeping the boy away into a black minivan, surrounded by other officers in commando gear, Elián's half-open mouth in a whimper, the operation executed amid gathering cries of family and supporters. There were live reports on the subsequent flashpoints of violence in Little Havana and police containment with tear gas; interviews with family members and lawyers; the landing of the plane that carried Elián to his father at Andrews Air Force Base. No one, certainly not Janet Reno, suspected that the beauty of TV resides not exactly in "what the facts are," but that it still buckles under the indelible power of the still image—as demonstrated so eloquently by AP photographer Alan Diaz. Having been invited into the González home when word began to leak of a possible "forcible removal," Diaz produced an image whose visual capital will far outlast all the hours of real-time television and all the piles of printed copy.

The photograph is positively unforgettable, and not only for reasons of content. In it, the domestic wood-panel sliding door and the clothes hanger pastel colors collide with the staggering gesture captured as a helmeted, commando-clad agent motions with a 9mm MP5 submachine gun—his other hand outstretched, his body poised as though about to snap, his eyes flaring behind the goggle-mask covering his flushed face, his mouth in a half-open frenzy. Behind him, another agent enters the door to the room. Two figures shrink away, barely contained by the right edge of the frame: Donato Dalrymple, the fisherman who had helped save Elián off the South Florida coast and who thereafter acted as his self-proclaimed protector, clutches a horrified Elián—his profile depicted in a wail of unadulterated fear.

The image is seared in memory because the show of institutional strength is so transparently misplaced. In the image, Dalrymple and Elián press back, in a failed attempt to secure a hiding spot, against the wardrobe of women's clothing in the closet. In no time the image was employed by protesters at the González's Miami home (caption: FEDERAL CHILD ABUSE) or lampooned on the internet (the heads of Clinton and Castro on the bodies of the two federal agents). Another photograph began to circulate—a snapshot of Elián cheerfully reunited with his father, stepmother, and half-brother; shortly, front pages and weekly news magazines betrayed their editorial intent with the visual hierarchies established between the two images, as variously cropped and Photoshopped.

Surprisingly, fewer still-images were derived from the footage of Miami fervor that followed in the wake of the INS raid. There was the American flag outside the González home tied down with a black garbage bag; there were vernacular placards with slogans like RENO TRAITOR and CLINTON'S JACK-BOOTED THUGS STRIKE AGAIN or FACT! CHILDREN FOR SALE IN THE WHITE HOUSE or WE DON'T FORGET. WE VOTE. The Miami violence shed inauspicious new light on the words of Joan Didion in her remarkably still-relevant 1987 book *Miami*, when she wrote of "a kind of collective spell, an occult enchantment, from that febrile complex of resentments and revenges and idealizations and taboos which renders exile so potent an organizing principle."[3] In the figure of Elián, Cuban immigrants projected their phantom image of the island not only as a birthplace, but "as a construct, the idea of birthright lost."[4] Correspondingly, and at the outset of the incident on that island of cherished birthright, "psychologists and other specialists" had gathered a month after Elián's retrieval from the sea for a panel discussion—"How Long Before the Mind of A Child Changes?" aired on Radio Rebelde and Radio Habana Cuba—to discuss the "grave consequences" in store for the "kidnapped boy" if not immediately returned to the *patria*, or fatherland.[5]

---

[3]   Joan Didion. *Miami* (New York: Vintage Books, 1998) p 17.

[4]   *Ibid.*

[5]   *¿En qué tiempo puede cambiare la mente de un niño?* (Havana: Casa Editorial Abril, 1999).

Prior to the Elián saga, U.S.-Cuba relations had reached a point at which an eventual lifting of the embargo was not unthinkable.[6] But with political divides again equated to the family institution, the struggle over Elián led to telecasts that were nothing if not a throwback to the Cold War rhetoric of freedom over indoctrination, now combined with ideological contradictions over family values and parental rights uttered in all manners of cartoonish commonplaces. Witness the exchange between John Fund of the *Wall Street Journal* and Victoria Jones of radio station WMAL in Washington, D.C. It aired on CNN's *TalkBack Live* on the Good Friday eve of the Elián grab, one of many television programs whose premise invites the democratic illusion of voiced opinion from live, virtual, and viewer audiences alike. These ranged from the naive to the monolithic, belying the convenient paternalism that is the short-hand attribute of the interactive mass media. Jeff, from North Carolina: "I really think we're asking the wrong question. People are saying who should he stay with? Should he be in the United States or should he be in Cuba? I think the real question is should he be with the father that loves him, assuming that's the case." Carlos, a Cuban immigrant, from Georgia: "It's not about politics...I mean it *is* about politics...not about parental rights." Jones and Fund, of course, were no significant improvement:

---

[6] Throughout the 1990s, the relative ease of U.S. travel back and forth to the island helped spark a renewed interest in things Cuban, both at the level of popular fascination and tourism—an industry the Cuban state was actively cultivating—and at the level of culture. Not only was there the obvious popular appeal of Cuban music—with its promotion by American champions, from David Byrne's Cuba Classics series to Ry Cooder's gig with The Buena Vista Social Club—but art-world interchange also began to take place between artists, curators and museum professionals who visited the Havana Biennials of the 1990s. Many Cuban artists had been officially allowed to leave the island at the onset of that decade—a ploy to keep them from venting their political dissent—and they headed primarily to Mexico, but also to Spain and elsewhere. U.S. high schools and universities had launched exchange programs. Increasingly more liberal Cuban-Americans—and their post-Ochoa generational counterparts on the island—were engaging critiques of the respective ideological givens of a prior term. The harsh reality of Cuba's "special period" and its lingering aftermath was equally pushing Castro to reconfigure the country's economic model. Speculation on the island was rampant, with Spain and Canada acting as particularly aggressive leaders in what is now a booming joint-venture tourist economy.

JOHN FUND: The American people really don't fully understand what a totalitarian country is like. Elián is going to be taken back to this special compound where supposedly he is going to be there with psychiatrists and psychologists to ease him into his transition back to Cuba. Was this the father's idea or is this Castro's idea? And that's really what's at the heart of this. Are we reuniting Elián with his father or reuniting him with Big Daddy Castro, who says that, quote, Elián is a possession of the Cuban government, unquote...

BOBBIE BATISTA (host, CNN *TalkBack Live*): But, what's the difference, though, between that, John, and the relatives making him do the videotape...

JOHN FUND: Look, first of all, I believe that Elián should be reunited with his father, but it should not be on Cuban soil in the United States. If he wants to be reunited with his father, have him move to a separate location, not the Cuban diplomatic compound, where if they pump him up with drugs and they bring in psychiatrists from Havana, we don't have any right to go in there, and don't think it hasn't happened before. There was a case of a Soviet ballerina in 1979 who was sent back and, after she had been drugged, told immigration officials she didn't want to stay in this country...

VICTORIA JONES: An awful lot of bad things happened during the Cold War. We also shouldn't forget, while we talk about what Castro's going to do to him, the thousands of unaccompanied minors who come to these shores from oppressive regimes, who have no lawyers, who are put in juvenile detentions, and then are shipped back by our government. Or the thousands of children who are taken away by a non-custodial foreign parent to another country and don't come back...

JOHN FUND: But let's make it very clear: what Elián is going back to is not a normal [!] poverty-stricken country like Haiti, which, as bad as that is, is a totalitarian system in which the government takes possession of children, puts them through youth camps, puts them through indoctrination, and Elián is going to become the mascot for the Communist Young Pioneer League....I would be much more sanguine about this Janet Reno operation if the child was not to be returned to the Cuban diplomatic compound. That is the worst possible outcome short of sending him to Cuba itself....

VICTORIA JONES: Well, I don't know, I think leaving him in a house with a convicted drunk driver and chain-smoker, whose sons are felons and whose daughter faints at the drop of a hat, doesn't seem very healthy to me [audience laughter and applause]....[7]

---

[7] *TalkBack Live*, CNN, April 21, 2000.

The lack of legitimate critical debate paled compared to the foreboding chance encounters between internet news and advertising. Above the CNN.com site for the dramatic April 22 posting of "Federal agents seize Elián in pre-dawn raid," an ad read "Isn't Your Future Worth the Investment? (click here)." On the *Miami Herald* website for Wednesday, May 17, a headline announced "Elián pictures anger exiles: Boy seen wearing communist symbol." Hovering above it, and in a telling comment on image-making and consumerism, was the following enticement: "Get 100 Free Prints With Select Digital Camera Purchases (click here for details)." At the end of a *Washington Post Online* story concerning the announced move by Elián's family and friends to the Cleveland Park area of Washington, D.C., the publicity box reads: "Mamma.com: The Mother of all Search Engines: Search Now!"— evoking in obscene irony no less than the largely unacknowledged memory of Elián's deceased parent, Elizabeth Brotons Rodríguez[8], over whose remains the saga may be said at last to rest.

"Saga" was the word used by the press to describe the unprecedented attention granted to the events variously constructed in the public sphere. The Elián story, not unlike other media blitzes before it, served as a reminder of TV's (and now the internet's) failed utopian promise of a peaceably united community of spectators in the form of televised entertainment or virtual transmission. There is poignancy to early discourses on the technology of the image in the household. In 1954, NBC executive Sylvester "Pat" Weaver spoke of television as having created:

> a situation new in human history in that children can no longer be raised within a family or group belief that narrows the horizon of the child to any belief pattern. There can no longer be a We-Group, They-Group under this condition. Children cannot be brought up to laugh at strangers, to hate foreigners, to live as man has always lived before.[9]

---

[8]   Sometimes spelled as "Broton Rodríguez" in American and British media.
[9]   Quoted by Lynn Spigel in "The Suburban Home Companion: Television and the Neighbourhood Ideal in Post-War America," *Feminist Television Criticism: A Reader*, ed. Charlotte Brunsdon, et al. (Oxford: Clarendon Press, 1997) p 216.

The Elián saga addressed, tellingly, adult-world delirium with regard to childhood—itself a kind of virtuality—a realm in which grown-up economies are utterly incompatible. The confounding of media event, with its looking-glass view to the real, and our common anxieties about childhood and representation, shared much in common with the sheer velocity and episodic absurdity of Lewis Carroll's *Alice in Wonderland*.[10] Commonplace notions on the subject of childhood are as vividly linked to how we choose to refigure our own personal narratives as they are informed by, and invariably bound to, shifting patterns of representation—and, now more than ever, to the ideologies of a capitalist consumerism contingent on image surfeit.

What kept this story going was this conflation of childhood writ large with the likeness of Elián on the television screen and other media platforms; and it was striking to count the number of times the word "image" was repeated during any given coverage. For childhood is still deemed, as a rule, the visual property of adulthood—in the dual sense of feature or virtue by right and ownership. To rhyme with the attendant question as to whether a child might not see the persecution the adult world imagines, there is the consequential actuality of the Elián saga where others would have viewed simulacrum.[11] In view of the media spectacle, one commentator suggested the following:

> Never a real child, though his childhood and the quality of it were the focus of thousands of lines of AP-feeds. Never a real human because he is contained in an image that is bounced from satellite to website and into your cranium. An image that is constructed of electrons and carbon residue, burn marks that never show up on the flesh of young Elián.[12]

---

[10]   Lewis Carroll. *Alice in Wonderland and Through the Looking Glass* (New York: Signet Classics, 2000) p 115 ("'Let the jury consider the verdict,' the King said, for about the twentieth time that day. 'No, no!' said the Queen. 'Sentence first—verdict afterwards.'")

[11]   For a sobering corrective to notions of social fact and childhood held exclusively in the realm of the simulacrum, one need only view the undeclared war on the underaged as captured in the photographs of Stan Grossfeld, recently gathered in *Lost Futures, Our Forgotten Children*, or to regard, otherwise, how conventional ideas equating childhood with innocence are complicated by photographers such as Julia Margaret Cameron, Lewis Hine, Weegee, Helen Levitt, Sally Mann, and Graciela Iturbide.

[12]   Chris Buzachero. "Elián González in Hyper-Space," in *C-Theory*, vol. 23, nos. 1–2 (http://www.ctheory.com).

Representation, both democratic and aesthetic, survive as future-driven, utopian—the "fullness of embodiment" by which late Cuban modernist José Lezama Lima saw possibility and meaning "surge into historical timeliness"[13]—and worthy of the kinds of battles mass-mediated across what another poet, Robin Blaser, called the "image-nation."[14] It was a conflict that implicated semblance's illusory dream of being contemporaneous with the present, the sacrosanct standing of the family institution, the pleasures and sense-giving attendant on watching television news. With all the public displays of histrionics and media overkill, it is easy to dismiss the symbolic relevance of how the spectacle of Elián González was played out in the public domain; easy to forget the real human bonds at stake, always enacted in a double movement as simulated soap opera and resonant human content. Can the act of surrendering to the melodramatic spectacle of media events be recognition of the complexity and conflict that are the givens to living in the mediated world? Is it too plain to overlook the "real" emotional involvement that is invested in identification with the protagonists of media events? Is Elián finally about the media's mode of determination, always positioned in advance, as we are, between cynicism and sincerity when our relation to the real and the political becomes a series of images and headlines? Is it possible no longer to imagine it otherwise?

Louis Althusser spoke of ideology as a representation of "the imaginary relationship of individuals to their real conditions of existence."[15] If we accept the desires and world outlooks that are presented in the palpable fictions of entertainment, in the "grotesque facts" and "exotic truths"[16] of the information industry or in the tantalizing overtures of advertising as the material means by which men and women "represent their real conditions of

---

[13]   José Lezama Lima. "26 de julio: Imagen y posibilidad," in *Imagen y posibilidad* (Havana: Editorial Letras Cubanas, 1981) p 19.

[14]   Robin Blaser. *The Holy Forest* (Toronto: Coach House Press, 1993). See the incredible serial poem, a contemporary masterwork, entitled "Image-Nations."

[15]   Louis Althusser. *Lenin and Philosophy* (New York: Monthly Review Press, 1972) p xiv.

[16]   Mary B. Campbell. *The Witness and the Other World: Exotic European Travel Writing, 400–1600.* (Ithaca: Cornell University Press, 1991) pp 3; 47.

existence to themselves in an imaginary form,"[17] then the high stakes involved in the Elián González display were the contradictions and impossibilities inherent in democracy itself.

In his routinely suggestive fusion of psychoanalysis and popular culture, Slavoj Žižek discussed the problem of formal democracy as a violent abstraction:

> There is in the very notion of democracy no place for the fullness of concrete human content, for the genuineness of community links: democracy *is* a formal link of abstract individuals. All attempts to fill out democracy with "concrete contents" succumb sooner or later to the totalitarian temptation, however sincere their motives may be. Critics of democracy are thus correct in a way: democracy implies a split between the abstract *citoyen* and the *bourgeois* bearer of particular "pathological" interests, and any reconciliation between the two is structurally impossible.... [Democracy] literally lives on the split between the "public" and the "private."[18]

What better image for the community of viewers than that of a child—an "enemy" boy—to embody the anxieties about our optimistically deluded faith in the democratic subject? What more effective effigy to posit the dream by which our manifold causes and claims can transcend the impossibility posed by representation so as to reconcile the incommensurate differences between the singular and the plural, between actual event and its mediation, between individual spectator and social audience? At risk is the illusory prospect of what Žižek calls the "democratic break"[19] by which all features of distinction are cast away in order to found the democratic subject—even as this purging is never complete, never without its necessary remainder. A boy delivered by dolphins from the sea.

"The image is the secret cause of history," wrote Lezama Lima,[20] I cannot help but return to these ideas when thinking of Elián; to

---

[17]   *Ibid*, 162–77.

[18]   Slavoj Žižek, *Looking Awry: An Introduction to Jacques Lacan Through Popular Culture* (Cambridge, MA: The MIT Press, 1997) pp 164–65.

[19]   *Ibid*.

[20]   José Lezama Lima. "26 de julio: Imagen y posibilidad," in *Imagen y posibilidad* (Havana: Editorial Letras Cubanas, 1981) p 19 [Author's translation].

what Lezama suggests when he says, that the "hypothesis of the image is possibility....But the image must side with death, must endure the opening of the ark as superlative enigma and fascination, that is, in the fullness of embodiment, so that possibility may achieve meaning and surge into historical timeliness."[21] Thinking of Elián, I am tempted to retrace what Lezama Lima means when he evokes Homer's Odysseus and his descent into the underworld in search of his shadow-mother who, after several withdrawals and elisions, urges her son to remain no longer in that somber valley, but to return without delay to the light. Lezama Lima claims that the "force of encounter... ascends toward the timely, occupies that space where light strikes its enemies and dispossesses the medusa of its infinite features."[22] Elián as image and possibility.

No. Elián the new millennium. Elián the spared-by-fortune. Elián the Second Coming, the dictator, the hostage, the alliance. Elián the venture capitalist. Elián the commercial sponsor is brought to you by Elián the movie-of-the-week. No. Elián the communist interior minister, president of the republic, counterrevolutionary; the true cross, scapegoat, trophy, freedom-fighter, the chief of staff. No. Elián the spoils of the battle, of the foreign menace, of the most beautiful drowned mother in the world. Elián the image-maker. Elián the hero with a thousand faces.

Awash in a sea of information that rose daily in ever-increasing proportions in the print and electronic media, it was the relentless contingency of images—the order of their disclosure and intensity as they were broadcast headlong into a calendar heavy with the weight of anniversary—that catapulted this undoubtedly amazing account into the operatic heights of the symbolic. Freud may not have imagined the unconscious in the vibrant color scale or flashing contours of our present-day mediascape, but the comparison is apt, at least for decoding the sweep of both the arbitrary and meaningful relations that the incident set into motion between text and image, and our relation as accomplice-consumers of these current events.

---

[21] *Ibid.*

[22] *Ibid.*

In a language not unlike the workings of the mind in excess of itself—very often a kind of phantasmagoria rising from the printed page of the popular press or on the screens and monitors of our televisions and workstations—the collective unconscious that is the media forced us as viewers to habitually second-guess the motives or to identify the symptoms in the onslaught of "dream-censorship and representation by symbols,"[23] its oversights and contradictions, and what remains of its ever-fleeting succession—this virtual democracy that it purports to represent. Possibly even at the risk of rehearsing the same scenes over and over again.

[23]   Sigmund Freud. *Introductory Lectures on Psychoanalysis* (New York: W.W. Norton, 1977) p 209.

Elián had already
become a phantom image
of himself; had already,
possibly much earlier
but never more clearly

◆

than in this footage,
slipped through the
looking glass of childhood
as it is represented in
the era of simulation...

S O T
H R
A E
W V

THE SYLLABIC RHYTHMS OF THE WORD "*ENERGÚMENO*" are a recital of the sort that Spanish—a language rich in proparoxytones—is especially equipped to enact. Etymological lines point back to Greek and Latin for a person possessed by the devil and prone to fury, even as subsequent uses modified the term over time to nominate the figure of a lunatic. To unleash those syllables from mouth and lips is already to inhabit the mad articulations of its referent, in gestures suspended between the half smirk of that inaugural "e" and the paroxysm of that accented antepenultimate vowel.

"What is a word?" Nietzsche asked. "It is the copy in sound of a nerve stimulus."[1] The "*energúmeno*" is, as well, a reappearing persona in Pablo Helguera's demanding and magnetic prose delirium *Onda corta*, a literary performance proper to such figures of speech—at once sleepless, unpredictable, and wholly devoted to the idiosyncratic exaltation of subjects unrestrained and on display. "As long as I can remember," the author recalls, "two methods have especially appealed to me: games of fiction and the play of the absurd. In the former, a truth is actually presented as a falsehood; in the latter, apparent nonsense suddenly bursts into meaning."[2]

---

[1]   Friedrich Nietzsche. "On Truth and Lies in a Non-Moral Sense" in *Philosophy and Truth; Selections from Nietzsche's Notebooks of the Early 1870s* (Atlantic Highlands, N.J.: Humanities Press, 1979) p 81.

[2]   Electronic correspondence with the artist, 18 July 2012.

This emphasis on the gestural possibility of language should come as no surprise to those familiar with this multimedia artist who rearranges the rules of the game in terms of material, method, and artistic identity. Diverse modes of staging meant to animate public actions have consistently structured his lectures, installations, sculpture, photography, drawing, and socially engaged art. For instance, in a sprawling road trip fueled by both critical inquiry and narrative wanderlust, Helguera's project The School of Panamerican Unrest (2003–2006) joined elements of a socialist-reform education campaign to those of a traveling theater troupe. The result was what the artist called "a nomadic think tank"[3] whose headquarters consisted of a roving minivan and pop-up schoolhouse that traveled, with twenty-seven urban stops along the way, from Anchorage, Alaska, to Tierra del Fuego. The schedule of events co-sponsored by a wide network of artists, activists, and educators prompted roundtable discussions (on topics ranging from "the uses and misuses of art" to "populism as cultural revolution"),[4] as well as screenings of documentary films and experimental videos; workshops in writing and performance; an array of information exchanges or civic ceremonies; and a web log that endures now as the record of that elaborate undertaking. If, for Pablo Helguera, "every artwork is a script"[5] of the kind enlivened by The School of Panamerican Unrest, then in concept and execution a counterpart complexity motivates the pages of *Onda corta* and other works in which language serves as cultural description and surface demonstration—statement as persona and action; itinerary along a path whose uncertain endpoint is the curvature of the earth as it appears to coincide with the simultaneous stages of a lunar eclipse.

Onda corta begins in Havana, Cuba, with ensuing geographies that span from Mexico City to Surabaya, Indonesia. Divided into forty-eight sections, none more than a page or two in length—

[3] Pablo Helguera, "Biographical note," artist website <http://pablohelguera.net/bio/>

[4] "Pablo Helguera: The School of Panamerican Unrest | La escuela panamericana de sosiego," press release, (New York: Americas Society, April 20, 2006) n.p.

[5] Pablo Helguera, Ohad Meromi, and Xaviera Simmons in conversation with Paul David Young. "Turning Theater into Art," *PAJ: A Journal of Performance and Art* 100 (2012) p 180.

a duration that invites comparison to that of a serial radio broadcast—
and framed by a preface and epilogue, each scene gives way to
overlapping assertions of place and time for the personae of this prose
account, invested in the completion of a pre-determined task. In what
constitutes, by comparison, a relatively transparent opening sequence,
set in the present backdrop of Cuba's urban capital, a national
imaginary and built environment at the crossroads of arrested time,
geographic isolation, and tourist traffic, there emerges a temporality
akin to the unfinished modern project of the aesthetic and social
avant-gardes: "Aquí el presente todavía se define por un conocimiento
de lo histórico, que es lo único que está a la mano de todos porque está
enterrado en el pasado."[6] This recognition activates a reverie about a
Blaupunkt short wave radio in the remote location of childhood, the
simultaneity of places made available by means of airwaves, and the
structure of memory as being parallel to the belatedness of history.

What follows, then, are the fever dreams of objects, people,
and places prompted by incitements that include travel and leisure
time; math, music, and medicine; geography and the natural
world; historical, literary, or mythic figures and various forms of
representation. *Onda corta* animates improbable assemblies into
scenes of material and ongoing metaphoric transmutations. The
likelihood of any stable portrayal is further diminished by a host of
subjects, animate and inanimate, committed to the accidental or
calculated gesture, as when "el energúmeno dejó de hablar pero
sus brazos cumplieron las funciones de trece ministerios."[7] These
rhetorical acrobatics disrupt the habits of grammar that submit
obligatory links between cause and effect, or that privilege the
sequential over other kinds of temporal alignments: "...ni tampoco
habría sido posible ni siquiera imaginar la posibilidad de pensar en
la remota posibilidad de pensar en que la posibilidad de imaginar la
remota posibilidad de imaginar lo posiblemente posible."[8] Such are

---

[6] "Here the present is defined by historical knowledge, the only thing within reach
because it is buried in the past." Pablo Helguera, *Onda corta* (New York: Jorge Pinto Books,
2012) p 4 [Translations mine].

[7] ..."the lunatic ceased to speak but his arms fulfilled the task of three ministers." *Ibid.*, p 9.

[8] "...nor was it even possible to imagine the remotest possibility of imagining the possibly
possible." *Ibid.*, p 6.

the perverse or excessive time-signatures of fantasy that find aim in the object world, that make necessary the laws of prohibitions, and the unwanted thoughts to which they give birth, if only in order to defy them: "El dieciocho brumario de mi oficina despuntaba pero el sol de la hora de comer iniciaba su escape."[9]

Here, any aspiration to a stable selfhood—"Seamos realistas: soy el presidente de este universo"[10]—is but an effect that proliferates at the speed, wavelength, and frequency of electromagnetic radiation: "Dejemos todas las tiendas abiertas toda la noche, con todas las luces encendidas, pero que nadie entre en ellas, y prendamos un radio universal que narre todo aquello que no está aconteciendo, lo cual será un gran acontecimiento."[11] This utopian universe squarely situates Pablo Helguera's work in the extended field of surrealist practice that values the ongoing potential of play as a structuring device. Surrealism endures to the degree that its accounts of experience are a chain of effects—multimedia and interdisciplinary—that rarely decline into mere negative critique, preferring happily instead to tell the lie about the metaphysics of depth.

Roger Caillois wrote that play "can consist not only of deploying actions or submitting to one's fate in an imaginary milieu, but of becoming an illusory character oneself, and of so behaving ... the subject makes believe or makes others believe that he is someone other than himself."[12] In Mexico, and as far back as 1988, Helguera began to locate serious play at the center of his practice. He turned at first to the palindrome, a language game that flirts with nonsense but whose mathematical value is measured by degrees of poetic accuracy—insofar as absolute incoherence would render them

---

9   "The eighteenth brumaire of my office glowed but the mealtime sun had begun its escape." *Ibid.*, p 8.

10   "Let us be realists: I am the president of this universe." *Ibid.*, p 13.

11   "Let's leave every store open all night, with all the lights on, but let no one enter, and let's switch on the universal radio that tells of all things not taking place, all of which would be a remarkable occurrence." *Ibid.*, p 32.

12   Roger Caillois. *Man, Play, and Games*, trans. Meyer Barash (New York: The Free Press of Glencoe, Inc., 1961) p 19.

pointless. Now living the United States, Helguera gave birth to a heteronym à la Fernando Pessoa[13]; a literary alter ego who provided the artist with permission to pen poems by means of automatic writing or "stream of consciousness" techniques; in this way he managed anonymously to contribute to literary journals under the pseudonym of Rodolfo Limonini.[14] Initially a joke that freed him from certain representational attachments, Limonini soon exposed the multiple facts and fictions of selfhood; truths in the non-moral sense that Nietzsche described as being the "residues of a metaphor," like coins that have "lost their embossing and are now considered as metal and no longer as coins."[15]

Following the logic of the unconscious with parallel techniques of condensation and displacement, the artist began to overwrite the assumption that private narratives submit original meaning, deranging instead the ideal forms that contain the muddle of allegedly defensible sentences. As by the surrealist procedure of definitions, or that of the question and answer,[16] a temporal clause

---

[13] In his manuscripts, and even in personal correspondence, Pessoa attributed much of his best writing to various fictional alter egos, which he called "heteronyms." Scholars have tabulated as many as seventy-two of these. His love of invented names began early: at the age of six, he wrote letters under the French name Chevalier de Pas, and soon moved on to English personae such as Alexander Search and Charles Robert Anon. But the major heteronyms he used in his mature work were more than jokey code names. They were fully fledged characters, endowed with their own biographies, philosophies, and literary styles. Pessoa even imagined encounters among them, and allowed them to comment on one another's work. If he was empty, as he liked to claim, it was not the emptiness of a void but of a stage, where these selves could meet and interact. —Adam Kirsch, "Fernando Pessoa's Disappearing Act." (*The New Yorker,* 2017).

[14] Helguera writes: "Rodolfo Limonini is my earliest heteronym. He was born around 1985 and his poems have appeared sporadically with an increase of production—always in Spanish—mostly between the years 1994 to 2001." Helguera, Pablo. "Rodolfo Limonini." Accessed June 2018. http://pablohelguera.net/1994/01/rodolfo-limonini/.

[15] Friedrich Nietzsche, "On Truth and Lies in a Non-Moral Sense" in *Philosophy and Truth; Selections from Nietzsche's Notebooks of the Early 1870s* (Atlantic Highlands, N.J.: Humanities Press, 1979) p 84.

[16] *A Surrealist Book of Games,* compiled and edited by Alastair Brotchie and Mel Gooding (Boston Shambhala Redstone Editions, 1995) pp 26–7.

such as "Ese fue el momento de..." unhinges into the seemingly unrelated consequence of "...las montañas rosas, todas leves presenciando una película sin importancia pero sin embargo cargada de especias árabes."[17]

Importantly, having lived for over 20 years in the United States—and having written all his lectures, essays, and art theory exclusively in English—Helguera has been mindful that this mode of writing remain uniquely tethered to the Spanish language. Related to this, and to the degree that surrealism in Latin America necessarily points back to the colonial archive and to the transitory circumstances of change that projected Western consciousness into modernity, Helguera began an ambitious project entitled "The Well-Tempered Exposition" (2011) whose method was to "translate" the structure of Bach's "The Well-Tempered Clavier" into discursive terms. With this acknowledgment of the baroque—where musical composition and rhetoric are of a piece, where violence and sensuality are productive of an open-ended system of meaning—Helguera sought to bring independent speaking parts into collective speech: a poetics akin to "Panamerican Unrest."

Panamerican Unrest is an apt definition, too, for those techniques capable of inaugurating an apotheosis out of everyday objects; for re-enchanting the raw material of language elsewhere put to instrumental use; for those methods that so enliven the arbitrary as to resist any totalizing account. Considering the artist's explorations of writing and in particular, metaphor—the multiplying language of unrest—allows us to understand Helguera's mode of interdisciplinary making as part of the *longue durée* of surrealism. Central to surrealism is the material fact of the body as a threshold container of departure and arrival, an exception to the laws of reason, and a zone of unexpected physical or chronological juxtapositions. Allergic to historicism and its comprehensive descriptions, surrealist drive proliferates into occasions of display meant to prompt commitments by further multiplying perceptual

---

[17] "That was the moment..." // "the rose-colored mountains, all of them weightless attending a film of no importance but nonetheless redolent of Arabic spices." Pablo Helguera, *Onda Corta* (New York: Jorge Pinto Books, 2012) p 8.

means. In this, Helguera aligns himself with the view of Cuban modernist José Lezama Lima who considered images to be "the secret cause of history,"[18] and with latter-day U.S. American surrealist Barbara Guest who spoke of poetry's shadow relation to gestural abstraction by which "art as reflection became more instantaneous, willful, enthusiastic, freed by action."[19]

As in André Breton's *Mad Love*, there is in *Onda corta* a counterpoint between the verbal performance and silent image. The dexterity of the prose and its forward motion are punctuated with visual interludes: drawings, prints, and photographs offer admission to concurrence and coincidence, the "objective chance" that Breton claimed makes "a mockery of what would have seemed most probable."[20] The iconography betrays a central point. Electromagnetic conductors, tuning forks, a kind of camera obscura, a game board, microphones and modulators, an acoustic laboratory or echo chamber, a humble observatory in a woodland clearing, photographic postcards from Surabaya, and diagrams depicting the manners of human motility: figures of a world measured only by the verifiable in physical experience. Martin Heidegger imagined an "endlessly extended emptiness of the purely quantitative" when he proposed that the "fundamental event of modernity is the conquest of the world as picture."[21]

How to assemble a present or future self as to procure relevance from within that visual authority over the quantifiable world? Toward the final scenes of *Onda corta*, its dramatis personae— child, physicist, *energúmeno*—suggest a horizon of possibility and deliverance: "En esos momentos entiendo, creo, la modernidad,

[18]   José Lezama Lima. "26 de Julio," *Imagen y posibilidad*, edited and compiled with a prologue by Ciro Bianchi Ross (Havana: Letras Cubanas, 1981) p 19.

[19]   Barbara Guest. "The Shadow of Surrealism," *Women's Studies: An Inter-Disciplinary Journal*, 30:1, p 9.

[20]   André Breton. *Mad Love* [1937], trans. Mary Ann Caws (Lincoln: University of Nebraska Press, 1987) p 87.

[21]   Martin Heidegger. "The Age of the World Picture," in *The Question Concerning Technology and Other Essays* [1938], trans. and ed. William Lovitt (New York, Harper Torchbooks, 1977) pp 133–4.

pero tal hecho no me salva; es el actuar de forma casi imperceptible entre el pensar y el no pensar, lo que nos volverá libres de nosotros mismos y de los otros que queremos ser."[22] In the intervals of word and image, of increase and decrease, of reason and unreason, there emerges a commitment to act in the world. Then again, maybe the task is only as tenable as the book's concluding image: a light beam traversing space onto the surface of a picture from an opening above, lasting until that moment when "En realidad ya no pertenecemos a este mundo."[23]

---

[22] "In those moments, I believe, I understand modernity, but the fact does not come to my rescue; it is the rehearsal of the almost imperceptible form between thinking and non-thinking, which will free us from ourselves and from the others we wish to be." *Ibid.*, pp 66–7.

[23] "In reality, we no longer belong to this world." *Ibid.*, p 99.

*Central to surrealism
is the material fact of
the body as a threshold
container of departure
and arrival,*

◆

*an exception to the laws
of reason, and a zone
of unexpected physical
or chronological
juxtapositions.*

VA

NISHING
ACTS

A MULETS THAT SHARE A SECRET KINSHIP in the history of light and language, with words like *glimmer* or *destello* sparks of intensity fade; splinters of duration evanesce. In a double life conjured by these vocables—[mm], [ll]—a zone of repetition glows at the origin, so making vision contingent at the material level of the letter, and all things abrupt ease into intermittency. There, claims to singularity are never less than overstatement, and resemblance comes into view out of joint with experience. These words remind us that in the developmental account, attributes of cataclysm and bliss reside not in the portentous totality, but in the unassuming detail. In a *glimmer* or *destello* is marked the ethics of attention required to tell narratives of sight and sound in transformation. Discrete words provide a partial view, but even as we link subject to predicate—"I surface"—the self remains at best a proposition, a reason we ascribe belatedly to a sequence of effects.

Nietzsche famously cautioned against the "habits of grammar" in which "I" am the cause of my thoughts.[1] But it was also, by contrast, the spell of words that enabled him precisely to submit in parables

---

1 The "habits of grammar...." Friedrich Nietzsche, *Beyond Good and Evil: Prelude to a Philosophy of the Future*, trans. R. J. Hollingdale, Baltimore, Maryland, Penguin Books, 1973, p 28.

a rejoinder to all those laws that set into motion the overarching systems. Today, under the pervasive audiovisual domains of high-speed communication, and in the psychopharmacology of everyday life, and by the flattened contours that make of a singular life another algorithm or dataset, there emerges the power of storytelling—in parables and other forms of living speech, as sights of embodiment with narrative consequence. They provide us with scripts of action, so we can navigate the intangible space of so much unprocessed information.

French psychoanalyst Jacques Lacan tells a story—"a true story" meant to join light and subjectivity—about an encounter with a "family of fisherman in a small port" on the coast of Brittany. Recalling his days as a budding writer in search of authentic experience ("something practical, something physical"), a youthful Jacques has thrown himself into the hard labor of fishing and into the "danger and excitement" of the open sea, even as a death marks the present tense of the story's telling.[2] Petit-Jean, the real-life protagonist of the parable, has since succumbed to "tuberculosis, which at that time was a constant threat to the whole of that social class..." But in the time that frames the story, on a day buoyant with sun and promise, in one of those frail crafts used for fishing, Petit-Jean, effusive and very much alive, turns to Jacques and then to a sardine can he glimpses afloat in the water, reflecting rays of sunlight. *"You see that can? Do you see it?"* He points to the object as he deridingly snickers, *"Well, it doesn't see you."* The narrator fails to see what is so amusing, perhaps because the scene submits a vision, independent of any particular body or volition: a visibility divergent from—or foreign to—human seeing; it swells into the picture as quickly as it recedes... and that ebb marks a constitutive rift. A glimmer prompts the necessary forethought for the storyteller to understand that "I was rather out of place in the picture."

To be in surplus of a scene is to be simultaneously attached to the setting and estranged from it. Looking back at the scene from his youth, Jacques Lacan viewed such excess as a value, as that which

[2]   Jacques Lacan. *The Four Fundamental Concepts of Psychoanalysis (Seminar XI)* trans. Alan Sheridan, New York, W. W. Norton & Company, 1978, pp 95–96.

makes something accessible to experience out of a general diminishing. The sun sparkle from a tiny metal shell—the stress point that Petit-Jean signaled to mean the cycle of community production and nameless consumption—allowed the psychoanalyst a glimmer into that unremarked violence at the picture's margin that gives surface reality a neutral semblance. A conflict underpins the misrecognition in the story, its incommensurability of viewpoint poised at an interface that determines inclusion in, or exclusion from, categories greater than the individual: an ethics. The glimmer from the sardine can—that which is outside the field of vision that makes me see myself seeing myself—so dislocates me from my surroundings as to resist too easy allocations of meaning. A person in the variability of place: Roger Caillois provided grounds to the claim that, insofar as I can assimilate into my surroundings, there is a decline in my feelings of personal attributes. To the degree that I generalize space, the more distinct become my feelings of mental and somatic sovereignty. The fate of indulging in fantasy may so lead to such mimetic incorporation of the animate in the inanimate, and vice versa, as for me to reconfigure the possibilities of my environs.[3] It led the poet Wallace Stevens—that "listener in the snow" in the frosty spaces of concept—to perceive "Nothing that is not there and the nothing that is."[4]

In the ether of global finance capital and its promise of an audiovisual "second life," there has been a turn to articulate the fractures of our social distribution. This artwork looks to the present political economy, the predicament of urban hyper-development, the effects of industrialism on the environment, and the contradictions of our cultural institutions. But there is also shadow line of image-making that so sees itself seeing itself as to be rendered "out of the picture" in some versions of contemporary poetry. This art enlivens objects with energies at the intersections of a self and its social stress points. It values a poetics of knowledge obtained in hidden spaces, or in the vicissitudes of language and other media, as the grounds

[3]   Roger Caillois. "Mimicry and Legendary Psychasthenia," trans. John Shepley, *October*, Vol. 31 (Winter, 1984) p 28.
[4]   Wallace Stevens. "The Snowman," *Collected Poems*, (New York, Knopf, 1954) p 10.

for public culture. It makes palpable a selfhood—if only for a lapse in time—that can modify the perception of an onlooker, alter the awareness of a situation, reframe the view to a familiar place, or invite an incremental engagement with one's immediate circumstance.

This kind of enactment seeks tonal ranges that speak to a social imaginary in arguments that apply pressure to image and cadence alike. It explores the potential of sight to convey internal striving as commensurate with the onrush of history. Like storytelling, it seeks rapport with a future listener to re-enchant the "communicability of experience" with rhetorical tension and critical timing.[5] It is suspicious of realisms that, in light of that which is most intimate and furtive, would limit our faculty to alter the order of things. It returns as that which is repressed in contemporary art, the disavowed underbelly that reinforces the art world institution.

Little triumph with a mirror, breath, or handprint.... humble habitats of ghosted flesh as on the threshold of speech.... viscous secretions, as well voluptuous. In the work I have in mind sex in abjection emerges as life enhancing: perverse enactments, the compulsion to repeat, and the spell of partial objects give shape to political emotions of a present, even as they belie the cover story of an alleged global citizenship. These scenes assume no less the particular language of materiality and gesture, like the structure of a sentence that is in perfect in keeping with its content. Artworks, inasmuch as they are propositions, locate a circumstance in the world, make claims about it, and offer alternate arguments.

Lezama Lima's poem "The Embrace" enlivens the polymorphous, engendering potential of non-reproductive sex between unspecified bodies. Pliable flesh and corporeal secretions proliferate into a network of analogies connecting human to non-human animal. Infinitesimal points are rendered as gaping mouths that now give rise to planetary systems, and contract again into horses, pheasants, devilfish, sea-owls, kangaroo tails, and sea-serpents. Such intercourse in the treacherous flux of life forebodes the destructive impact of human activity on atmospheric and biological processes here on earth, and

---

5   Walter Benjamin. "The Storyteller," in *Illuminations: Essays and Reflections*, trans. Harry Zohn, (New York, Schocken Books, 1969) p 86.

it points to the insignificance of our human moment in terms of geological time.

> The two bodies disappear
> into a point now opening its mouth.
> Wetness, softness,
> the infinitely-expanding sponge
> all responding at the door
> glowing with the ointment
> of horses at daybreak and the flicker
> of pheasants, their eyes barely a memory.

> The dolmen bestows gifts
> at the anointed door,
> its old wood silently creaking.
> The two bodies disappear
> and unite on the edge of a cloud.
> That devilfish, a sea-owl,
> dries the starry perspiring
> the bodies exhale in crucifixion.
> Tree and phallus
> know nothing of resurrection,
> they surface and ebb with the half-moon
> and the blazing sulfur of the sun.
> The two engirded bodies,
> kangaroo tail
> and sea-serpent,
> knot and rustle in the boreal casque.

In another posthumously published poem entitled "Octavio Paz," Lezama Lima choreographed attitudes and attributes disposed to narrow the distance between shifting tableaux, between known and unknowable things; between aesthetic understanding and the experimental imagination:

> Everything everywhere looming.
> It is the deer that sees the snake in the calls
> of the river; nature slipping
> on the scales that invoke an inaugural rhythm.
> Naming and name-making in a groping blindness.

The masked voice commanding the kings of Greece,
the blood adverse to the nocturnal tongs
returning to the original whirling sphere.
Asleep on the terrace, the priest
awakens with each word he slings
at the partridge falling into its steel mirror.
The word in motion
at the instant of release, parading
now through the resistant numbers,
in the plausible city
built for the formless inhabitants beginning
to breathe. Deep in the wood the dances
arrived in costume—but the fire
by then had already uprooted the horizon.
The dormant city evaporates its language,
the fire roaming like water
along the rungs of my arms.
The new, illegible ordinance
lifted the head of a mumbling Crusoe.
Only the fire mirrored
the silent mass of the shipwreck.[6]

"Naming and name-making" constitute "inaugural rhythms" able to create an environment for the cohabitation of the material, mythic, and historical structure of the imagination; a place for "words in motion" inclined to "uproot the horizon" into the "illegible ordinances" and "shipwrecks" that are the varieties of life processes and of ceaseless transfiguration. Statements reflect an energy and outline in excess of subject matter. Something in the artwork is exhausted neither by its enunciation nor by its form of address. Walter Benjamin called this the "expressionless,"[7] irreducible to content, sustaining the difference between surface effect and essence so as to prevent the conflation of essence with truth. There is no mystery other than the meanings a self attributes to the situational world where, under a dimming glow, symbolic actions have a stake in escaping the instrumental life.

---

6   José Lezama Lima. "Octavio Paz," trans. Roberto Tejada, *Sulfur* (38) Spring 1996, p 111.
7   Walter Benjamin. "Goethe's *Elective Affinities*," in *Selected Writings, 1913–1926*, trans. Stanley Corngold. (Cambridge, Massachusetts, Harvard University Press, 1996) p 350.

There is a rip in the web of meaning that artworks cast and draw. But owing to that gash—the fear and desire in light of seeing and knowing—carefulness of thought or gesture emboldens and persuades. The limberness of what we call poetry untangles the strict partitions of subject and object, of self and other, with the kind of intuitive leaps that only metaphor makes plausible. These moments of poetic elucidation cannot be generalized, nor are they easily earned, nor is it possible to isolate them without jeopardizing the architecture specific to lyric intimacy. The quality of light and subjectivity that is a provisional glimmer reminds us, as did Marx, that the world can be readily stripped of its halo. When "all that is solid melts into air" and we are made to see the "real conditions" of our lives, the ethical self seeks reflection in settings of experimentation that cover a ground if only as a temporary residence.[8] The transience may quicken us to substitute the vanishing with so many constituent parts, reanimated. Even as they are deprived of a halo, even as they are released from fixity and essence, some works are not without the radiance of a convenient forgetting. They are visual equivalents of the hypothetical enunciation—"what if" or "as though"—when we comprehend that in any quest-account the amulet found "is really a refinding."[9] This art exacts an unhurried measure, inasmuch as speed for speed's sake endangers the sensual opportunity of the world and, everyday—because so beckoning—its recurring custody. It encompasses speculative objects and symbolic acts that bind us together in mindfulness, around which we congregate, and over which we're inclined to argue... and then we vanish.

---

[8]   Karl Marx. "Communist Manifesto" (1888) in Marshal Berman, *All That is Solid Melts into Air*, (New York, Simon & Schuster, 1982). p 95.

[9]   Sigmund Freud. *Three Contributions to the Theory of Sex*, trans. A. A. Brill, New York. (E. P. Dutton & Company, 1962) p 79.

SOUNDS

POSTSCRIPT: NEIGHBORING

THE WRITINGS ASSEMBLED IN THIS BOOK are synchronized now to a time of staggering global and regional transformations. The enormity of our moment defies individual understanding of the potential outcome, inducing a paralysis of the political imagination. With each day going seven degrees further than what we experienced yesterday as unprecedented, the here and now begins to feel so inextricable, immersive, and devoid of a definable or future shape, as to be unavailable to any predictive sense, be it hope or despair. A lifetime ago abruptly surfaces.... As an adolescent in Los Angeles, in the years hinging between the late 1970s and early 1980s, I received instruction from educators committed, in one form or another, to an ethics in keeping with contemporary life and culture, social equity, and introspection for the sake of others. From them I learned a method of discernment; a double movement of distress and plenitude for persons who—"sometimes consoled by Heaven ... sometimes a prey to desolation"[10]—endure the internal antagonism.

---

[10]   St. Ignatius of Loyola. *Manresa: Or, the Spiritual Exercises of St. Ignatius, for General Use* (London: Burns, Oates & Washbourne, 1881) p 6. Loyola's exercises are a series of image techniques that make of embodiment and speech the media enabling of authentic identification with the lives of others. Those Jesuit priests in Cold War California provided encouraging lessons in the values of striving for collective integrity

Its twin structure unites prospection with a tenor of mind that seeks the attainment of justice. My attentions thereafter attuned, as later informed by the work of Michel de Certeau, to culture in the plural, to place as relating a viewpoint, and to a walkabout sensibility that shows up the dubious project of any foregone conclusion. To listen and act in relation to the past—to its vicinities far and near—is to view history and metaphor as a "discourse of the dead," but whose hidden figures serve as an "exchange among the living."[11]

The reflections gathered here were written over a span of twenty-seven years, from 1991 to the present. In the walking tour of my personal past—and in materials encompassing diverse time periods, geographies, and rhetorical tones; an autobiography by other means—contradictory pleasures emerged from the occasion to regard a life, now in alignment, now in a complicated relationship to belonging. In *Alternating Current,* Octavio Paz wrote: "The poem is the trajectory between [ ] two silences—between the wish to speak and the silence that fuses the wishing and the speaking."[12] In the selection, arrangement, editing, and occasional rewriting of these essays—composed in Mexico City; Buffalo, New York; San Diego and Los Angeles; Austin, Dallas, and Houston; as well as during brief periods of research in São Paulo, Brazil—I found myself resisting other varieties of silence: the twofold hesitations of ambivalence and belatedness. I heard inflections of the present in the many pauses of a former self, and encountered again the experience of personhood as displacement, the leitmotif that unites many of these written rehearsals. As I returned to my early reflections on illusory truths described in the *relaciones* of Spanish colonizers, and in subsequent travel writing—to those "exotic truths" and "grotesque facts" about the original inhabitants of these lands—U.S. officials of the current administration had already bankrupted the language of demonstrable experience with a depraved agenda of "alternative facts." The executive officer of the nation continued to pursue his

---

by means of a critical standpoint that neither forfeits the legitimate potential of the passions, nor that views commitment and uncertainty as incompatible.

[11] Michel de Certeau. *The Writing of History*, trans. Tom Conley (New York: Columbia University Press, 1988) p 46.

[12] Octavio Paz. *Alternating Current*, trans. Helen Lane (New York: Viking Press, 1973) p 68.

dehumanizing assault on African Americans, Muslims, Mexicans, Central Americans, women, queer communities, immigrants, and asylum-seekers, among others, while calling for the construction of a U.S.-Mexico border wall to make good on his campaign promise. It shed now belated light on the verbal and visual attitudes surrounding the 1846 U.S. War on Mexico—on such images as James Walker's 1847 *The Storming of Chapultepec*—and on the perverse eventualities of that rhetoric uniting territorial speculation, war, travel, and tourism.

In an earlier 1844 image, *Castle at Tuloom* [sic], Frederick Catherwood depicted the laboring bodies of indigenous men as they perform the back-breaking work of clearing the overgrowth around an ancient Maya ceremonial site. Catherwood renders the native figures in various degrees of undress while the American diplomat and explorer John Lloyd Stephens reclines in the foreground as the custodian of the undertaking. It is a scene of amazement in the presence of Mesoamerican antiquity, but no less the placeholder for Western cultural supremacy.[13] This nineteenth-century image reverses time and rushes back to be continuous with the earliest "expropriation of New World lands and the subsequent reduction of the indigenous peoples to being a landless, rightless, neo-serf work force."[14] Sylvia Wynter relates how, in recursive descriptions of this kind, "the accelerated mass slave trade out of Africa to the Americas

---

[13]   John L. Stephens. *Incidents of Travel in Yucatan* (New York: Harpers & Brothers, 1843), Vol. II, p 390–1.

The plate opposite represents the front of the Castillo. A few of the trees which grew around it appear in the engraving, and one is left growing on the top of the lower range, with its gnarled roots binding the front wall and obstructing the doorway, but no words and no drawing could convey a true idea of the solemnity of its living shroud, or of the impression made upon us when the ring of the axe first broke the stillness that had so long prevailed around.

The Library of Congress print differs importantly from the engraving published in John Lloyd Stephens' account: in the book's pages the scene is precisely the same but the laboring bodies are eerily absent. The description continues: ".... and again on the walls we found the mysterious prints of the red hand."

[14]   Sylvia Wynter, "Unsettling the Coloniality of Being/Power/Truth/Freedom: Towards the Human, After Man, Its Overrepresentation—An Argument," *CR: The New Centennial Review* 3.3 (2003) p 290.

and the Caribbean," and the "large-scale slave plantation system" it unleashed were made, in representation, "to seem just and legitimate to its peoples."[15]

The narratives in this book take place across the residual landscapes of that original haunting. First figures and belated counterparts loom over time in geographies of trespassing and entitlement; in scenes of an ambivalent hospitality that arises between the autochthonous and foreign. Small wonder that my fascination in these essays is so often with culture and authority, with deracinated experience, with the privilege of travel, and with dubious attitudes and actions around ownership of space in the American continent. In my role here as protagonist-antagonist of my former selves, I could stage my own indebtedness to kinship and foreignness. Hospitalities welcomed my alien status. Communities made room for me and for *Mandorla: Nueva Escritura de las Américas / New Writing from the Americas*, a multi-lingual journal of poetry, poetics, and translation that I founded in Mexico City with the purpose of bringing multiple sites of cultural activity into print form. "It was a publishing effort that, over the course of two decades (1991–2013) and a handful of editorial fluctuations, navigated the literary geographies of the American continents.... Mexico City, where the first five issues were edited and printed, was an advantageous site for the cultural debates connecting north and south in the face of privatization, trade agreements, labor flows, and other emergent realities in the region."[16]

---

[15]   *Ibid*, p 291. In my wishful reading of the Catherwood image, the moment hangs on the muscular indigenous male in the lower right foreground of the scene. As he reaches his right arm back, machete in hand, he will fell the tree but likewise stage the uprising that, hereinafter, will have altered the historical record.

[16]   Gabriel Bernal Granados, Kristin Dykstra, and Roberto Tejada. "Poetry in Translation: Hemispheric Perspectives," *Literary Publishing in the Twenty-First Century*, eds. Travis Kurowski, Wayne Miller & Kevin Prufer (Minneapolis, Minnesota: Milkweed Editions, 2016) p 78–9. Also: "As the magazine shape-shifted over the years, it grew from a modest independent annual, produced by a single editor (Roberto Tejada) and one guest editor (Esther Allen) to a long period of co-editorship [Gabriel Bernal Granados, Kristin Dykstra, and Roberto Tejada] (2004–2013), with a substantial editorial board and issues as voluminous as 662 pages in length."

I try to acknowledge that moment and others, but I cannot detach today from the news cycle appearing on my screen—images by Reuters photographer Mike Blake of the detention camp in Tornillo, Texas. In that aerial perspective, the immigrant children below, already separated from their families, become further dehumanized as ordered to march in formation from one end of the barracks to the military quarters containing the chain-link cages we have knowledge of in other photographs—a place of punishment obscenely peddled by officials as protection. The image produces horror in excess of what it depicts as an incommensurable gap opens up between a viewer and the arena for action. Detached, disembodied, at a mediated distance from the absolute malice unleashed, it makes palpable the degraded values of a democracy at its most endangered. The brutality of the state reappears to terrorize the most vulnerable, as when Elián González served as symbol of our anxious faith in the democratic subject.

This book is a condensation of curiosities, compassions, and anxieties about the relationship of artists and intellectuals to society, and about the imaginary form of national anatomies among the Americas, particularly the U.S., Mexico, and Cuba. The essays examine a tradition that questions U.S. cultural and political selfhood, sometimes open to what Lezama Lima knew as the "rift in response"—a method of uncertainty. That self-severance sets into motion the excitations of desire at the center of my writing. While I have no proprietary claim on appeals to passion, I mean to hold fast to the particularity of form while seeking the evasive qualities of subject matter. Shifts in mood and register are commensurate with the intervals between the contemplated object and the analogies that make present the past and its belongings; with the difference between the embedded and embodied perspectives of a desiring personhood.

In keeping with a subject recursive in my thought, I wonder whether this is really not a book about what it means to be a neighbor. Pierre Mayol suggested that to "leave one's home, to walk in the street, is right away to commit a cultural, non-arbitrary act... The relationship between entrance and exit, inside and outside, intersects with others such as between home and work, known and unknown, hot and cold, humid and dry weather, activity and passivity, masculine and feminine...."[17] The neighboring perspective delights in the both the stupefying and affirmative capacity of analogy, in the faith of estrangement and wonder; in the difficult optimisms that energize. As in the commitments of Muriel Rukeyser,[18] it views poetic forms as cultural propositions, meant to bridge the gap between imaginative ideals and the material means available to dwellers in language against a backdrop of possibility; an art whose arguments are for speaking the "general conflict of our culture" and as a "meeting place" that prepares us for thought.[19]

And yet *Still Nowhere in an Empty Vastness* fails miserably—its limits betrayed by a title whose metaphor is but another brutal irony undermining the concrete histories of dispossession. Commitments to indigenous methods of "critical place inquiry" have foregrounded

---

[17] Pierre Mayol, "The Neighborhood." In Michel de Certeau, Luce Giard, Pierre Mayol, and Timothy J. Tomasik, The Practice of Everyday Life: Volume 2, trans. Timothy J. Tomasik (Minneapolis: University of Minnesota Press, 1998) p 12. Mayol writes:

> The neighborhood is also the space of a relationship to the other as a social being, requiring a special treatment.... [It] is always a relationship between oneself and the physical and social world; it is the organizer of an inaugural and even archaic structure of the urban 'public subject' through the unflagging, because everyday, stomping around, which buries in a determinate soil the elementary seeds (decomposable into discrete units) of a dialectic constitutive of the self-awareness that, in this come-and-go movement, in this move between social mixing and intimate withdrawal, finds the certainty of itself as immediately social.

[18] Edward Hirsch. *Poet's Choice.* (Mariner Books, 2007) p 269.

> Rukeyser's way of blending the personal and the political looks backward to Walt Whitman and forward to Grace Paley, Jane Cooper and Adrienne Rich, who has now edited a first-rate version of Rukeyser's Selected Poems for the American Poets Project at the Library of America. Rukeyser's commitments were adamant and clear. She was determined to be politically aware without any sacrifice of poetic craftsmanship. "To live as a poet, woman, American, and Jew—this chalks in my position," she wrote in 1944. "If the four come together in one person, each strengthens the other."

[19] Muriel Rukeyser. *The Life of Poetry*, with a new foreword by Jane Cooper (Ashfield, Massachusetts: Paris Press, 1996) p 75; 78.

the need for non-abstractions of land, and for sovereignty as the refusal of communities to be the subjects of knowledge.[20] In "Not Nowhere: Collaborating on Selfsame Land,"[21] and in her podcast *The Henceforward*, Eve Tuck proposes the practice of "contingent collaboration" and cautions against the use of metaphor in historical and present-day articulations of land and place. There are abundant reasons to hesitate. In episode ten of *The Henceforward*, Eve Tuck, an indigenous scholar (Unangax̂), and Rinaldo Walcott, a Canadian black and queer studies scholar, rehearse an imperative—the unlearning of land conceived as vacant space or elsewhere.

RINALDO WALCOTT: Because the question of land is again not only a thorny issue but is one in which certain kinds of bodies and histories, certain kinds of persons, are immediately in forms of alienation to the land, or what we mark as land. So these create some significant tensions around how we might think of forms of contemporary debates within indigenous studies and around the notion of indigeneity, but also coming out of a region in the Caribbean where the question of alienation is central to how one begins to think about what one might be, and therefore how one might begin to think about other processes of indigeneity... . How does one become indigenous to the place that you are not from? How does one become indigenous to a place that you are alienated from? How does one become? This question of becoming is, for me, central to the kind of dialogue we are trying to forge.

EVE TUCK: Why is the goal to try to become indigenous to a place and not to become 'belonged' to a place? So this process of becoming, to me, it seems is a settler obsession to be obsessed with trying to become indigenous to a place, but I'm not sure why that is a way that it necessarily needs to be understood. I had an interview with Kim Tallbear recently where she was talking about kinship and the significance, the growing significance of kinship in her work, and what she talked about was ... we need to be in relationship and that relationship needs to exist outside of the ways that we have available to us—talking about black and indigenous people needing to be in relationship with each other—black

---

[20]   Eve Tuck and Marcia McKenzie. *Place in Research: Theory, Methodology, and Methods* (New York: Routledge, 2015) pp 146–9.

[21]   Eve Tuck, Allison Guess, and Hannah Sultan, "Not Nowhere: Collaborating on Selfsame Land," *Decolonization: Indigeneity, Education & Society*, 26 June 2014.

and indigenous people in Turtle Island,[22] needing to be in relationship to each other outside of how those relationships have already been constructed within settler states, already been constructed within settler colonial configurations of race. She said [she is] not interested in a relationship in which people are interested in trying to become indigenous, because I do not consent to that; it needs to be mutually consensual and I do not consent to that being somebody's endgame. And so I wonder what productive differences there could be between projects of becoming 'belonged,' if we want to stay with becoming, or projects of becoming indigenous which I'm far less interested in consenting to.

RINALDO WALCOTT: How do we make sense of this group of people for whom homeland is a mirage; but who, because of the current arrangements of how human life [is] organized must also claim a place of belonging. And so some of the ways in which we deploy notions of indigeneity actually say to those people that you have nowhere in the world.

EVE TUCK: I want to think about how indigenous desires to... recognize the ways in which place, in which land and water are significant, is an exception and is exceptional from the kinds of demands on black people to account, account in every kind of public encounter, about where they are from, because "they can't possibly be from here." We have to be able to set aside the way that that is working in larger mainstream settler society and to be able to fathom that the questions of centering land and place in indigenous frameworks [have] a different set of terms [and] conditions. Why do our relations have to inherit something that... actually works in very good ways in order to tell black people that they won't ever belong?— and to tell indigenous people that they don't belong anymore, "because you are already dead?" How do we not inherit something that never came from our relations? How does saying we're all indigenous from some place, or some of us are indigenous, elide the ways in which some of us are indigenous to this place, and that that sets into motion a set of obligations about how we relate and how we make sense in this place?[23]

---

[22] "Turtle Island is a reference to the continent of North America, which in many Eastern Woodlands origin accounts is built on the back of a giant turtle floating in a world ocean, with the soil having been brought from the depths by a smaller creature and spread across the turtle's back to create the foundation of the lands...." Daniel Heath Justice. *Why Indigenous Literatures Matter* (Wilfrid Laurier University Press, 2018) p 6.

[23] "Writing into the Henceforward." *The Henceforward* from the Indian & Cowboy Podcast Media Network, 2 May 2017, <http://www.thehenceforward.com/episodes/2017/5/2/episode-10-writing-into-the-henceforward>.

My meanings for an empty vastness have been those of history and analogy, always insufficient to the cruel fortunes and joyful vitality of irreducible human experience. I take leave of the figures in this landscape wondering whether "history is a record of survivors,"[24] one that is actually able to provide a shelter in poetry for the counted and the uncounted; for the belonged and the alienated from belonging. The perspectives I offer here compel a desire to host neighboring voices and parting words proper to such places assumed wrongly to be self-estranging or always already...

—Houston, July-August 2018

[24]   Susan Howe. *The Birth-Mark: Unsettling the Wilderness in American Literary History* (Hanover: University Press of New England, 1993) p 47.

WORKS

CONSULTED

Acevedo, Esther. "Annotations," Documents of 20th-Century Latin American and Latino Art: A Digital Archive and Publications Project, ICAA-812445.

Adams, Rachel. *Continental Divide: Remapping the Cultures of North America.* Chicago: University of Chicago Press, 2010.

Alcalá, Rosa. *The Lust of Unsentimental Waters.* Bristol, U.K: Shearsman Books, 2012.

Alvarado Leticia. "Asco's *Asco* and the Queer Affective Resonance of Abjection." *Aztlán: A Journal of Chicano Studies* 40:2 Fall 2015.

Althusser, Louis. *Lenin and Philosophy.* New York: Monthly Review Press, 1972.

Antin, David. "Words into type: David Antin on Vito Acconci." *Artforum International*, vol.44 no.7 March 2006, pp 51–52.

Anzaldúa, Gloria. *Borderlands: The New Mestiza.* San Francisco: Spinsters/ Aunt Lute, 1987.

Anreus, Alejandro, Robin A. Greeley, and Leonard Folgarait. *Mexican Muralism: A Critical History.* Berkeley: University of California Press, 2012.

Arendt, Hannah. *The Human Condition*, University of Chicago Press, 1958.

Ashton, Dore. "Mexican Art of the Twentieth Century," in *Mexico: Splendors of Thirty Centuries*. New York: The Metropolitan Museum of Art, 1990.

Barragán, Luis. "Una poética del espacio," *Artes de México* 23, 1994.

Bataille, Georges. *Theory of Religion*, Robert Hurley, trans., New York, Zone Books, 1992.

Baudrillard, Jean. *Jean Baudrillard: Selected Writings*, ed. Mark Poster. Stanford, California: Stanford University Press, 1988.

Baudrillard, Jean. *Simulacra and Simulation*. Michigan: University of Michigan Press, 1994.

Baudrillard, Jean. *Simulations*. New York City: Semiotext(e), Inc, 1983.

Bauman, Zygmunt. "Life on Credit," *Soundings*. London, England. 41:1.

Bauman., Zygmunt "Modernity and Ambivalence," *Theory, Culture & Society* Vol. 7, London, 1990.

Bedoya, Roberto. Personal Interview. 17 June 2018.

Bedoya, Roberto. "'Scene One,' from Decoto," *Writers Who Love Too Much: New Narrative Writing 1977–1997*, eds. Kevin Killian and Dodie Bellamy. Nightboat Books, 2017.

Behar, Ruth (ed). *Bridges to Cuba / Puentes a Cuba*. Ann Arbor, University of Michigan Press, 1995.

Bejel, Emilio. *Gay Cuban Nation*. Chicago: The University of Chicago Press, 2001.

Benjamin, Walter. "Goethe's *Elective Affinities*," in *Selected Writings, 1913–1926*, trans. Stanley Corngold. Cambridge, Massachusetts, Harvard University Press, 1996.

Benjamin, Walter. *Illuminations: Essays and Reflections*, trans. Harry Zohn. New York: Schocken Books, 1969.

Benvegnù, Damiano. "Images of Narcissus: Figuring Identity in José Lezama Lima and Pier Paolo Pasolini." *Comparative Literature Studies*, Vol. 52, No. 4 (2015), pp 818–842.

Bernal Granados, Gabriel, Kristin Dykstra and Roberto Tejada. "Poetry in Translation: Hemispheric Perspectives," *Literary Publishing in the Twenty-First Century,* eds. Travis Kurowski, Wayne Miller & Kevin Prufer. Minneapolis, Minnesota: Milkweed Editions, 2016.

Blaser, Robin. *The Holy Forest.* Toronto: Coach House Press, 1993.

Bleys, Rudi. *Images of Ambiente: Homotextuality and Latin American Art, 1810–Today,* London and New York: Continuum, 2000.

Bobes, Marilyn. "Dangers of Speaking and Staying Quiet. Language of Silence," trans. Ruth Behar. *Bridges to Cuba / Puentes a Cuba,* ed. by Ruth Behar. Ann Arbor, University of Michigan Press, 1995,

Brenner, Anita. *Idols Behind Altars: Modern Mexico and its Cultural Roots.* Mineola, New York: Dover Publications, Inc., 2002.

Brenner, Anita. *The Wind That Swept Mexico.* Austin: University of Texas Press, 1984.

Breslauer, Jan. "The Forces Behind Bedoya's Resignation." *Los Angeles Times* Dec 27 1990, p F6.

Breton, André. *Mad Love,* trans. Mary Ann Caws. Lincoln: University of Nebraska Press, 1987.

Bronk, William. *Life Supports: New and Collected Poems.* San Francisco: North Point Press, 1981.

Bronk, William. *Selected Poems.* New York: New Directions, 1995.

Bronk, William. *Vectors and Smoothable Curves: Collected Essays.* San Francisco: North Point Press, 1985.

Brotchie, Alastair and Mel Gooding (ed). *A Surrealist Book of Games.* Boston: Shambhala Redstone Editions, 1995.

Bruce, Edward. "Implications of the Public Works of Art Project." *The American Magazine of Art,* Vol. 27, No. 3. March 1934.

Burke, Kenneth. Introduction. *Testimony,* by Charles Reznikoff, Objectivist Press, 1934.

Butterick, George F. "Charles Olson and the Postmodern Advance," *The Iowa Review*, Vol. 11, Issue 4 Fall 1980.

Buzachero, Chris. "Elián González in Hyper-Space," *C-Theory*, vol. 23, nos. 1–2 http://www.ctheory.com.

Cabeza de Vaca. Directed by Nicolás Echeverría. Concorde Pictures, 1991.

Cabeza de Vaca, Álvar Núñez. *Adventures in the Unknown Interior of America*, Cyclone Covey, trans. Albuquerque: University of New Mexico Press, 1983.

Cabeza de Vaca, Álvar Núñez. *Naufragios*. Juan Francisco Maura, ed. Madrid: Ediciones Cátedra, 1989.

Caillois, Roger. *Man, Play, and Games*, trans., Meyer Barash. New York: The Free Press of Glencoe, Inc., 1961).

Caillois Roger. "Mimicry and Legendary Psychasthenia," trans. John Shepley. *October*, Vol. 31 (Winter, 1984).

Calvino, Italo. *Invisible Cities*. New York: Mariner Books, 2013.

Cámara, Madeline. "Third Option: Beyond the Border," *Bridges to Cuba/Puentes a Cuba*, ed. Ruth Behar. Ann Arbor, University of Michigan Press, 1995.

Campbell, Bruce. *Mexican Murals in Times of Crisis*. Tucson: University of Arizona Press, 2003.

Campbell, Mary B. *The Witness and the Other World: Exotic European Travel Writing, 400–1600*. Ithaca: Cornell University Press. 1991.

Carroll, Lewis. *Alice in Wonderland and Through the Looking Glass*. New York: Signet Classics, 2000.

Castaways, The Narrative of Álvar Núñez Cabeza de Vaca, Enrique Pupo-Walker, ed. Frances M. López-Morillas, trans. Berkeley: University of California Press, 1993.

Chavoya, C. Ondine."Internal Exiles: The Interventionist Public and Performance Art of Asco," *Space, Site, Intervention: Situating Installation Art*, ed. Erika Suderburg. University of Minnesota Press, 2000.

Chavoya, C. Ondine and Harry Gamboa Jr. "Social Unwest: An Interview with Harry Gamboa Jr." *Wide Angle* 20:3 (1998) 55–78.

Clifford, James. *The Predicament of Culture: Twentieth-Century Ethnography, Literature, and Art*. Cambridge: Harvard University Press, 1988.

Clifford, James and George E. Marcus. *Writing Culture: The Poetics and Politics of Ethnography*. Berkeley: University of California Press, 1986.

Colón, Cristóbal. *Relaciones y cartas*. Madrid: Librería de la Viuda e Hijos de Cuesta, 1892.

Coffey, Mary K. *How a Revolutionary Art Became Official Culture: Murals, Museums, and the Mexican State*. Durham: Duke University Press, 2012.

Coffey, Mary and Tejada, Roberto. Introductory note to "The Cosmic Race" by José Vasconcelos; *Modern Art in Africa, Asia, and Latin America: An Introduction to Global Modernisms*. Ed Elaine O'Brien. Chichester, West Sussex: Wiley-Blackwell, 2013.

Conger, Amy. *Edward Weston in Mexico, 1923–1926*. Albuquerque: University of New Mexico Press, 1983.

Crane, Hart. *The Complete Poems and Selected Letters and Prose of Hart Crane*, ed. Waldo D. Frank. Washington, D.C.: Library of America, 2006.

Crane, Hart. *The Letters of Hart Crane, 1916–1932*, ed. Brom Weber, New York: Hermitage House, 1952.

Curtis, Erin M., Jessica Hough, and Guisela Latorre. ¡Murales Rebeldes!: L.A. Chicana/Chicano *Murals under Siege*. Angel City Press, 2017.

Davenport, Guy. *Geography of the Imagination*. Berkeley: North Point Press, 1982.

Davidson, Michael. Introduction, *New Collected Poems*, by George Oppen. New York, New Directions, 2002.

Davis, Mike. *City of Quartz: Excavating the Future in Los Angeles*. New York: Vintage Books, 1992.

Debaene, Vincent. *Far Afield: French Anthropology Between Science and Literature*, trans. Justin Izzo, University of Chicago Press, 2014.

Debaene, Vincent. "Levi-Strauss: What Legacy?" *Rethinking Claude Lévi-Strauss (1908–2009)* ed. Robert Doran, Yale University Press, 2013.

Debois, W.E.B. *The Souls of Black Folk*. New York: Washington Square Press, 1970.

De Certeau, Michel. *The Writing of History*, trans. Tom Conley. New York: Columbia University Press, 1988.

De Certeau, Michel. "Vocal Utopias." *Representations*, no. 56, 1996, pp 29–47.

Dembo, L. S. "'The Objectivist' Poet: George Oppen," *Contemporary Literature*, 10.2, Spring 1969.

Deleuze, Gilles. *The Logic of Sense*. New York: Columbia University Press, 1990.

De Orellana, Margarita. *Filming Pancho: How Hollywood Shaped the Mexican Revolution*. London; New York: Verso, 2009.

Derrida, Jacques. *The Ear of the Other*. Lincoln: University of Nebraska Press, 1988.

Dewey, John. *Experience and Education*, New York: Simon & Schuster, 1997.

Díaz del Castillo, Bernal. *The Conquest of New Spain*, trans. J. M. Cohen. Baltimore: Penguin, 1963.

Didion, Joan. *Miami*. New York: Vintage Books, 1998.

Donne, John. *The Major Works*. Oxford: Oxford University Press, 1990.

DuPlessis, Rachel Blau. "Oppen from Seventy-Five to a Hundred, 1983–2000," *Jacket* 36, 2008.

DuPlessis, Rachel Blau, editor. *The Selected Letters of George Oppen*. Durham and London, Duke University Press, 1990.

Echavarren, Roberto, José Kozer, and Jacobo Sefamí. *Medusario: muestra de poesia Latinoamericana*. Mexico City: Fondo de Cultura Económica, 1996.

Eder, Rita "Two Aspects of the Total Work of Art: Experimentation and Performativity," *Defying Stability: Artistic Processes in Mexico 1952–1967*, ed. Rita Eder, translation, Elisa Schmelkes, Mexico, 2014.

¿En qué tiempo puede cambiare la mente de un niño? Havana: Casa Editorial. Abril, 1999.

Foster, Sesshu. "Interview with Juan Fish (Supposedly); photographs by Arturo Ernesto Romo-Santillano." *Mandorla: New Writing from the Americas*, no 12, 2009.

Foster, Sesshu and Arturo Ernesto Romo-Santillano. *ELA Guide.*
   (www.elaguide.org). Accessed 20 June 2018.

Foucault, Michael. *The Order of Things: An Archeology of the Human Sciences.*
   New York: Vintage Books, 1994.

Foucault, Michel. *Power/Knowledge: Selected Interviews and Other Writings
   1972–1977,* ed. Colin Gordon. Brighton, Sussex: Harvester Press, 1980.

Fox, Claire F. *Making Art Panamerican: Cultural Policy and the Cold War,*
   University of Minnesota Press, 2013.

Frank, Waldo. "Pilgrimage to Mexico," *New Republic.* Vol. 67, Issue 865,
   July 1, 1931.

Freud, Sigmund. *Introductory Lectures on Psychoanalysis.* New York:
   W.W. Norton, 1977.

Freud, Sigmund. *Three Contributions to the Theory of Sex,* trans. A. A. Brill.
   New York: E. P. Dutton & Company, 1962.

Gabara, Esther. *Errant Modernism: The Ethos of Photography in Mexico and Brazil.*
   Durham: Duke University Press, 2008.

Galeano, Eduardo. *Open Veins of Latin America: Five Centuries of the Pillage
   of a Continent,* trans. Cedric Belfrage, Monthly Review Press, 1997.

Gamboa Jr. Harry. "A Matter of Record: An Interview by Roberto Tejada
   with Harry Gamboa Jr.," *Spot,* 2017.

Gamboa Jr. Harry. *Urban Exile.* Minnesota: University of Minnesota Press, 1998.

Gamboa Jr. Harry. Personal Interview. 20 April 2017.

"George Biddle papers, 1910–1969, Reel 3621," *Archives of American Art,*
   Smithsonian Institution, Washington D.C. Viewed 26 May 2018.

https://www.aaa.si.edu/collections/george-biddle-papers-7126.

Gerbi, Antonello. 1955. *La disputa del Nuevo Mundo: Historia de una polémica,
   1750–1900.* Trans. Antonio Alatorre. Mexico: Fondo de Cultura
   Económica, 1987.

Gilderhus, Mark T. R. "United States-Mexican Relations since 1910: A Survey,"
     Twentieth-Century Mexico, eds. W. Dirk Raat and William H. Beezley,
     Lincoln: University of Nebraska Press, 1986.

Giménez Smith, Carmen. "Make America Mongrel Again." *Harriet*,
     The Poetry Foundation, 19 April 2018.

Ginsberg, Allen. *Reality Sandwiches 1953–1960*. San Francisco: City
     Lights Books, 1963.

Glusker, Susannah Joel. *Anita Brenner: A Mind of Her Own*. Texas: University
     of Texas Press, 1998.

Goeritz, Mathias. "La integración plástica en el C.U. Presidente Juárez,"
     Arquitectura,1952.

González-Casanovas, Roberto J. *Imperial Histories from Alfonso X to Inca Garcilaso:
     Revisionist Myths of Reconquest and Conquest* Potomac, Maryland:
     Scripta Humanistica, 1997.

González Mello, Renato and Diane Miliotes. *José Clemente Orozco in the
     United States, 1927–1934*. New York: W. W. Norton & Company, 2002.

Greenblatt, Stephen. "Towards a Poetics of Culture." *The New Historicism*,
     ed. H. Aram Veeser. New York: Routledge, 1989.

Grossfeld, Stan. *Lost Futures, Our Forgotten Children*. New York: Aperture, 1997.

Grosz, Elizabeth. *Volatile Bodies: Toward a Corporeal Feminism*. Bloomington:
     Indiana University Press, 1994.

Guest, Barbara. "The Shadow of Surrealism." *Women's Studies: An Inter-Disciplinary
     Journal*, 30:1.

Gunn, Giles. *The Interpretation of Otherness: Literature, Religion, and the American
     Imagination*. New York: Oxford University Press, 1979.

Harris, Kaplan Page. "Bay Area Poetics,1944–1981," *A History of California
     Literature*, ed. Blake Allmendinger. Cambridge University Press, 2015.

Heidegger, Martin. *The Question Concerning Technology and Other Essays*,
     trans. William Lovitt. New York, Harper Torchbooks, 1977.

Helguera, Pablo. *Onda Corta*. New York: Jorge Pinto Books, 2012.

Helguera, Pablo. "Rodolfo Limonini." Accessed June 2018.
http://pablohelguera.net/1994/01/rodolfo-limonini/.

Helguera, Pablo & Meromi, Ohad & Simmons, Xaviera & Young, Paul David.
"Turning Theatre Into Art." *PAJ: A Journal of Performance and Art*,
vol. 34 no. 1, 2012, pp 169–182. Project MUSE, muse.jhu.edu/
article/463553.

Heller, Ben A. *Assimilation/Generation/Resurrection: Contrapuntal Readings
in the Poetry of José Lezama Lima*. Lewisburg, PA: Bucknell University
Press, 1997.

Hernández, Robb. "Drawing Offensive/Offensive Drawing: Toward a Theory
of Mariconógraphy." *MELUS*, Volume 39, Number 2 (Summer 2014).

Herring, Adam. *Art and Writing in Maya Cities, A.D. 600–800: A Poetics of Line*,
Cambridge University Press, 2005.

Hinton, Laura. "The Return of Nostalgia: A Fetishistic Spectator in Leslie
Scalapino's *The Return of Painting* and the Hudson River School of Art,"
Textual Practice, 24:2, 2010.

Hirsch, Edward. *Poet's Choice*. Mariner Books, 2007.

Hokin, Jeanne. "Volcanoes and Pyramids: Marsden Hartley." *Latin American Art*.
Winter, 1990.

Horsman, Reginald. *Race and Manifest Destiny*. Cambridge: Harvard University
Press, 1982.

Howe, Susan. *The Birth-mark: Unsettling the Wilderness in American Literary
History* Hanover: University Press of New England, 1993.

Hulburt, Laurance P. *The Mexican Muralists in the United States*. Albuquerque:
University of New Mexico Press, 1989.

Hughes, Langston. *The Collected Poems of Langston Hughes*, ed. Arnold
Rampersad. New York: Vintage: Random House, 1995.

Hughes, Langston. *The Collected Works of Langston Hughes, Volume 14,
Autobiography: "I Wonder as I Wander."* Edited with an Introduction
by Joseph McLaren. Missouri: University of Missouri Press, 2003.

Indych-López, Anna. *Muralism without Walls: Rivera, Orozco, and Siqueiros in the United States, 1927–1940*. Pittsburgh: University of Pittsburgh Press 2009.

James, Daniel. "Sears, Roebuck's Mexican revolution," *Harper's Monthly*, 1959.

Justice, Daniel Heath. *Why Indigenous Literatures Matter*. Wilfrid Laurier University Press, 2018.

Kadir, Djelal. *Columbus and the Ends of the Earth: Europe's Prophetic Rhetoric as Conquering Ideology*. Berkeley: University of California Press, 1992.

Kaplan, Caren. *Questions of Travel, Postmodern Theories of Displacement*. Durham: Duke University Press, 1996.

Kelly, Mary. "Re-Viewing Modernist Criticism," *Art After Modernism: Rethinking Representation*, ed. Brian Wallis. New York: New Museum of Contemporary Art, New York, 1984. Previously published in *Screen*, Volume 22, Issue 3, 1 September 1981.

Killian, Kevin and Dodie Bellamy. *Writers Who Love Too Much: New Narrative Writing 1977–1997* (New York: Nightboat Books, 2017)

Kirsch, Adam. "Fernando Pessoa's Disappearing Act." *The New Yorker*. September 2017. https://www.newyorker.com/magazine/2017/09/04/fernando-pessoas-disappearing-act.

Kofman, Sarah. *Camera Obscura: Of Ideology*, NewYork, Cornell University Press, 1999

Kutzinski, Vera M. *Against the American Grain: Myth and History in William Carlos Williams, Jay Wright and Nicolas Guillén*. Baltimore: Johns Hopkins University Press, 1987.

Kurowski Travis, Wayne Miller and Kevin Prufer. *Literary Publishing in the Twenty-First Century*. Minneapolis, Minnesota: Milkweed Editions, 2016.

Lacan, Jacques. *The Four Fundamental Concepts of Psychoanalysis (Seminar XI)*, trans. Alan Sheridan. New York: W. W. Norton & Company, 1978.

Latorre, Guisela. *Walls of Empowerment: Chicana/o Indigenist Murals of California*. Austin: University of Texas Press, 2008.

Lee, Anthony. *Painting on the Left: Diego Rivera, Radical Politics, and San Francisco's Public Mural*. Berkeley: University of California Press, 1999.

Levinson, Brett. *Secondary Moderns: Mimesis, History, and Revolution in Lezama Lima's "American Expression."* Lewisburg, Pennsylvania: Bucknell University Press, 1996.

Lezama Lima, José. "A Chinese Battle" (p. 8); "An Appetite" (pp. 9–11); "Goat and Cherub" (p. 12); "The Birth of Day" (pp. 13–19); "Universality of Touch" (pp 20–21); and "Waiting for Absence" (pp. 22), trans. Roberto Tejada. *White Wall Review* 36 (2012): 8–22.

Lezama Lima, José. *Analecta del reloj.* Havana: Orígenes, 1953.

Lezama Lima, José. *Cartas a Eloísa y otra correspondencia.* Madrid: Verbum, 1998.

Lezama Lima, José. *Con Cuba: An Anthology of Cuban Poetry of the Last Sixty Years,* trans. Elinor Randall et al. Ed Nathaniel Tarn. London: Cape Goliard, 1969.

Lezama Lima, José. "Confluences," trans. James Irby. *Sulfur* (25) Fall 1989.

Lezama Lima, José. *Cartas a Eloísa y otra correspondencia.* Verbum, 1998.

Lezama Lima, José. *El reino de la imagen*, ed. Julio Ortega. Caracas: Biblioteca Ayacucho, 1981.

Lezama Lima, José. *Imagen y posibilidad.* Havana: Editorial Letras Cubanas, 1981.

Lezama Lima, José. *José Lezama Lima: Selections.* California: University of California Press, 2004.

Lezama Lima, José. *La expresión americana*, ed. Irlemar Chiampi. Mexico City: Fondo de Cultura Económica. 1993

Lezama Lima, José. "Dissonance" and "Octavio Paz," trans by Roberto Tejada. *Sulfur* (38) Spring 1996.

Lezama Lima, José. *Paradiso*, trans. Gregory Rabassa. New York: Farrar, Strauss and Giroux, 1974.

Lezama Lima, José. "Ten Prose Poems," trans. James Irby. *Sulfur* (3) 1982.

Limón, José E. *American Encounters: Greater Mexico, the United States and the Erotics of Culture.* Boston: Beacon Press, 1998.

Logenbach, James, "A Test of Poetry," *Nation*, 286.5, 2008, p 29. Web. 12 March 2015.

Loyola, St. Ignatius. *Manresa: Or, the Spiritual Exercises of St. Ignatius, for General Use*. London: Burns, Oates & Washbourne, 188.

Lowry Malcolm. *Under the Volcano*. Philadelphia and New York: J. B. Lippincott Company, 1965.

Mandorla: Nueva escritura de las Américas / New Writing from the Americas. eds. Roberto Tejada (nos. 1–5), Esther Allen (no. 6) and Robero Tejada, Kristin Dykstra, and Gabriel Bernal Granados (nos. 7–16), Mexico City, Los Angeles, New York; Normal, Illinois, et al.,1991–2013.

Marx, Karl. *Capital: A Critique of Political Economy*, trans. Samuel Moore and Edward Aveling, New York: The Modern Library, 1906.

Marx, Karl. "Communist Manifesto" (1888), *All That is Solid Melts into Air*. New York, Simon & Schuster, 1982.

Mayers, Kathryn. "Of Third Spaces and (Re)localization: Critique and Counterknowledge in Nicolas Echeverria's Cabeza de Vaca," *Confluencia: Revista Hispánica de Cultura y Literatura*, vol. 24, no. 1. 2008. p 2–16.

Mayol, Pierre, "The Neighborhood." Michel de Certeau, Luce Giard, Pierre Mayol. *The Practice of Everyday Life: Volume 2*. Minneapolis: University of Minnesota Press, 1998.

Medusario: Muestra de poesía latinoamericana, ed. Roberto Echavarren, José Kozer, and Jacobo Sefamí. Mexico City: Fondo de Cultura Económica, 1996.

Mesa-Bains Amalia. "Domesticana: The Sensibility of Chicana Rasquache." *Distant Relations: A Dialogue among Chicano, Irish, and Mexican Artists*. Santa Monica, Calif.: Smart Art Press, 1995, pp 156–63.

Mignolo, Walter. *Local Histories / Global Designs: Coloniality, Subaltern Knowledge and Border Thinking*. Princeton, New Jersey: Princeton University Press, 2000.

Modern Architecture, International Exhibition: New York, Feb 10 to March 23, 1932, Museum of Modern Art (catalog), New York, 1932.

Montoya, José. "El Louie." *Aztlán: An Anthology of Mexican American Literature*, ed. Luis Valdez and Stan Steiner. New York: Vintage Books, 1972.

Nahui Olin: Una mujer de los tiempos modernos. Mexico City: Instituto Nacional de Bellas Artes, 1992.

Nicholls, Peter. "George Oppen in Exile: Mexico and Maritain (For Linda Oppen)," *Journal of American Studies*, 39, 2005.

Nietzsche, Friedrich. *Beyond Good and Evil: Prelude to a Philosophy of the Future*, trans. R. J. Hollingdale. Baltimore, Maryland: Penguin Books, 1973.

Nietzsche, Friedrich. *Philosophy and Truth; Selections from Nietzsche's Notebooks of the Early 1870s*. Atlantic Highlands, N.J.: Humanities Press, 1979.

Núñez Pineda y Bascuñá, Francisco. *El cautiverio feliz*, ed. Ángel C. González, (Santiago: Ediciones Zig- Zag, n/d).

Oles, James, and Marta Ferragut. *South of the Border: Mexico in the American Imagination, 1917–1947*. Washington: Smithsonian Institution Press, 1993.

Olin, Nahui (Carmen Mondragón). *Óptica verbal: poemas dinámicos*. Mexico City: Ediciones Mexico Moderno, 1922.

Olson, Charles. *The Collected Poems of Charles Olson: Excluding the Maximus Poems*. Berkeley: University of California Press, 1987.

Olson, Charles. *The Collected Poems of Charles Olson: Excluding the Maximus Poems*. Berkeley: University of California Press, 1997.

Olson, Charles. *The Maximus Poems*. Berkeley: University of California Press, 1983.

Olson, Charles, Robert Creeley, George F. Butterick, and Richard Blevins. *Charles Olson & Robert Creeley: The Complete Correspondence*. Santa Barbara: Black Sparrow Press, 1980, vol 1–10.

Oppen, George. *New Collected Poems*. New York: New Directions, 2008.

Oppen, George. "Selections from George Oppen's 'Daybook'" ed. Dennis Young, *The Iowa Review*, Vol. 18, No. 3, 1988.

Oppen, George. Interviewed by David Gitin and Charles Amirkhanian, 30 March 1970, KPFA broadcast 19 April 1971.

Oppen, George. "Philosophy of the Astonished," Selections from the Working Papers Ed. Rachel Blau du Plessis, *Sulfur* 27, 1990.

Oppen, Linda. "Photographs of G. Oppen furniture and carvings." 4 October 2015.

Oppen, Mary. "Mary Oppen Papers, 1913–1990." University of California, San Diego, Special Collections Library, MSS 0125, Box 4, Box 4Box Oversize FB-090, Oversize AB-002-F, Oversize FB-094.

Oppen, Mary. *Meaning A Life: An Autobiography*. Santa Barbara: Black Sparrow Press, 1978.

Paz, Octavio. *Alternating Current*. New York: Viking Press, 1973.

Paz, Octavio. *El ogro filantrópico: historia y política (1971–1978)*, Madrid: Seix Barral 1979.

Paz, Octavio. *México en la obra de Octavio Paz* (3 vols.). Mexico: Fondo de Cultura Economica, 1987.

Pérez, Omar. *Algo de lo sagrado: Something of the Sacred: A Book in Two Parts*, trans. Kristin Dykstra and Roberto Tejada. New York: Factory School, 2007.

Phillips, Adam and Barbara Taylor. *On Kindness*. New York: Farrar, Straus and Giroux, 2009.

Porter, Katherine Anne. *Letters of Katherine Anne Porter*, New York: The Atlantic Monthly Press, 1990.

Pratt, Mary Louise. *Imperial Eyes: Travel Writing and Transculturation*. London: Routledge, 1992.

"Projected Invasion of Texas by Mexico." The New Yorker, Feb 1, 1840, vol. 8; no. 20, p 315.

Rexroth, Kenneth. *An Autobiographical Novel*. Garden City, New York: Doubleday & Company, Inc., 1966.

Rexroth, Kenneth. *The Collected Shorter Poems*. New York: New Directions, 1966.

Rich, B. Ruby. "Queering the Social Landscape." *New Queer Cinema: The Director's Cut*. Duke University Press Books, 2013.

Ríos-Ávila, Rubén. *Coloquio internacional sobre la obra de José Lezama Lima: Poesía*. Madrid: Editiorial Fundamentos, 1984.

Robles, Concepción Christlieb. "Biblioteca 'Lino Picaseño' de la Facultad de Arquitectura," http://www.posgrado.unam.mx/sites/default/ files/2016/05/2806.pdf.

Rodríguez, Israel. "Imaginaries: Introduction," *Defying Stability: Artistic Processes in Mexico 1952–1967*, ed. Rita Eder, translation, Elisa Schmelkes, Mexico, 2014.

Rodríguez, Reina María. *Cuando una mujer no duerme*. Havana: UNEAC, 1982.

Rodríguez, Reina María. *En la arena de Padua*. Havana: Ediciones Union, 1992.

Rodríguez, Reina Maria. *La detención del tiempo: Time's Arrest*, trans. Kristin Dykstra. Indiana, Pa.: Factory School, 2005.

Rodríguez, Reina María. *Para un cordero blanco: poesía*. Havana: Casa de las Américas, 1984.

Rodríguez, Reina María. "Two Poems," trans. Roberto Tejada. *Mandorla: Nueva escritura de las Américas / New Writing from the Americas*, no. 4, 1995.

Rodríguez, Reina Maria. *Violet Island and Other Poems*, trans. Kristin Dykstra and Nancy Gates Madsen. Copenhagen & Los Angeles: Green Integer, 2004.

Rojas, Rafael. "México en Lezama." *La jornada seminal*. No. 787, 4 April 2010.

Rukeyser, Muriel. *The Life of Poetry*, Current Books, 1949.

Ruiz Barrionuevo, Carmen. "'Enemigo rumor', de José Lezama Lima," *Coloquio Internacional sobre la obra de Jose Lezama Lima: Poesía*. Ed. Cristina Vizcaino. Madrid: Editorial Fundamentos, 1984.

Rukeyser, Muriel. *The Life of Poetry*. Ashfield, Massachusetts: Paris Press, 1996.

Salazkina, Masha. *In Excess: Sergei Eisenstein's Mexico*. Chicago: The University of Chicago Press, 2009.

Salván, Marta Hernández. *Minima Cuba: Heretical Poetics and Power in Post-Soviet Cuba*. New York: SUNY Press, 2015.

Sánchez, Osvaldo. "Los hijos de la utopia." *Blancomovil*, No. 49, June/July 1991.

Sánchez, Osvaldo. *Matar al último venado.* Havana: Unión de Escritores y Artistas de Cuba, 1982.

Sánchez, Osvaldo. "Utopia Under the Volcano: The Cuban Avant-Garde in Mexico," *Sulfur* (32) Spring 1993.

Sandweiss, Martha A; Rick Stewart and Ben W. Huseman. *Eyewitness to War: Prints and Daguerrotypes of the Mexican War.* Washington D.C.: Smithsonian Institution Press, 1989.

Sandweiss, Martha A. *Laura Gilpin: An Enduring Grace.* Fort Worth: Amon Carter Museum, 1986.

Schreiber, Rebecca Mina. *Cold War Exiles in Mexico: U.S. Dissidents and the Culture of Critical Resistance*, University of Minnesota Press, 2008.

Segalen, Victor. *Essay on Exoticism: An Aesthetics of Diversity*, trans. and ed. Yaël Rachel Schlick; forward Harry Hartoonian. Durham: Duke University Press, 2002.

Sennett, Richard. "What Do We Mean by Talent?" *The Political Quarterly*, Vol. 77, June 2006.

Smith, Dale. *American Rambler.* Austin, Texas: Thorp Springs Press, 2000.

Snow, Shauna. "Roberto Bedoya: A New Face at LACE—and a New Direction." *Los Angeles Times*, May 17 1990, p OCF4.

Soja, Edward. "The City and Spatial Justice," Spatial Justice Conference, 12–14 March, 2008, Nanterre, Paris.

Spicer, Jack, *My Vocabulary Did This to Me: The Collected Poetry of Jack Spicer.* eds. Peter Gizzi, and Kevin Killian. Middletown, Conn: Wesleyan University Press, 2008.

Spigel, Lynn. "The Suburban Home Companion: Television and the Neighbourhood Ideal in Post-War America," *Feminist Television Criticism: A Reader*, ed. Charlotte Brunsdon, et al. Oxford: Clarendon Press, 1997.

Stephens, John L. *Incidents of Travel in Central America, Chiapas, and Yucatan.* New York: Harpers & Brothers, 1843.

Stevens, Wallace. *Collected Poems.* New York, Knopf, 1954.

TalkBack Live. CNN. April 21, 2000.

Tejada, Roberto. "Assault on the Quiet Continent: Oppen in Mexico," 31st annual George Oppen Memorial Lecture, *The Poetry Center Digital Archive*, San Francisco State University. https://diva.sfsu.edu/collections/poetrycenter/bundles/227959.

Tejada, Roberto. *Exposition Park*. Middletown, Conn: Wesleyan University Press, 2010.

Tejada, Roberto. *National Camera: Photography and Mexico's Image Environment*. Minneapolis: University of Minnesota Press, 2009.

"To Be a Good Finder: Dale Smith in conversation with Kent Johnson." *Jacket*. December 2001

Todorov, Tzvetan. *The Conquest of America*, trans. Richard Howard. New York: Harper and Row, 1984.

Tuck, Eve, Allison Guess, and Hannah Sultan. "Not Nowhere: Collaborating on Selfsame Land." *Decolonization: Indigeneity, Education & Society*, 26 June 2014.

Tuck, Eve and Marcia McKenzie. *Place in Research: Theory, Methodology, and Methods*. New York: Routledge, 2015.

Turner, Victor W. and Edward M. Bruner, eds. *Anthropology of Experience*. Urbana: Illinois University Press, 1986.

Vallejo, César. *Desde Europa: Crónicas y artículos (1923–1938)*, ed Jorge Puccinelli. Lima: Ediciones Fuente de Cultura Peruana, 1987.

Van Der Beets, Richard. *The Indian Captivity Narrative: An American Genre*. Lanham: University Press of America, 1984.

Vaughn, Alden T., and Edward W. Clark, eds. *Puritans Among the Indians: Accounts of Captivity and Redemption, 1676–1724*. Cambridge, Massachusetts: Belknap Press, 1981.

Voigt, Lisa. *Writing Captivity in the Early Modern Atlantic: Circulations of Knowledge and Authority in the Iberian and English Imperial Worlds*. Chapel Hill: University of North Carolina Press, 2009.

Wallach, Alan. "For a Social History of the Hudson River School," *American Art*, Vol. 31, No. 2, Summer 2017.

"Was the Gun Pointed At Elian?" *CBSNEWS.COM*. 2000. https://www.cbsnews.com/news/was-the-gun-pointed-at-elian/

Weinberger, Eliot, *Works on Paper*. New York: New Directions, 1986.

Weiss, Mark. *The Whole Island: Six Decades of Cuban Poetry, a Bilingual Anthology*. Berkeley: University of California Press, 2009.

Weston, Edward. "Letter to Alfred Stieglitz, 21 February 1923, Box 51, Folder 1234, YCAL MSS 85," Alfred Stieglitz / Georgia O'Keeffe archive, Beinecke Rare Book and Manuscript Library, Beinecke Digital Collections, Yale University Libraries, New Haven, CT. Viewed 26 May 2018. https://brbl-dl.library.yale.edu/vufind/Record/3667903

Weston, Edward. *The Daybooks of Edward Weston*, ed. Nancy Newhall. Millerton, N.Y.: Aperture, 1973.

Williams, Reba and Dave. *The Mexican Muralists and Prints* (Catalogue). New York: The Spanish Institute, 1990.

Williams, William Carlos. *In the American Grains*. New York: Albert & Charles Boni, 1925.

Williams, William Carlos. *The Collected Poems of William Carlos Williams, Volume II 1939–1962*, ed. Christopher J. MacGowan. New York: New Directions, 1986.

Wright, Jay. *Dimensions of History*. Kayak, 1976.

Wright, Jay. "Zapata and the Egúngún Mask," *Callaloo*, No. 19, Jay Wright: A Special Issue, Autumn, 1983.

"Writing into the Henceforward." *The Henceforward* from the Indian & Cowboy Podcast Media Network, 2 May 2017, <http://www.thehenceforward.com/episodes/2017/5/2/episode-10–writing-into-the-henceforward>.

Wynter, Sylvia. "Unsettling the Coloniality of Being/Power/Truth/Freedom: Towards the Human, After Man, Its Overrepresentation—An Argument." *CR: The New Centennial Review* 3.3 (2003).

Ybarra-Frausto, Tomás. "Rasquachismo: A Chicano Sensibility." *Chicano Art: Resistance and Affirmation, 1965–1985*. eds. Richard Griswold del Castillo, Teresa McKenna, and Yvonne Yarbro-Bejarano. Los Angeles: Wight Art Gallery, University of California, 1991, pp 156–162.

Young, Iris Marion. *Throwing Like a Girl and Other Essays in Feminist Philosophy and Social Theory*. Bloomington: Indiana University Press, 1990.

Zavala, Adriana. *Becoming Modern, Becoming Tradition: Women, Gender, and Representation in Mexican Art*. University Park, Pa: Pennsylvania State University Press, 2010.

Zinn, Howard. *A People's History of the United States*. New York: Harper and Row, 1980.

Žižek, Slavoj. *Looking Awry: An Introduction to Jacques Lacan Through Popular Culture*. Cambridge, MA: The MIT Press, 1997.

Zúñiga, Francisco. "La decadencia de las escuelas de arte," *Esmeralda: Órgano independiente*, no.1, 1954.

ACKNOWLE

DGMENTS

"Limitrophe" previously appeared in a slightly different version in *boundary 2*, Vol. 26, No. 1, 99 "Poets/1999: An International Poetics Symposium" (Spring, 1999), pp 253–255. My thanks to Charles Bernstein for the invitation to participate in that conversation.

"The Logic of Elsewhere" was commissioned by The Poetry Project at St. Mark's Church, New York, and delivered as a talk entitled "The Image of the Other: The Presence of Mexico in North American Arts and Writing," November 18, 1990. Thereafter, it was only published in Spanish, first as "En alguna otra parte," translated by Jaime Moreno Villarreal, Vuelta (Mexico City) vol. 15, no. 176, 1991, 32–39; then in revised form as the critical essay to the anthology I edited: En algún otro lado: Mexico en la poesía de lengua inglesa (Mexico City: Libros Vuelta, 1992). This essay and others owe a debt to Eliot Weinberger who made possible paths that led elsewhere to Mexico.

"Assault on the Quiet Continent: The Oppens in Mexico" was originally written for and delivered as the 31st George Oppen Memorial lecture, sponsored by The Poetry Center, San Francisco State University (Unitarian Center, 1187 Franklin Street, San Francisco December 12, 2015) with generous support from the Dorothy A. Fowler Trust.

My thanks to Steve Dickison and the staff at The Poetry Center; to Natalia Brizuela, who provided a forum for presenting a early draft at our Latin American and Latinx visual studies working group in October 2015 at UC Berkeley; to Lynda Claassen, director and chief curator of the Mandeville Special Collections Library at UC San Diego, and Rob Melton, curator at UCSD's Archive for New Poetry; and to Linda Oppen, who patiently answered many questions and who shares a gratitude for "this in which" one is shaped by years and days in Mexico.

Some passages from "Translating the Counter-Conquest" appeared as notes to frame my translations of poems by José Lezama Lima: "Translator's Note," *Sulfur* (38) Spring 1996, 118–119, 219; "José Lezama Lima: Two Poems from *Enemy Rumor*," *a.bacus* (Bedford, Massachusetts: Potes and Poets Press, no. 149, 2002). My thanks to poet Dan Featherston.

"Avant-Garde in Crisis" first appeared on the *Lana Turner* blog (2013), then in print format as originally commissioned for *The Force of What's Possible: Writers on Accessibility & the Avant-Garde*, eds. Lily Hoang and Joshua Marie Wilkinson (New York: Nightboat Books, 2014). My thanks to the aforesaid editors, as well as to Calvin Bedient and David Lau.

"The Zone is Immanence" was first published as "In Relation: The Poetics and Politics of Cuba's Generation-80," in Reina María Rodríguez, *La detención del tiempo / Time's Arrest* trans. Kristin Dykstra (Indiana, Pa.: Factory School, 2005).

In an earlier version, "Strategic Dissolutions of Identity" was included in a limited-edition chapbook featuring work by Gabriel Gomez, J. Michael Martínez, Carmen Giménez Smith, Rosa Alcalá, and Roberto Tejada. Gabriel Gomez and J. Michael Martínez (eds), *Breach*, (Boulder: Breach Press, 2009).

"Elián Through the Looking Glass" saw print as "Democracy, Virtual and Otherwise: Elián Through the Looking Glass" in *Camerawork*, vol. 27, no. 2, Fall/Winter, 2000, 27–35. The essay owes its genesis, with gratitude, to David Levi Strauss.

"Short Wave" appeared in Spanish as the prologue to Pablo Helguera, *Onda Corta* (New York: Jorge Pinto Books, 2012).

"Vanishing Acts" originally appeared in English ("Vanishing") and Spanish ("Disolvencia," trans. Gabriel Bernal Granados) in *Destello*, exhibition and catalog curated and edited by Osvaldo Sánchez (Ecatepec de Morelos, México: Fundación Colección Jumex, 2011). It appeared, in edited form, as "Vanishing Acts," *English Language Notes* (Boulder: University of Colorado) 50.1 Spring / Summer 2012, 5–8. Thanks to John-Michael Rivera.

Deep gratitude to the following who assisted in obtaining rights to authoritative images: Stephanie Ball (Amon Carter Museum); DeCarlos Boyd (Library of Congress); Tammy Carter (Center for Creative Photography, University of Arizona); Lynda Claassen (Mandeville Special Collections Library, University of California, San Diego); Rebecca Frazier (UCLA Chicano Studies Research Center); Carolyn Gibbs (California State University, Sacramento); Harry Gamboa Jr. (artist's archive); Peter Huestis (National Gallery of Art, Washington); Rob Melton (Archive for New Poetry, Mandeville Special Collections Library, University of California, San Diego); Elaine O'Brien Ph.D. (California State University, Sacramento); Marcia L. Schiff (Associated Press); Katherine Strickland (University of Texas Libraries); Alexis Valentine (Library of Congress); Shandi Wagner (Center for Creative Photography, University of Arizona), with special thanks to The University of Houston Libraries

Ghosted among the pages of this book are belated self-syllables in the acoustic uncanny. Warmest thanks to Rosa Alcalá, Esther Allen, Joel Bettridge, Susan Briante, Mary Coffey, Kristin Dykstra, Joshua Escobar, Claire Fox, Esther Gabara, Alan Gilbert, Andrea Giunta,

Lise Goett, Gabriel Bernal Granados, Timothy Liu, Peter Ramos, Dale Smith, Matthew Stadler, and Dorothy Wang: their generosity and judgment allowed me, at crucial junctures along the way, to rehearse lost voices in regenerate encounters with the estrangement of time. I reserve a very dear line of gratitude to Lalitha Gopalan whose elective affinities resolve and make favorable the critical entanglements; and to Ann Lauterbach whose acts of thought and faith in poetic purpose discern the coordinates of life. My thanks to Douglas Kearney, whose design imagination inspires the cover and pages of this book in mood, matter, and method. I'm indebted to the publishers and editors of Noemi Press, especially to Suzi F. García and R. Bruno; their editorial intelligence gave shape to the hidden figures far and near.... The historical view is an intimacy, a living space, a future in the making. I'm thankful each day to dwell there with Michael Bryan; now on the side of amazement and curiosity, now on the side of gladness, care, and possibility.

INDEX OF POEMS

"A Bridge, A Remarkable Bridge" (José Lezama Lima)
"Abstract #1, Yucatán" (Charles Olson)
"A Language of New York" (George Oppen)
American Rambler (Dale Smith)
"An Obscure Meadow Lure Me" [Una oscura pradera me convida] (José Lezama Lima)
"Birth of Day" [Nacimiento del día] (José Lezama Lima)
"Blood from the Stone" (George Oppen)
"Carpenter's Boat" (George Oppen)
"Coastal Strip" (George Oppen)
Dador (José Lezama Lima)
Death of Narcissus [Muerte de Narciso] (José Lezama Lima)
"Deleted to Meet You" (Harry Gamboa Jr.)
Dimensions of History (Jay Wright)
Discrete Series (George Oppen)
"Dissonance" (José Lezama Lima)
"Eclogue" (George Oppen)
"El Louie" (José Montoya)
"Fourth Eclogue" (Virgil)
"Gradualism" (Kenneth Rexroth)
"Image of the Machine" (George Oppen)
"Image-Nations" (Robin Blaser)
"Insular Night: Invisible Gardens" (José Lezama Lima)
"Loss of the Love Poem Called 'Mist'" (Luis Rogelio Nogueras)
"Mexican Market Woman" Langston Hughes

"Oaxaca 1925" (Kenneth Rexroth)
"Octavio Paz" (José Lezama Lima)
"Opposing Fast Lanes" (Harry Gamboa Jr.)
"Paradise. Storefront. Monte Street" (Reina María Rodríguez)
"Pavilion of Nothingness" [El pabellón del vacío] (José Lezama Lima)
"Plastic Poem" (Mathias Goeritz)
"Population" (George Oppen)
"Primitive" (George Oppen)
"Purgatorio" (Hart Crane)
"Resort" (George Oppen)
"Self-Recognition of the Fish" (Roberto Tejada)
"Siesta in Xbalba" (Allen Ginsberg)
"Tenochtitlan" by William Bronk
"The Broken Tower" (Hart Crane)
"The Circumstance" (Hart Crane)
"The Desert Music" (William Carlos Williams)
"The Embrace" (José Lezama Lima)
"The Gods" (José Lezama Lima)
"The Greeks, the Chinese, or Say the Mayans" (William Bronk)
"The Kingfishers" (Charles Olson)
The Maximus Poems (Charles Olson)
"The Mayan Ground" (George Oppen)
"The Neck" (José Lezama Lima)
"The Sad Indian" (Hart Crane)
"The Snowman" (Wallace Stevens)
"They Slip Through the Night" (José Lezama Lima)
"The Zone" (Reina María Rodríguez)
"Thing Language" (Jack Spicer)
"To the Countess of Huntingdon" (John Donne)
"Tourist Eye" (George Oppen)
"Un hombre sin élite" ["A Man Without an Elite"] (Omar Pérez)
"Untitled" (Osvaldo Sánchez)
"Zapata and the Egúngún Mask" (Jay Wright)

INDEX

Roberto Tejada is the author of poetry collections that include *Full Foreground* (Arizona, 2012), *Exposition Park* (Wesleyan, 2010), *Mirrors for Gold* (Krupskaya, 2006), and a selected poems in Spanish translation, *Todo en el ahora* (Libros Magenta, 2015). He was the founder and co-editor of the journal *Mandorla: New Writing from the Americas*, a multilingual annual of poetics and poetry in translation (1991–2014). He has published art histories that include *National Camera: Photography and Mexico's Image Environment* (Minnesota, 2009); a monograph on pioneering Chicana conceptual artist *Celia Alvarez Muñoz* (Minnesota, 2009), writings on photographers Manuel Álvarez Bravo, Graciela Iturbide, and Luis Gispert, and such catalog essays as "Los Angeles Snapshots" in *Now Dig This!: Art and Black Los Angeles, 1960–1980* (Hammer Museum, 2011). He is the Hugh Roy and Lillie Cranz Cullen Distinguished Professor in Creative Writing and Art History at the University of Houston.